THE OLD
FARMER'S
ALMANAC

FLOWER
GARDENER'S
HANDBOOK

The Old Farmer's Almanac Books
PUBLISHER: Sherin Pierce
EDITOR: Janice Stillman
CREATIVE DIRECTOR: Colleen Quinnell
MANAGING EDITOR: Jack Burnett
EDITORIAL STAFF: Benjamin Kilbride, Sarah Perreault, Heidi Stonehill

V.P., NEW MEDIA AND PRODUCTION: Paul Belliveau
PRODUCTION DIRECTOR: David Ziarnowski
PRODUCTION MANAGER: Brian Johnson
PRODUCTION ARTISTS: Jennifer Freeman, Rachel Kipka, Janet Selle

SENIOR DIGITAL EDITOR: Catherine Boeckmann
ASSOCIATE DIGITAL EDITOR: Christopher Burnett
SENIOR WEB DESIGNER: Amy O'Brien
DIGITAL MARKETING SPECIALIST: Holly Sanderson
E-COMMERCE MARKETING DIRECTOR: Alan Henning
PROGRAMMING: Peter Rukavina

CONTRIBUTORS: Catherine Boeckmann, Lynn Coulter, Betty Earl, Larry Hodgson, Doreen G. Howard, Mare-Anne Jarvela, Sarah F. Price, Shirley Remes, Sally Roth, Robin Sweetser, Cynthia Van Hazinga, Kris Weatherbee, Evelyn Weibye

COVER PHOTO CREDITS: See page 224 for credits from Flowers chapter profiles.
BACK COVER PHOTOS, CLOCKWISE FROM TOP LEFT: KarenMassier/Getty Images; kongxinzhu/Getty Images; Edita Medeina/Shutterstock; schnuddel/Getty Images; kschulze/Getty Images; seaonweb/Shutterstock

For additional information about this and other publications from The Old Farmer's Almanac, visit ALMANAC.COM or call 1-800-ALMANAC.

Distributed in the book trade by HarperCollins in the United States and by Thomas Allen & Son Ltd. in Canada.

Yankee Publishing Inc., An Employee-Owned Company
P.O. Box 520, 1121 Main Street, Dublin, New Hampshire 03444

Thank you for buying this book! Thanks, too, to everyone who had a hand in it, including printers, distributors, and sales and delivery people.

ISBN: 978-1-57198-928-4
First Edition
Printed in U.S.A.

DAHLIAS

A FLOWERING FUTURE

Welcome, friends:

Thank you for your enthusiasm for flower gardening and for your interest in this book! Our intent in curating this collection is to provide guidance, inspiration, and entertainment along with timesaving tips, practical advice, and ideas to spark your imagination.

We had a range of folks in mind when developing the content: novice gardeners with germinating curiosity, budding growers who want to add color and variety to their yard or containers, and seasoned horticulturists whose cutting beds are the envy of the neighborhood.

Here you will all find help and solutions for planning and preparing pots and plots; choosing and maintaining plants—natives and non-; and enjoying the endless benefits of flowering plants and shrubs, from spectacular fresh or dried blooms to beneficial pollinators (calling all butterflies and hummingbirds!) to the beauty of birds seeking shelter and sustenance and bees spreading pollen and collecting nectar.

Dozens of plants are named on these pages, and 32 are profiled with specific details, such as their reputation in the plant world, tips on how to start them successfully and care for them to maturity (while thwarting pests and diseases!), and recommended varieties. For many, we also include fascinating facts about them in folklore and/or history.

Some plants in which you have an interest may not be included; in consultation with experienced gardeners, we chose these 32 because they are popular and common to most areas of the United States and/or Canada and have generated a great number of questions by visitors to Almanac.com. You'll find many more flowering plants, with suggestions on how to use them, in the "Inspiration" section of this book.

Because this is an *Old Farmer's Almanac* publication and we love to share our passion for plants and gardening, we have included flower lore, flower gardening quotes, and anecdotal tales from gardeners. We welcome stories about your flowers, too—your beauties, your deadheads, your floricultural unforgettables. Share them— and ask questions about other plants—at Almanac.com or on our social media.

We believe that with this book, you'll have a flowering future ahead. Now, let's head to the garden!

–Janice Stillman

CONTENTS
PART 1

GROUND RULES

Getting Started . . . 10
Perennial, Biennial, and Annual Flowers . . . 12
Natives vs. Non-natives . . . 16
Contain Your Enthusiasm! . . . 20
Soil Matters . . . 22
The Dirt on Dirt . . . 24
The pH-enomenal Effects of pH . . . 26
Make the Most of Compost . . . 28
How to Start Seeds . . . 30
U.S. Frosts and Growing Seasons . . . 34
Canadian Frosts and Growing Seasons . . . 35
When to Plant . . . 36

FLOWERS

Aster 42
Astilbe 45
Bee Balm 48
Black-Eyed Susan 50
Bleeding Heart . . 53
Canna 55
Chrysanthemum . 60
Clematis 63
Columbine 66
Coneflower 68
Coreopsis 72
Dahlia 74
Delphinium 79
Dianthus 82
Foxglove 85
Hollyhock 87
Hydrangea 90
Iris 96
Jasmine 100
Lavender 103
Lilac 107
Lily 111
Lily-of-the-Valley 115
Lupine 117
Peony 120
Rhododendron. . 124
Rose 127
Salvia 133
Sunflower 137
Tulip 141
Viburnum 145
Wisteria 148

CONTENTS
PART 2

INSPIRATION
Expert Advice for Constant Color . . . 156
Perennials for Every Region . . . 160
Tiny Bulbs . . . 162
9 Summer-Flowering Shrubs . . . 166
Feather Your Nest . . . 172
Hear the Buzz? . . . 176
Enjoy More, Labor Less . . . 178
Cut Flower Care . . . 182
How to Dry Flowers . . . 186

GROWING CONCERNS
Dealing With Flower Diseases and Pests . . . 190
Facts About Fertilizers . . . 202
Be Water Wise . . . 206
Putting the Garden to Bed . . . 208

LORE AND MORE
Interpreting Plant Names . . . 214
The Language of Flowers . . . 216
Birth Month Flowers . . . 218

JOURNAL PAGES
Flower Tracker . . . 15
Natives in My Garden . . . 19
My Soil's pH . . . 27
My Seed-Starting Record . . . 33
My Planting Record . . . 39
How Does My Garden Grow? . . . 152, 153
My Color Inventory . . . 159
My Bulb Inventory . . . 164, 165
My Shrubs . . . 171
Observations and Reminders . . . 181, 219
My Cutting Flowers . . . 185
Disease and Pest Record . . . 201
My Fertilizer Record . . . 205
Cleanup Checklist . . . 211

INDEX . . . 220

GROUND RULES

GETTING STARTED

Plants with an asterisk (*) are profiled in this book.

IN HIS GARDEN EVERY MAN MAY BE HIS OWN ARTIST WITHOUT APOLOGY
OR EXPLANATION. . . . EVER A SEASON AHEAD OF US FLOATS
THE VISION OF PERFECTION AND HEREIN LIES ITS PERENNIAL CHARM.
–Louise Beebe Wilder, American garden writer and designer (1878–1938)

We all dream of a lush, lovely flower bed full of colorful blooms all season long. What we end up with is often something else: The color runs out when the heat hits; the plants clash instead of complement; the tall plants crowd out the short ones. By late summer (or sooner!), it all looks sad and shabby.

Don't despair! With planning and preparation, the garden of your dreams is possible— and it starts right here.

LET THE SUN SHINE

Give careful consideration to where you site your garden. Before digging, evaluate your garden area: Note microclimates (very small, localized weather conditions) created by trees and walls. Watch the path of the Sun, noting the winds and soil conditions. Soil types can greatly affect water penetration: Soil near walls and fences and under overhanging trees tends to be too dry for good plant growth.

Most flowering plants need at least 6 hours of sunlight per day, although some will grow well in more shade. In general, the more sunlight flowering plants receive, the more abundant and lush their blooms. Avoid planting flowers and shrubs near large trees. These will cast shade and compete with your plants for nutrients and water.

BE READY WITH WATER

Have water readily available. Consider installing a soaker or drip hose. These use a fraction of the water used by a sprinkler and deliver it where it is needed.

CAPTURE YOUR IDEAS

Sketch your garden on the back of an envelope, keep each year's plan in a notebook, or use an app on an electronic device, but plan your garden and retain the notes—they will serve as a guide to adding or replacing plants in future years.

Pencil and paper never go out of fashion, but an app adds a new dimension to the garden, whether it's in a plot or a pot. We realized the benefits of electronic planning years ago and now use and recommend The Old Farmer's Almanac Garden Planner. This app helps with planning your garden's size; knowing the number of plants that a space will support successfully; planting and watering schedules; archiving plans; journaling; and a whole lot more—personalized to your zip or postal code. Learn more and try it free for 7 days at Almanac .com/gardenplanner.

Group plants according to their water needs. Set plants with higher water needs in a hollow that collects rainwater. Remember that warmer southern or western exposures use the most water.

ENCOURAGE AIR TRAVEL
Good airflow will encourage sturdy plant growth and help to keep diseases at bay. It also makes the garden less hospitable to insect pests.

BE WARY OF THE WINDS
Solid walls or fences may provide shelter, but they can also cause the wind to form destructive turbulence on the leeward sides; do not plant too close to them.

IMAGINE THE POSSIBILITIES
Ever wonder why some gardens look great all season long? In most cases, it's because the gardener understands and executes the following basic principles.

A garden is a multilayered community of plants. A combination of bulbs, perennials, annuals, and shrubs will provide four-season interest. It's important to pay attention to heights. Even in a small garden, there is room for short, medium, and tall plants.

Spring-blooming bulbs offer the earliest color. These include snowdrops, crocuses, tulips, and daffodils; turn to page 162 for more.

Perennials offer a diversity of flowers and foliage, and you have to plant them only once! By staggering the bloom times, you can have color all season long. Once a perennial is done flowering, it still needs to look good. Plants with interesting foliage colors or

FOXGLOVE

textures will continue to add something to your garden even when not in bloom.

Consider some of these tried-and-true perennials: black-eyed Susan,* coreopsis,* daisies, daylilies, certain foxgloves,* cranesbill geraniums, heuchera, lady's mantle, phlox, sedum, and yarrow.

Look for native perennials if you want to make your garden a bee-, butterfly-, and hummingbird-friendly habitat. Some natives to include are agastache, or anise hyssop; asclepias (milk- or butterfly weed), asters,* bee balm,* columbine,* and coneflowers.*

Annuals are great for bridging the gaps in the perennial garden. They will give you season-long color if kept deadheaded. Since they are not permanent additions to the garden, you can change them every year, giving your garden a new look.

READY FOR YOUR IDEAS TO BLOSSOM? SHARE AND LEARN ON 📌 @ALMANAC

These are easy to grow and put on a good show: browallia, calendula, cleome, cosmos, dahlias,* nasturtiums, purpletop verbena, and 'Profusion' zinnia.

Shrubs add needed structure and year-round interest. Options include dwarf conifers, hedges, and broadleaf evergreens. Shrubs with colorful bark or twisty shapes serve as focal points. Those that also offer flowers, fruit, and fall color are welcome additions, too. Turn to page 166 for more.

Finally, seriously think about how much time you have to devote to your garden. A plan will help you to choose plants wisely and enjoy the experience for years to come.

PERENNIAL, BIENNIAL, AND ANNUAL FLOWERS

Plants marked with an asterisk (*) are profiled in this book.

ANNUAL PLANTS ARE NATURE'S EMERGENCY MEDICAL SERVICE, SEEDED IN SOUNDS AND SCARS TO HOLD THE LAND UNTIL THE PERENNIAL COVER IS RE-ESTABLISHED.
–Wendell Berry, American novelist and farmer (b. 1934)

Know the life expectancy of a plant before you purchase and plant it. You may be surprised, but you will not be disappointed.

PERENNIALS

Perennials, which usually form the backbone or foundation of a garden, are flowers that return reliably year after year. They live in the ground for more than 2 years and die back to the ground every fall. Their roots survive the winter, and plants resprout in the spring.

Once established, many perennials need minimal upkeep in the form of watering and fertilizing because their roots reach farther for nutrients than those of annual plants. Many perennials spread readily, filling out garden spaces and providing more color each year. This does not necessarily mean that all perennials are carefree. In some cases, you might need or want to control their spread by dividing the plants or eliminating their

WHY DO PLANTS BEHAVE SO DIFFERENTLY?

Ecologists believe that a plant's environment—its native habitat—determines its growth habit. Annuals develop in stressed, open environments where the soil has been recently disturbed. Perennials thrive in closed, protected areas. Biennials grow best in semi-open, intermittent habitat—places where the soil has been disturbed and then lain fallow for 1 to 3 years.

root spread or suckers.

Perennials can be planted at any time, but the best times are fall, well before winter's chill sets in, and spring, before the hot, dry summer. We prefer fall because the soil is warmed. You can plant in summer, but you will probably need to water frequently. The goal is to allow the plant the time and conditions to get established.

Perennials need well-draining soil that is amended with compost or organic matter. Most perennials grow best in soil with a pH of 6.0 to 7.0.

For the best outcome, choose native perennials when possible and be wary of beautiful flowers that are not meant for your growing zone.

Examples of perennials include aster,* bearded iris,* bee balm,* black-eyed Susan,* (purple) coneflower,*

12

PERENNIAL CONEFLOWER

coreopsis,* daylily, false indigo (baptisia), hosta, peony,* phlox, Russian sage, salvia,* sedum, and yarrow.

BIENNIALS

In a class of their own, biennials live for two growing seasons before setting seed.

They form roots, stems, and leaves in Year 1. Usually, the plant's stem is very short and its leaves grow low to the ground, forming a rosette—a tight complex of leaves at ground level. Then, in colder months, the plant enters a period of dormancy, a factor essential for bloom.

During the following spring or summer, Year 2, the stem elongates and flowers form. Next, it produces seeds, self-sowing as it dies. A biennial plant needs to produce four

times as many seeds as a perennial and twice as many as an annual just to survive. Biennial seeds are usually larger than those of annuals and perennials.

Blooming biennials are among the best old-fashioned garden favorites, adding color and interest to any bed. Examples

BUYING TIPS

• In fall, many nurseries sell their perennials stock at bargain prices.

• Don't balk at small pots: Perennials in 4-inch pots cost less and catch up to larger perennials within 1 year after planting!

include forget-me-not, most foxgloves,* hollyhock,* and lunaria. Consider allotting extra space in your garden for biennials to naturalize through self-seeding.

ANNUALS

Annuals are wonderfully versatile: They grow for one season, filling "holes" in a garden bed while providing spots of color. Annuals complement perennials well!

Annuals bloom, produce seeds, and then die in the same growing year. They need to be replaced every spring—and this is your opportunity to try something new! You can go from bold and bright to soft

BIENNIAL HOLLYHOCK

SHADE ANNUAL LOBELIA

pastel or from cottage garden to tropical paradise by switching out your annual plants. Annuals' other advantages include adding color to containers and providing cut flowers all season long.

Annuals exist for almost any situation. Here are a few:

ANNUALS FOR HOT, DRY SOIL
Hot, dry soil a problem? Try growing . . .
■ cactus-like, low-growing *Portulaca grandiflora,* aka **moss rose,** with its festive pastel flowers
■ 4- to 6-foot-tall tithonia, aka **Mexican sunflower,** with its orangey-red daisylike blooms
■ stiff-stemmed gomphrena, aka **globe amaranth,** with ball-shape flowers for

cutting and dried flower arrangements

ANNUALS FOR SHADE
You can brighten up shady sites in your garden or elsewhere with . . .
■ the colorful flower clusters and foliage of **begonias,** which are deer- and rabbit-resistant
■ the true-blue blooms of **lobelia**
■ the lavender-blue blooms of shrubby browallia, aka **bush violet**

ANNUALS FOR MOIST SOILS
Moist soil is no problem for . . .
■ tall (1 to 6 feet), heat-loving cleome, aka **spider flower** for its form
■ bushy torenia, aka **wishbone**

flower for its tubular, bicolor blooms
■ **monkey flower** (in the native genus *Mimulus*), whose monkey-face blooms host larvae of Baltimore and common buckeye butterflies and are beloved by bees

ANNUALS AS ARCHITECTURAL PLANTS
Tall plants add a touch of drama to the landscape as centerpieces, against a wall, or in clusters. Consider . . .
■ 3- to 5-foot-tall *Nicotiana sylvestris,* aka **flowering tobacco** or **white shooting stars**
■ towering (up to 16 feet tall) **sunflowers***
■ 3- to 5-foot-tall **elephant head amaranth,** with striking magenta seed heads

FLOWER TRACKER

PERENNIALS: YEAR PLANTED/VARIETY	BIENNIALS: YEAR PLANTED/VARIETY	ANNUALS: YEAR PLANTED/VARIETY

NATIVES VS. NON-NATIVES

Plants marked with an asterisk (*) are profiled in this book.

GARDENERS DON'T HAVE TO DO A BIG CONVERSION TO A NATIVE LANDSCAPE.
EVERY NATIVE PLANT HELPS. IT'S A MATTER OF AWARENESS FOR THE
FUTURE. . . . THERE ARE BEAUTIFUL PERENNIALS TO INCORPORATE
INTO FLOWER BEDS AND LOVELY SHRUBS TO ADD TO FOUNDATIONS.
–Bringing Nature Home: How You Can Sustain Wildlife With Native Plants (*2009*),
by Prof. Douglas W. Tallamy, chair, Dept. of Entomology and Wildlife Ecology, University of Delaware–Newark

It happens to every gardener, especially beginners. You want to grow everything! Maybe you could, and maybe you should. Or maybe you should think again. Consider growing plants that are suited to your area, environment, and zone. Think "natives." And think seriously about how much time you have to devote to your garden.

WHAT IS A "NATIVE" PLANT?

All plants are native to the earth, and many that we think of as all-American (such as lilacs and forsythias) are not native to this continent at all but crossed the ocean with the first European settlers.

A native plant is one that thrives naturally in a region, ecosystem, or habitat and was not introduced by humans. Neil Diboll, president of the Prairie Nursery in Westfield, Wisconsin, defines "native" as "those plants in place 150 to 200 years ago."

"Non-native" plants are considered to be those introduced, accidentally or purposefully, to an area in which they did not exist.

Native plants offer many advantages:

■ Once established, they require little to no maintenance or water, being adapted to the climate and soil.
■ Fertilizer and pesticides are seldom needed with natives; insects and diseases are infrequent challenges.
■ They provide nectar for native pollinators (bats, bees, birds,

SUIT PLANTS TO YOUR SITUATION

Thousands of native species grow all across America—plants that exist for a vast range of growing conditions. Some of them—prairie plants, for instance—thrive in lean or poor soil. Others are drought-tolerant, and some prefer wet or boggy spots; there are natives for almost every type of soil, as well as those that can withstand searing heat, bitter cold, and gale-force winds. You need only choose wild plants that suit your situation.

Before you design a garden or spend any money on plants or seeds, understand the character of your site and your soil. If you don't know whether your soil is acid or alkaline, get it tested by your local Cooperative Extension service. See page 22.

BLUESTAR

COMPASS PLANT

CUP PLANT

butterflies, moths, and more).
- They provide habitat or shelter for birds and mammals.
- They promote biodiversity and, through their deep roots, help to maintain healthy soil.

WHAT IS A "NATURALIZED" PLANT?

A "naturalized" plant is a non-native plant that can reproduce and maintain itself in an area without benefit of human intervention. Naturalized plants do not become natives. Some invasive plants—non-native plants that become established, spread without human help, and disrupt or harm (even destroy!) plant communities or ecosystems—become naturalized.

NATIVES THAT YOU MIGHT NOT KNOW
Perennials

Bluestar (*Amsonia hubrictii*), native to Okla. and Ark.

Compass plant (*Silphium laciniatum*), native to all of North America

Cup plant (*S. perfoliatum*), native to eastern and central North America

Indian pink (*Spigelia marilandica*), native to the southeastern United States

Large coneflower (*Rudbeckia maxima*), native to the central and southern United States

ARE YOUR PETALS
TO THE METTLE? TAG US
IN A PIC ON 📷
@THEOLDFARMERSALMANAC

New England aster* (*Symphyotrichum novae-angliae*), native to all of North America

Nodding ladies' tresses orchid (*Spiranthes odorata*), native to the southeastern United States

Wild ginger (*Asarum shuttleworthii*), native to the southeastern United States

Wild stonecrop (*Sedum ternatum*), native to eastern North America

Bulbs

Bloodroot (*Sanguinaria canadensis*), native to the eastern and central United States and central Canada

Canada lily* (*Lilium canadense*), native from Ontario to Nova Scotia and

INDIAN PINK

NODDING LADIES' TRESSES

WILD GINGER

BLOODROOT

JACK-IN-THE-PULPIT

YELLOW TRILLIUM

south to Georgia and Alabama

Desert lily *(Hesperocallis undulata)*, native to desert areas of southwestern North America

Dutchman's breeches *(Dicentra cucullaria)*, native to eastern North America

Jack-in-the-pulpit *(Arisaema triphyllum)*, native to the eastern United States and eastern and central Canada

Little sweet Betsy *(Trillium cuneatum)*, native to the southeastern United States

Southern swamp lily *(Crinum americanum)*, native from Texas to North Carolina

Spider lily *(Hymenocallis liriosme)*, native to Texas, Louisiana, Oklahoma, Arkansas, Mississippi, and Alabama

LET YOUR PHOTOS FLOWER!
TAG US IN A PIC ON 📷
@THEOLDFARMERSALMANAC

Yellow trillium *(Trillium luteum)*, native to the Great Smoky Mountains region

Ferns

Broad beech fern *(Phegopteris hexagonoptera)*, native to eastern North America

Deer fern *(Blechnum spicant)*, native to western North America

Glade fern *(Diplazium pycnocarpon)*, native to North America

Goldie's fern *(Dryopteris goldiana)*, native to eastern North America

Interrupted fern *(Osmunda claytoniana)*, native to eastern North America

Kunth's maiden fern *(Thelypteris kunthii)*, native to the southern United States

Lady fern *(Athyrium filix-femina)*, native to eastern North America

Male fern *(Dryopteris filix-mas)*, native to northern temperate regions

Narrow beech fern *(Phegopteris connectilis)*, native to the Northern Hemisphere

Rusty woodsia *(Woodsia ilvensis)*, native to North America

Western maidenhair fern *(Adiantum aleuticum)*, native to western North America

GLADE FERN

LADY FERN

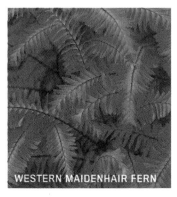

WESTERN MAIDENHAIR FERN

NATIVES IN MY GARDEN

VARIETY	PLANTING DATE	NOTES

CONTAIN YOUR ENTHUSIASM!

Plants marked with an asterisk (*) are profiled in this book.

ALL GARDENS ARE A FORM OF AUTOBIOGRAPHY.

−Robert Dash, American artist and gardener (1934–2013)

Containers enable you to make flowers a part of any landscape—even a deck, patio, porch, or balcony! Plus, when you garden in containers, you have more control over growing conditions and, overall, have a lot less work to do!

POT-TICULARS

Large plants need lots of space, and most roots need room to grow. Just as important, the bigger your container, the greater the number of plants you can grow in it.

Anything that holds soil can support plants. Just be sure that any container has drainage holes in the bottom. Plastic pots won't dry out as fast as unglazed terra-cotta will, and black pots absorb heat when they are sitting in the sun, which can also dry out the soil more quickly.

Place saucers underneath pots to catch runoff or rainwater and protect a deck or other surface. Remember to pour off standing water so that your plants don't drown.

Do not fill pots with soil from the garden: It is too heavy, can become waterlogged, and brings disease and insects with it. Instead, choose prepared potting mixes, aged compost, or a soilless mixture combined with organic matter. Not only are soil-free potting mixes light, but also the fluffy blend allows roots to access more oxygen and nutrients.

Do not fill the bottom of a pot with pebbles unless the extra weight is needed to keep the pot from tipping over. Instead, cover the drainage holes with a piece of plastic

PERENNIALS AND ANNUALS FOR CONTAINERS

Perennials produce some of the most beautiful flowers, plus they'll come back every year! Here are some of our favorites suitable for containers:

- Astilbe*
- Bee balm*
- Bergenia
- Bleeding heart*
- Coneflower*

- Daylily hybrids
- Evening primrose
- Hosta (dwarf or miniature)

- Maltese cross
- Salvia*
- Speedwell (Veronica)

Annuals are stunning and easy to mix and match. If you don't like how they look, just try different ones in the next year! Some of the best annuals for containers include:

- Begonia
- Browallia
- Coleus
- Coreopsis*
- Dusty miller
- Fuchsia

- Lobelia
- Marigold
- Morning glory
- Nasturtium
- Pansy
- Petunia

- Portulaca
- Snapdragon
- Statice
- Sweet alyssum
- Sweet pea

PETUNIA

screening to prevent clogging.

Wind and warmth draw moisture from plant leaves, drying them out, so many plants must be watered as often as twice a day. Consider using self-watering containers, which have a water reservoir in the bottom for conveying water to the dry soil as needed.

To keep potted plants adequately cool and moist, double-pot them by placing a small pot inside a larger one and filling the space between them with sphagnum moss or crumpled newspaper. When watering the plant, also soak the filler between the pots. The moist filler acts as insulation.

CONTAINER CAPACITIES

Potting mix is sold by volume. Most pots are described by their diameter. Use this table to see how much a pot holds.

Container size	Potting mix
8-inch	3 quarts
10-inch	1½ gallons
12-inch	2 gallons
14-inch	3 gallons
16-inch	5 gallons
20-inch	6 gallons
24-inch	7 gallons
30-inch	18 gallons
36-inch	24 gallons

Basic Potting Mix

2½ gallons peat moss†

2½ gallons vermiculite or perlite

1¼ gallons screened compost or composted cow manure

2 cups fine sand (not beach sand)

2 cups time-release fertilizer pellets

½ cup lime (to counter the acid of the peat and keep the pH level near neutral)

Mix thoroughly. Makes enough to fill two 14-inch tubs or five 12-inch hanging baskets. Double or triple recipe for bigger containers.

†Replace peat moss with coco coir, if desired. Both ingredients have similar moisture-retention qualities. If using coir, eliminate the lime; if you do not, your soil will be too alkaline, aka basic. Coco coir has an almost-neutral pH, while peat is more acidic. Lime is added to counteract the peat.

VOICES OF EXPERIENCE

I have added coffee grounds, tea leaves, and crushed eggshells to my potting mix to plant all of my annuals. They seem to do really well here where I live, in the Tennessee area climate. I have these items daily, so it stretches my potting mixture and adds lots of potassium and other minerals.   –Debbie, on Almanac.com

I never knew how important it is to have good potting soil. I am just a beginner, and I have always planted things since I was young. Some thrived and others did not. I had never thought that different plants need different soil. I had thought that plants are planted and that they will grow no matter what the soil. This comes from school experiments where you went and got your own soil and hoped that your little plant would survive. Thank you so very much for your tips. They help immensely.   –Max, on Almanac.com

GET DOWN TO EARTH–
TAG US IN A PIC ON 📷
@THEOLDFARMERSALMANAC

SOIL MATTERS

ALL THROUGH THE LONG WINTER, I DREAM OF MY GARDEN.
ON THE FIRST DAY OF SPRING, I DIG MY FINGERS DEEP INTO THE SOFT EARTH.
I CAN FEEL ITS ENERGY, AND MY SPIRITS SOAR.

–Helen Hayes, American actress (1900–93)

Good soil is the secret to a successful garden. Even though soil covers the ground, it is not of the same quality everywhere. Fortunately, the structure, texture, and/or nutrients in most soils can be improved. By identifying the characteristics of your soil, you can properly amend it.

TEST, DON'T GUESS

The first step in assessing your soil is to test it. The results will reveal what it lacks and what to add. Soil that does not suit the plants that you want to grow will cause them to underperform or even fail. Why risk it?

The Laboratory Soil Test

A lab test provides the most thorough analysis of soil. Most state Cooperative Extension services (usually affiliated with colleges or universities) can help. Find the one nearest to you at Almanac.com/cooperative-extension-services.

Expect to pay a nominal fee and to receive a customized report with suggested amendments to suit whatever you plan to grow—flowers, grass, shrubs, trees, or vegetables.

Soil continually changes, so test yours every 2 to 3 years. Keep records of test results, fertilizer applications, and any other soil amendments.

The DIY Soil Test Kit

A do-it-yourself soil test kit generally reveals the soil's pH level and nitrogen, phosphorus, and potassium (N, P, K) content. It's simple to do at home, and instructions for amending the soil are usually included. Basic kits, available at garden centers, hardware stores, and online, run from $10 to $25; more comprehensive versions can cost more.

The DIY Pantry pH Test

This procedure gives you a quick clue to your soil's pH:
■ Combine 2 tablespoons of soil and ½ cup of vinegar in a bowl. If the mixture fizzes, you have alkaline soil.
■ Place 2 tablespoons of soil in a bowl. Moisten it with distilled water. Add ½ cup of baking soda. If the mixture fizzes, you have acidic soil.

If your soil does not react to either test, it has a neutral pH.

The Earthworm Test

This test will indicate your soil's tilth, or richness. In spring, when the soil temperature has reached 50°F and its surface is moist, grab a shovel and dig up about 1 cubic foot of it. Put the soil on a piece of cardboard and break it apart. If you find at least 10 earthworms, your soil is healthy; if fewer, add more organic matter to it.

THE WEED TEST
Some plants are themselves telltale signs of soil conditions.

IF YOU HAVE . . .	YOUR SOIL IS . . .
bracken fern, dock, horsetail, nettle, Virginia creeper	acidic
broom sedge, burdock, horsetail, stinging nettle	calcium-deficient
cattail, horsetail, Joe Pye weed, marsh mallow	wet or poorly draining
common mullein, mugwort	infertile
crabgrass, field bindweed, plantain, quackgrass	hardpan or compacted
dead nettle, lamb's-quarter, pigweed, purslane	nutrient-rich
knapweed	nutrient-deficient
lamb's-quarter, wild mustard	alkaline
lamb's-quarter, ox eye daisy, wild buckwheat	phosphorus-deficient

IF YOU HAVE . . .	YOUR SOIL HAS . . .
comfrey	nitrogen, potassium, and phosphorus
dandelions	iron, potassium, and phosphate
legume-type weeds, such as vetch and clover	nitrogen
nettle	iron and nitrogen
yarrow	iron and phosphate

THE DIRT ON DIRT

IN THE SPRING, AT THE END OF THE DAY, YOU SHOULD SMELL LIKE DIRT.
—Margaret Atwood, Canadian writer (b. 1939)

The texture of your soil is as important as its nutrient and pH levels. Soil texture—the amount of sand, silt, and clay, collectively known as mineral components—affects water and nutrient retention, air exchange, chemical reactions, and more.

Topsoil, aka loam, is the ideal medium for growing most plants. It is a combination of soil mineral particles (sand, silt, and clay), organic matter (decayed plant matter), air, and water. These ingredients in combination result in soil that is fertile, free-draining, and easy to work.

THE UNDERSIDE OF TOPSOIL

Topsoil is exactly what its name suggests: surface dirt. Depending on location, topsoil may be nonexistent to up to 12 inches deep. It is impossible to judge its quality by looking at it. State and local regulations of the quality for sale vary greatly (if they exist at all). If you plan to buy topsoil, take this advice.

■ **Ask gardeners to recommend suppliers.**
■ **Tell the supplier how you are going to use the soil.**

SOIL FIXES

IF YOU HAVE THIS SOIL TEXTURE . . .	AMEND WITH THIS . . .
sandy	compost; humus; aged manure; sawdust with extra nitrogen; heavy, clay-rich soil
silt	coarse sand (not beach sand) or gravel and compost, or aged horse manure mixed with fresh straw
clay	coarse sand (not beach sand) and compost

TO IMPROVE YOUR SOIL, ADD THE PROPER AMENDMENT(S) . . .

bark, ground: made from various tree barks; improves soil structure

compost: an excellent conditioner

leaf mold: decomposed leaves, which add nutrients and structure to soil

lime: raises the pH of acidic soil and helps to loosen clay soil

manure: best if composted; never add fresh ("hot") manure; is a good conditioner

coarse sand (not beach sand): improves drainage in clay soil

topsoil: usually used with another amendment; replaces existing soil

24

■ **Ask for test data.** If the topsoil hasn't been tested, ask for a small sample and have it tested yourself.

■ **Learn the soil pH and the soil texture classification.** It's possible to raise or lower pH, but it takes work to change a soil's texture. Texture classification is based on the relative percentages of sand, silt, and clay particles in the soil; "loam" or "sandy loam" is best.

■ **Ask whether the soil has been screened.** Unscreened topsoil can be full of rocks and roots that you will have to rake out.

HELP YOUR GARDENING IMAGINATION BLOOM ON 🅿 @ALMANAC

■ **Don't buy a product that has a chemical smell or other off-odor.** It could contain soils contaminated by petroleum or other potentially toxic waste products.

■ If you have any concerns about herbicide residues, **take home a sample of the topsoil and sow a few seeds of different plants in it.** See how well the seeds germinate. This process will also help you to determine whether the soil is infested with perennial weeds.

HOW TO TURN TOPSOIL INTO TIP-TOP SOIL

Any topsoil needs organic matter for holding moisture, improving soil structure, and retaining plant nutrients. Add plenty of organic matter to purchased topsoil, whatever its source, in the form of compost and composted animal manure. Be sure to incorporate the new soil into the top few inches of your existing soil. This will promote plant root growth better than if you had simply spread it on top.

25

THE pH-ENOMENAL EFFECTS OF pH

Plants marked with an asterisk (*) are profiled in this book.

SOIL IS THE HOME OF THE FLOWER. ALL FLOWERS MUST LIVE
IN THEIR HOMES, NOT IN SOMEWHERE ELSE; NOT IN A WOMAN'S HAIR OR
NOT IN A LOVER'S HANDS OR NOT ON A DINNER TABLE!
–Mehmet Murat İldan, Turkish writer (b. 1965)

Essentially, pH is a snapshot of the acidity (sourness) or alkalinity (sweetness) of the soil. On a scale of 0 to 14, the low numbers indicate acidity; the high numbers, alkalinity. Soil levels usually range from about 4.5 to about 9.5. The number at the center, 7, is the neutral point.

Acidic, or sour, soil (below 7.0) is counteracted by applying finely ground limestone; alkaline, or sweet, soil (above 7.0) is treated with ground sulfur.

A soil test will indicate your soil's pH and specify the amount of lime or sulfur that is needed to reach the proper level.

A pH of 6.5 is just about right for most home gardens, since most plants thrive in the pH range of from 6.0 to 7.0, slightly acidic to neutral. There are exceptions; refer to the list of common plants for each one's pH range.

SELECTED pH PREFERENCES

Alyssum 6.0–7.5
Aster,* New England . . 6.0–8.0
Astilbe* 6.0–8.0
Baby's breath 6.0–7.0
Bachelor's button. 6.0–7.5
Bee balm* 6.0–7.5
Begonia. 5.5–7.0
Black-eyed Susan* 5.5–7.0
Bleeding heart* 6.0–7.5
Canna* 6.0–8.0
Chrysanthemum* 6.0–7.5
Clematis* 5.5–7.0
Columbine* 6.0–8.0
Coneflower,* purple . . 5.0–7.5
Coreopsis* 5.0–6.0
Cosmos. 5.0–8.0
Crocus 6.0–8.0
Daffodil 6.0–6.5
Dahlia* 6.0–7.5
Daisy, Shasta. 6.0–8.0
Daylily. 6.0–8.0
Delphinium* 6.0–7.5
Dianthus*. 6.0–7.0
Foxglove* 6.0–7.5
Geranium. 5.5–6.5
Geranium, cranesbill. . 6.0–8.0
Gladiolus 5.0–7.0
Hibiscus 6.0–8.0
Hollyhock* 6.0–8.0

Hyacinth. 6.5–7.5
Hydrangea,* blue. 4.5–5.5
Hydrangea,* pink 6.0–7.0
Iris,* blue flag. 5.0–7.5
Jasmine* 5.5–7.0
Lavender* 6.5–7.5
Lilac*. 6.0–7.0
Lily* 6.0-7.0
Lily-of-the-valley* 4.5–6.0
Lupine*. 5.0–6.5
Marigold. 5.5–7.5
Morning glory 6.0–7.5
Narcissus, trumpet . . . 5.5–6.5
Nasturtium. 5.5–7.5
Pansy. 5.5–6.5
Peony* 6.0–7.5
Petunia 6.0–7.5
Phlox, summer. 6.0–8.0
Poppy, oriental. 6.0–7.5
Rhododendron*. 4.5–6.0
Rose,* hybrid tea 5.5–7.0
Rose,* rugosa 6.0–7.0
Salvia*. 5.5–6.5
Snapdragon 5.5–7.0
Sunflower* 6.0–7.5
Tulip* 6.0–7.0
Viburnum*. 5.5–8.0
Wisteria*. 6.0–7.0
Zinnia 5.5–7.0

MY SOIL'S pH

DATE	TEST RESULTS/GOAL	AMENDMENTS

MAKE THE MOST OF COMPOST

**I FIND THAT A REAL GARDENER IS NOT A MAN WHO CULTIVATES FLOWERS;
HE IS A MAN WHO CULTIVATES THE SOIL.**
–The Gardener's Year *(1929/1931), by Karel Čapek, Czech writer (1890–1938)*

Consisting of decomposed plant material, compost is the gardener's best friend. Its ability to fix almost any soil problem has earned it the nicknames "black gold" and "the great equalizer."

Compost is also a soil conditioner that helps to stabilize pH levels in the soil. As organic matter, it attracts earthworms, which thrive in it, and their presence makes more nutrients available from deep in the soil. Perhaps the best part of all: You can make compost yourself!

HOW TO MAKE HOT COMPOST

Many people think that composting is as simple as throwing all food and garden waste into a container and leaving it there for a couple of years. While you will indeed get compost in this way, you can produce much better compost and get it much more quickly if you follow these simple guidelines for hot compost.

Fancy compost bins are not necessary. You can just pile up your ingredients on the ground. Ideally, the pile should be at least 4 feet high, 4 feet wide, and 4 feet long. Below a certain size, a pile will not heat up.

You need four ingredients for good hot compost: greens, browns, air, and moisture. The green and brown ingredients contain carbon and nitrogen. The ratio of carbon to nitrogen determines whether we label the ingredient a "green" or a "brown":

■ **Greens are ingredients with a relatively high nitrogen content** (a carbon-to-nitrogen ratio of less than 30:1). Greens include grass clippings (that have not been sprayed with weed killer), vegetable waste, fruit peelings, annual weeds before they develop seeds, and old bedding plants. A word about grass clippings: Never add a lot all at once, as they will just form a slimy, matted layer. In fact, piles of any greens will result only in a soggy, smelly mess.

■ **Browns are ingredients**

with a lower nitrogen content (a higher carbon-to-nitrogen ratio). Browns include straw, wood materials (e.g., sawdust, chippings, and shredded brown cardboard), and fallen leaves. Bedding from herbivorous pets, such as guinea pigs, is ideal, as their manure adds a bit of nitrogen into the mix.

Color is not always a reliable indicator of whether something is a green or brown material. For example, fresh grass clippings that are spread out and left to dry are still considered to be a green ingredient even though they have turned a brownish color; all that they've really lost is moisture. However, straw is always considered a brown because before it was cut, the main stems had died and much of the plant's nitrogen had gone into the seeds as protein.

■ **Air is vital to the process.** Air is introduced when you

THE SECRET TO SPEEDY DECAY

Both green and brown ingredients decompose much more quickly if you chop them up: Cut up kitchen scraps, shred woody materials, and tear up cardboard. This allows more surface area to be exposed to the microbes.

turn or mix the compost; this speeds up decomposition. Ingredients should never be squashed down.

■ **Water.** If you stockpile brown materials, water the pile to get things going when first mixing it. Build up the pile with layers of browns and greens and water where necessary to produce a moist (but not soggy) mixture.

These four ingredients—greens, browns, air, and water—need to be balanced correctly for best results. Aim for two to three parts browns to one part greens, at least initially; more greens can be added as the compost "cooks." With air and moisture, you're giving the microbes that decompose the materials the best working conditions. As they break down the organic matter, they give off heat; this speeds up decomposition. In a well-mixed heap, temperatures can reach over 150°F.

A good compost heap has a slightly sweet smell. If it smells sour or rotten, then it has too many greens or is too wet. The remedy is to mix in more brown materials. If you follow this recipe, you should get a fine, crumbly-texture compost.

Any remaining large pieces can be sieved or screened out and put into the next compost heap, leaving you with the very best food possible for your plants.

A VOICE OF EXPERIENCE

I love all of the composting instructions that seem to assume that we all have a large quantity of "stuff" to compost all at once. Except for autumn leaves, I expect that most people are like me: I have food prep "stuff" to add almost every day. So I keep a large plastic coffee canister by the kitchen sink. Peels, cores, oops-that-lettuce-is-past-its-prime, tea bags, coffee grounds (*with* the filter), dead leaves from houseplants—you get the idea. When it's full (1 to 3 days), I carry it out to the compost "bin," which is a 30-gallon plastic can that is split slightly on the bottom. I usually layer in some grass clippings that have been drying in the sun for a couple of days. I rinse the coffee canister and add that water. Now and then I turn the garbage can on its side and roll it around a few times—a technique I found in an Almanac article that works surprisingly well to "stir" the pile.   –*Georgia, on Almanac.com*

HOW TO START SEEDS

THINK ABOUT A SEED. ONCE IT LANDS, IT'S STUCK. IT CAN'T MOVE TO FIND BETTER SOIL, MOISTURE, OR SUNLIGHT. IT'S ABLE TO CREATE EVERY PART OF ITSELF TO GROW AND REPRODUCE WITH THE HELP OF AIR, WATER, AND SUN.
–David Suzuki, Canadian environmentalist (b. 1936)

For a successful start indoors, seeds need air, water, and sun, yes, but they also need your time and attention.

Here's how to grow seedlings:

1. Make a list of the plants that you want to grow. (Plan for good spacing between plants by imagining your garden to be one-quarter of its actual size.)

2. Purchase seeds. One seed packet often yields much more than you will need; consider sharing the seeds or, later, the seedlings.

3. Read the seed packet for the best time to plant. Then estimate the time of the last average spring frost in your area by using the Frosts and Growing Seasons table (page 34 or 35), or going to Almanac.com/frostdates for dates specific to your zip or postal code. Start seeds indoors no more than 6 to 7 weeks before the last spring frost.

PREPARE TO PLANT

The growing medium (soil) should be weed- and disease-free, absorbent, and fluffy.

■ Avoid garden soil; it is too heavy and contains weed seeds.

■ Avoid potting soil; it is too dense.

■ Although the use of peat can be considered non–environmentally friendly, peat moss pellets are easy to use for this purpose. After being soaked, they expand and soften. Later, each one can be planted with the seedling in it.

■ If you purchase a bag of sterile seed-starting mixture, note the ingredients. If vermiculite, perlite, and crumbled sphagnum moss are not included, add them to help with drainage.

PLAN FOR POTS

Ideal seed containers are 2 to 3 inches deep. Clean recycled milk cartons, plastic or aluminum "take-out" trays, and yogurt cups work well

GOT OLD SEEDS?

Before you discard old seeds, test their viability. Wet two paper towels with warm water, wring them out, and spread them on a plate. Note each seed type and lay the seeds in rows, 5 to 10 seeds to a row. Cover the plate with plastic wrap and seal it at the edges. Set it on top of the refrigerator. Check occasionally to be sure that the towel does not dry out. Mist it, if necessary.

In about a week, viable seeds should show signs of germination. The percent that germinate should provide a clue to the germination rate of the remaining seeds in the packet.

if you add drainage holes. Commercial trays or pots are another option.

DIY STARTER SOIL

You can make your own medium. You will need:
compost
coir (coconut fiber) or
   well-rotted leaf mold
perlite

Break up or screen the compost, retaining the fine-textured portion. If using coir, soak until it is fibrous and can be easily pulled apart. Mix together 2 parts compost, 2 parts coir (or leaf mold), and 1 part perlite. Store in a covered container in a cool, dry place.

START THE SEEDS

Perform any specific instructions on the seed packets—soaking, scratching, or chilling seeds—before planting.

Start more seeds than you need. (Some will not germinate or will inexplicably die off.) Dampen the medium: Mist and mix it, or put some medium into a plastic bag, add water, and then knead the bag.

Gently but firmly press the damp medium into the containers.

Carefully read the seed packet instructions (again).

Place the seed on the medium, then sprinkle with dry medium two to three times the seed's thickness, or per the instructions on the seed packet. Press gently.

SHARE YOUR BUDS
WITH YOUR "BUDS"
WITH A GARDEN PIC
ON 📌 @ALMANAC

Resist the temptation to sow thickly; seedlings need space. Sow large seeds singly in containers. When sowing fine seeds, press them into the medium; don't cover them.

If the medium has been presoaked, you should not need to water it. If the medium is dry, water carefully. Water poured from a pitcher may come out too forcefully. A mist sprayer is gentle but can take time. A meat-basting syringe dispenses water without causing too much soil disruption. Always use room-temperature water.

Label the containers. Cover them with plastic (a sheet or a bag) and put them in a place that is consistently about 70°F—

atop a refrigerator, behind a woodstove, in a sunny window, or under a light.

Check them every day! When you see green growth, remove the plastic. Transfer the container(s) to a place that is at about 60°F, with increasing light, especially if the seedlings have been in darkness.

SHED A LITTLE LIGHT

Many gardeners succeed in starting seeds on windowsills, rotating them a quarter-turn every day and monitoring moisture. However, even in south-facing windows, the light may be inadequate. Cloudy days or a Sun that is low in the sky—causing too much warmth and too little light—can lead to spindly seedlings.

To get more light on the leaves, you could try homemade reflectors: foil-wrapped cardboard or flat white–painted surfaces behind the plants.

An increasingly popular option is to use compact fluorescent lamp (CFL) or light-emitting diode (LED) lights. Hang CFLs 3 to 6 inches above the containers or LEDs 12 to 24 inches above during the entire growth process. (Can't adjust the height of the light? Raise the containers by putting boxes, books, or pans under them.) Leave the lights on for 16 hours per day, with an 8-hour period of darkness. Maintain the room at about 60°F.

As seedlings develop, water less often—only when the top half of the medium is dry—and from the bottom. Once germination is achieved, provide nutrients. Any all-purpose fertilizer solution mixed at half-strength will do. Apply with a mister. (Seeds contain enough nourishment for a seedling's early days, so when seeds are just starting, nutrients are not necessary.)

THE DISTRESS OF DAMPING OFF

Sometimes seedlings collapse and die for no apparent reason. Often, the problem is "damping off," a disease caused by several fungi and fungus-like organisms and encouraged by poor drainage (too much moisture or dampness), little to no air circulation, and cool soil. To

prevent damping off . . .
■ Avoid overseeding and overwatering.
■ After setting seeds, cover the medium with $1/8$ inch of milled sphagnum moss.
■ Mist seedlings occasionally

THE MISFORTUNE OF MILDEW

The most common cause of mildew on soil is high humidity. Increase the air circulation by lifting the cover on your seedlings. Try to scrape off the mildew without harming the seedlings. To avoid this problem, use starting medium that is viable, new, and soilless. The "lightness" of the material encourages air circulation.

BOOST THE ROOTS

Phosphorus promotes strong root development. To ensure the availability of it in the root zone of new transplants, mix 2 tablespoons of a 15-30-15 starter fertilizer into 1 gallon of water and give each seedling a cup of the solution after transplanting.

with a fish or kelp (seaweed) solution.
■ Increase air circulation by setting a fan on "Low" near the seedlings.

HARDENING OFF

Before transplanting seedlings—homegrown or from a nursery—prepare them for the outdoors. During the plants' last 7 to 10 days indoors, withhold fertilizer and water less often. Each day, set the seedlings outdoors for a few hours in dappled shade, out of the wind. Gradually increase their exposure to full sun and wind. This is the hardening-off period. Keep the soil moist at all times during this stage. Dry air and spring breezes can result in rapid transpiration.

After this experience, your seedlings will be ready for transplanting, but to minimize the risk of losing them . . .
■ Transplant on overcast days or in the early morning, when the sunlight is not too harsh.
■ Set transplants into loose, well-aerated soil. It will capture and retain moisture, drain well, and allow easy penetration by seedling roots.
■ Soak the soil around new seedlings immediately after transplanting.
■ Spread mulch to reduce soil moisture loss and control weeds. Do not put mulch on or near seedlings' stems.

MY SEED-STARTING RECORD

DATE PLANTED	SEED/VARIETY	MEDIUM	DAYS UNTIL TRANSPLANT

U.S. FROSTS AND GROWING SEASONS

Dates given are normal averages for a light freeze; local weather and topography may cause considerable variations. The possibility of frost occurring after the spring dates and before the fall dates is 30 percent. The classification of freeze temperatures is usually based on their effect on plants. **Light freeze:** 29° to 32°F—tender plants killed. **Moderate freeze:** 25° to 28°F—widely destructive to most plants. **Severe freeze:** 24°F and colder—heavy damage to most plants.

–dates courtesy of National Centers for Environmental Information

STATE	CITY	GROWING SEASON (DAYS)	LAST SPRING FROST	FIRST FALL FROST	STATE	CITY	GROWING SEASON (DAYS)	LAST SPRING FROST	FIRST FALL FROST
AK	Juneau	171	Apr. 26	Oct. 15	NC	Fayetteville	212	Apr. 5	Nov. 4
AL	Mobile	269	Mar. 3	Nov. 28	ND	Bismarck	126	May 19	Sept. 23
AR	Pine Bluff	230	Mar. 22	Nov. 8	NE	Omaha	174	Apr. 23	Oct. 15
AZ	Phoenix	354*	Jan. 9	Dec. 30	NE	North Platte	131	May 16	Sept. 25
AZ	Tucson	309*	Feb. 2	Dec. 9	NH	Concord	136	May 15	Sept. 29
CA	Eureka	268	Mar. 4	Nov. 28	NJ	Newark	211	Apr. 6	Nov. 4
CA	Sacramento	281*	Feb. 17	Nov. 26	NM	Carlsbad	223	Mar. 27	Nov. 6
CO	Denver	154	May 4	Oct. 6	NM	Los Alamos	149	May 9	Oct. 6
CO	Grand Junction	159	May 3	Oct. 10	NV	Las Vegas	292*	Feb. 11	Dec. 1
CT	Hartford	165	Apr. 27	Oct. 10	NY	Albany	159	May 2	Oct. 9
DE	Wilmington	199	Apr. 13	Oct. 30	NY	Syracuse	158	May 5	Oct. 11
FL	Orlando	337*	Jan. 30	Jan. 3**	OH	Akron	174	Apr. 30	Oct. 22
FL	Tallahassee	238	Mar. 19	Nov. 13	OH	Cincinnati	179	Apr. 23	Oct. 20
GA	Athens	217	Mar. 31	Nov. 4	OK	Lawton	206	Apr. 7	Oct. 31
GA	Savannah	253	Mar. 12	Nov. 21	OK	Tulsa	207	Apr. 5	Oct. 30
IA	Atlantic	142	May 6	Sept. 26	OR	Pendleton	155	Apr. 30	Oct. 3
IA	Cedar Rapids	155	May 4	Oct. 7	OR	Portland	260	Mar. 6	Nov. 22
ID	Boise	166	Apr. 30	Oct. 14	PA	Franklin	160	May 9	Oct. 17
IL	Chicago	193	Apr. 17	Oct. 28	PA	Williamsport	167	May 1	Oct. 16
IL	Springfield	177	Apr. 20	Oct. 15	RI	Kingston	148	May 8	Oct. 4
IN	Indianapolis	172	Apr. 26	Oct. 16	SC	Charleston	305*	Feb. 17	Dec. 20
IN	South Bend	159	May 7	Oct. 14	SC	Columbia	235	Mar. 21	Nov. 12
KS	Topeka	182	Apr. 19	Oct. 19	SD	Rapid City	144	May 9	Oct. 1
KY	Lexington	185	Apr. 20	Oct. 23	TN	Memphis	229	Mar. 24	Nov. 9
LA	Monroe	238	Mar. 14	Nov. 8	TN	Nashville	206	Apr. 6	Oct. 30
LA	New Orleans	311*	Feb. 8	Dec. 17	TX	Amarillo	184	Apr. 20	Oct. 22
MA	Boston	208	Apr. 8	Nov. 3	TX	Denton	235	Mar. 21	Nov. 12
MA	Worcester	167	Apr. 29	Oct. 14	TX	San Antonio	267	Mar. 2	Nov. 25
MD	Baltimore	192	Apr. 16	Oct. 26	UT	Cedar City	119	May 31	Sept. 28
ME	Portland	160	May 1	Oct. 9	UT	Spanish Fork	162	May 2	Oct. 12
MI	Lansing	151	May 7	Oct. 6	VA	Norfolk	239	Mar. 23	Nov. 18
MI	Marquette	152	May 15	Oct. 15	VA	Richmond	204	Apr. 9	Oct. 31
MN	Duluth	129	May 19	Sept. 26	VT	Burlington	158	May 3	Oct. 9
MN	Willmar	149	May 4	Oct. 1	WA	Seattle	246	Mar. 12	Nov. 14
MO	Jefferson City	193	Apr. 14	Oct. 25	WA	Spokane	158	May 1	Oct. 7
MS	Columbia	243	Mar. 13	Nov. 12	WI	Green Bay	148	May 7	Oct. 3
MS	Tupelo	218	Mar. 30	Nov. 4	WI	Sparta	133	May 15	Sept. 26
MT	Fort Peck	135	May 13	Sept. 26	WV	Parkersburg	186	Apr. 20	Oct. 24
MT	Helena	132	May 15	Sept. 25	WY	Casper	105	June 1	Sept. 15

*In leap years, add 1 day   **In following year

CANADIAN FROSTS AND GROWING SEASONS

Dates given are normal averages for a light freeze; local weather and topography may cause considerable variations. The possibility of frost occurring after the spring dates and before the fall dates is 33 percent. The classification of freeze temperatures is usually based on their effect on plants. **Light freeze:** −2° to 0°C (29° to 32°F)—tender plants killed. **Moderate freeze:** −4° to −2°C (25° to 28°F)—widely destructive to most plants. **Severe freeze:** −4°C (24°F and colder)—heavy damage to most plants.

–dates courtesy of Environment Canada

PROV.	CITY	GROWING SEASON (DAYS)	LAST SPRING FROST	FIRST FALL FROST	PROV.	CITY	GROWING SEASON (DAYS)	LAST SPRING FROST	FIRST FALL FROST
AB	Athabasca	103	May 28	Sept. 9	NT	Fort Simpson	81	May 31	Aug. 21
AB	Calgary	99	May 29	Sept. 6	NT	Norman Wells	91	May 29	Aug. 29
AB	Edmonton	123	May 15	Sept. 16	NT	Yellowknife	102	May 31	Sept. 11
AB	Grande Prairie	106	May 22	Sept. 6	ON	Barrie	147	May 12	Oct. 7
AB	Lethbridge	108	May 25	Sept. 11	ON	Brantford	151	May 5	Oct. 4
AB	Medicine Hat	118	May 18	Sept. 14	ON	Hamilton	160	May 3	Oct. 11
AB	Peace River	96	May 28	Sept. 2	ON	Kapuskasing	75	June 18	Sept. 2
AB	Red Deer	108	May 24	Sept. 10	ON	Kingston	161	Apr. 28	Oct. 7
BC	Abbotsford	168	Apr. 30	Oct. 16	ON	London	141	May 15	Oct. 4
BC	Castlegar	141	May 8	Sept. 27	ON	Ottawa	135	May 13	Sept. 26
BC	Chilliwack	191	Apr. 19	Oct. 28	ON	Owen Sound	147	May 14	Oct. 9
BC	Coombs	139	May 13	Sept. 30	ON	Peterborough	137	May 12	Sept. 27
BC	Dawson Creek	76	June 8	Aug. 24	ON	Sudbury	124	May 21	Sept. 23
BC	Kamloops	152	May 3	Oct. 3	ON	Timmins	86	June 13	Sept. 8
BC	Kelowna	150	May 8	Oct. 6	ON	Toronto	161	May 4	Oct. 13
BC	Nanaimo	163	May 4	Oct. 15	ON	Wawa	97	June 6	Sept. 12
BC	Prince George	120	May 20	Sept. 18	ON	Windsor	172	Apr. 28	Oct. 18
BC	Prince Rupert	145	May 14	Oct. 7	PE	Alberton	122	May 31	Oct. 1
BC	Vancouver	180	Apr. 21	Oct. 19	PE	Charlottetown	142	May 20	Oct. 10
BC	Victoria	208	Apr. 14	Nov. 9	PE	Summerside	154	May 13	Oct. 15
MB	Brandon	92	June 6	Sept. 7	QC	Baie-Comeau	103	June 2	Sept. 14
MB	Lynn Lake	87	June 10	Sept. 6	QC	La Tuque	101	June 5	Sept. 15
MB	The Pas	106	May 31	Sept. 15	QC	Magog	129	May 19	Sept. 26
MB	Thompson	58	June 18	Aug. 16	QC	Montréal	168	Apr. 25	Oct. 11
MB	Winnipeg	116	May 21	Sept. 15	QC	Québec	129	May 17	Sept. 24
NB	Bathurst	101	June 4	Sept. 14	QC	Rimouski	140	May 18	Oct. 6
NB	Fredericton	125	May 22	Sept. 25	QC	Roberval	117	May 25	Sept. 20
NB	Miramichi	115	May 27	Sept. 20	QC	Thetford Mines	128	May 20	Sept. 26
NB	Moncton	103	June 3	Sept. 15	QC	Trois-Rivières	128	May 19	Sept. 25
NB	Saint John	165	Apr. 30	Oct. 13	SK	Moose Jaw	110	May 24	Sept. 12
NL	Corner Brook	129	May 27	Oct. 4	SK	North Battleford	108	May 26	Sept. 12
NL	Gander	115	June 6	Sept. 30	SK	Prince Albert	88	June 7	Sept. 4
NL	Grand Falls	105	June 8	Sept. 22	SK	Regina	91	June 1	Sept. 1
NL	St. John's	117	June 11	Oct. 7	SK	Saskatoon	126	May 15	Sept. 19
NS	Halifax	164	May 8	Oct. 20	SK	Weyburn	107	May 26	Sept. 11
NS	Kentville	122	May 26	Sept. 26	SK	Yorkton	106	May 26	Sept. 10
NS	Sydney	135	May 27	Oct. 10	YT	Dawson	62	June 9	Aug. 11
NS	Truro	103	June 7	Sept. 19	YT	Watson Lake	83	June 6	Aug. 29
NS	Yarmouth	162	May 4	Oct. 14	YT	Whitehorse	72	June 12	Aug. 24

WHEN TO PLANT

Plants marked with an asterisk (*) are profiled in this book.

ANYONE WHO THINKS THAT GARDENING BEGINS IN THE SPRING
AND ENDS IN THE FALL IS MISSING THE BEST PART OF THE WHOLE YEAR.
FOR GARDENING BEGINS IN JANUARY, BEGINS WITH THE DREAM.
– The Country Garden *(1970), by Josephine Nuese, American writer (1901–74)*

When do you plant flowers in the garden? It depends! There is no single day on which everyone everywhere can start planting; local and regional conditions vary greatly. But a few traditional beliefs and practices have proven favorable just about anywhere for centuries.

THE MUD CAKE PRINCIPLES
In spring, grab a handful of garden soil:
■ If you can form it into a ball and it holds its shape, the soil is too wet for planting. It's likely that seeds planted in it will rot.
■ Make a ball of soil and drop it. If it breaks into two clumps, it's still too wet for planting. If the ball crumbles, your garden

is ready for seeds.
■ If the soil sticks to your tools, it's too wet.
■ If the soil crumbles through your fingers like chocolate cake, it's ready for planting.

As soon as the soil crumbles, give it a good stirring and let it sit for several days. Then top-dress it with compost or aged manure.

ANNUAL FLOWERS

Because most annuals are frost tender, you'll need to wait until after the last spring frost date to transplant them into your garden. Below, you'll find a table listing common annuals, when to start their seeds indoors, and when to plant homegrown or purchased seedlings outdoors. Remember to harden off plants—expose them for a few hours per day to outdoor sun and wind—before moving them outside permanently.

FLOWER	START SEEDS INDOORS (WEEKS BEFORE LAST FROST DATE)	TRANSPLANT OUTDOORS
AGERATUM	6-8 weeks	On last frost date
ALYSSUM	6-8 weeks	1-2 weeks before last frost
AMARANTH	6-8 weeks	After last frost
BACHELOR'S BUTTON	6-8 weeks	On last frost date
CALENDULA	6-8 weeks	1-2 weeks before last frost
CELOSIA	6-8 weeks	On last frost date
COLEUS	8-10 weeks	1-2 weeks after last frost
COSMOS	6-8 weeks	On last frost date
DELPHINIUM*	6-8 weeks	1-2 weeks before last frost
GOMPHRENA	6-8 weeks	On last frost date
MARIGOLD	6-8 weeks	On last frost date
MORNING GLORY†	3-4 weeks	After last frost
NICOTIANA	6-8 weeks	On last frost date
PANSY	8-10 weeks	On last frost date
PETUNIA	8-10 weeks	On last frost date
PHLOX	8-10 weeks	On last frost date
PORTULACA	6-8 weeks	On last frost date
SALVIA*	6-8 weeks	On last frost date
SCABIOSA	6-8 weeks	On last frost date
SNAPDRAGON	8-10 weeks	On last frost date
STATICE	6-8 weeks	On last frost date
STOCK	8-10 weeks	On last frost date
STRAWFLOWER	6-8 weeks	On last frost date
SUNFLOWER*†	3-4 weeks	1-2 weeks after last frost
VERBENA	8-10 weeks	On last frost date
ZINNIA†	4-6 weeks	1-2 weeks after last frost

†These fast-growing annuals are often started outdoors after the danger of frost has passed.

PERENNIAL FLOWERS

Starting perennials from seed can be an inexpensive way to fill up a flower bed. Certain plants may be more challenging than others: Some seeds need a period of cold temperatures before they will germinate and some may also take longer to germinate. Always follow the instructions on your seed packet. Apply the transplant guidance below to homegrown and purchased seedlings.

FLOWER	START SEEDS INDOORS (WEEKS BEFORE LAST FROST DATE)	TRANSPLANT OUTDOORS
ANISE HYSSOP	8-10 weeks	On last frost date
BEE BALM*	8-10 weeks	On last frost date
BLACK-EYED SUSAN*	8-10 weeks	1-2 weeks before last frost
BLANKET FLOWER	8-10 weeks	On last frost date
CATMINT	8-10 weeks	On last frost date
COLUMBINE*	8-10 weeks	On last frost date
COMMON MILKWEED	10-12 weeks	1-2 weeks after last frost
CONEFLOWER*	8-10 weeks	On last frost date
COREOPSIS*	8-10 weeks	On last frost date
DAISY	10-12 weeks	1-2 weeks before last frost
DELPHINIUM*	10-12 weeks	1-2 weeks before last frost
DIANTHUS*	10-12 weeks	1-2 weeks before last frost
FOXGLOVE*	10-12 weeks	1-2 weeks after last frost
HELIOPSIS	10-12 weeks	1-2 weeks after last frost
HIBISCUS	8-10 weeks	1-2 weeks after last frost
HOLLYHOCK*	8-10 weeks	On last frost date
PHLOX	10-12 weeks	1-2 weeks after last frost
VIOLA	8-10 weeks	1-2 weeks before last frost
YARROW	8-10 weeks	On last frost date

THE FOOTPRINT TEST
Step into the garden and then step back and look at the footprint in the soil.
■ If it's shiny, then there's too much water near the soil surface to dig and plant.
■ If it's dull, excess water has drained away and it's time to plant.

KNOW YOUR FROST DATE
Whether you start your seeds or purchase seedlings, it's best to pay attention to your area's last spring (and first fall) frost dates because young plants are more susceptible to a freeze. Use the frost dates on pages 34 and 35 to determine when it's safe to plant outdoors. For dates specific to your zip or postal code, go to Almanac .com/frostdates.

MY PLANTING RECORD

PLANT	LOCATION	DATE PLANTED

FLOWERS

ASTER

Aster spp., *Symphyotrichum* spp.

THE ASTER HAS NOT WASTED SPRING AND SUMMER BECAUSE
IT HAS NOT BLOSSOMED. IT HAS BEEN ALL THE TIME PREPARING
FOR WHAT IS TO FOLLOW, AND IN AUTUMN IT IS THE GLORY
OF THE FIELD, AND ONLY THE FROST LAYS IT LOW.
–Henry Ward Beecher, American Congregational minister (1813–87)

Asters are daisylike perennials with star-shape flower heads that range in color from white to blue to purple. They enliven the garden in late summer and autumn, when many summer blooms are fading.

Even though there are more than 600 aster species, the two most commonly encountered for the home garden are the native New England aster (*Symphyotrichum novae-angliae,* formerly *Aster novae-angliae*) and the native New York aster (*S. novi-belgii,* formerly *A. novi-belgii*). A number of hybrid varieties are available in showy pinks, blues, and purples, yet "wild-type" species native to specific locales are generally a wise choice despite not being as flashy as the cultivated varieties.

Aster is versatile: Depending on the variety, its height can range from 8 inches to 6 feet, making it suitable for borders, rock gardens, or wildflower gardens. The flowers attract bees and butterflies, providing them with an important late-season supply of nectar. Its tasty seed heads are sought by cardinals, chickadees, finches, nuthatches, and many other seed eaters.

PLANTING

Asters prefer areas with cool, moist summers as well as cool nights, in sites with full to partial sun. In warmer climates, they do not like the hot midday sun.

Soil should be loamy and moist but well-draining. Mix 2 to 3 inches of compost into it prior to planting.

Asters can be grown from seed, but germination can be uneven. If desired, plant seeds outside in the fall or start them indoors in winter: Sow seeds 1 inch deep in pots or flats and refrigerate them for 4 to 6 weeks to simulate winter dormancy. This cold period will kick-start germination.

Seven to 8 weeks before planting, place the pots/flats in a sunny spot with a temperature of 60° to 62°F. Transplant seedlings outside in mid- to late spring after the danger of frost has passed.

Plant mature, potted asters as soon as they become available at garden centers (typically, in the fall). Space plants 1 to 3 feet apart, depending on the type and size.

Water well and spread mulch around the plants to keep the soil cool and prevent weeds.

CARE

Add a thin layer of compost (or a portion of balanced fertilizer) with a

RECOMMENDED VARIETIES

New England asters *(Symphyotrichum novae-angliae)*: many varieties, with flower colors from magenta to deep purple and white; sizes vary

New York asters *(S. novi-belgii)*: many varieties, with flower colors from bright pink to bluish-purple; may be double, semidouble, or single

Blue wood (or heartleaf) aster *(S. cordifolium)*: bushy with small, blue to white flowers; tolerates shade

Heath aster *(S. ericoides)*: a low-growing ground cover, with small, (usually) white flowers

Smooth aster *(S. laeve)*: tall and upright, with small, lavender flowers

'Mönch' Frikart's aster *(Aster x frikartii)*: a Swiss hybrid; large, lilac-blue flowers; Zones 5 to 10, but not reliably winter-hardy in Zone 5

'Nanus' Rhone aster *(A. sedifolius)*: native to Europe; small, lilac-blue flowers; compact growth

WIT & WISDOM

● *The name "aster" comes from the ancient Greek word for "star"—*
a reference to its flower shape.

● *Asters are called "Michaelmas daisies" because they bloom*
around September 29, which is the ancient feast day of St. Michael and
a "quarter day," marking the transition to autumn.

off-season interest. Note that fully mature flowers may reseed themselves, but resulting asters may not bloom true to the parent.

To maintain plant vigor and flower quality, divide every 2 to 3 years in spring.

DISEASES/PESTS (*see pages 190–200*)
Diseases: aster yellows; blight, Botrytis; leaf spot, fungal; mildew, powdery; rust; rot, Rhizoctonia root and stem; smut, white; wilt, Fusarium; wilt, Verticillium. *Pests:* aphids; nematodes, foliar; slugs/snails; Tarsonemid mites.

2-inch layer of mulch around the plants in spring to encourage vigorous growth.

If less than 1 inch of rain falls per week in summer, water regularly. But beware: Many asters are sensitive to too much or too little moisture. They will lose their lower foliage or not flower well. Watch for stress and try a different watering method if your plants are losing flowers.

Stake the tall varieties to keep them from falling over.

Pinch back asters once or twice in early summer to promote bushier growth and more blooms.

In winter, cut back asters after the foliage has died or retain it to provide

HARVEST
Cut asters for flower arrangements when blooms are just beginning to open. Vase life is 5 to 10 days.

A VOICE OF EXPERIENCE

I planted some aster flowers last fall, so I started to get flowering from the beginning of summer. A few of them started drying up, so I bought a net to prevent excess sunlight. Now they are doing well. Thank you!
–Steve, on Almanac.com

ASTILBE

Astilbe spp.

ASTILBE MY HEART!
—Anonymous

Astilbe (*Astilbe* spp.) produces spikes of showy flowers atop glossy, fernlike foliage beginning in late spring. The flower clusters, in pale to dark pinks or white, vary in size from 6 inches to 2 feet, and the plant height ranges from 6 inches to 5 feet, depending on the variety. Astilbes add perennial color and texture to a shady place.

PLANTING

Astilbes prefer light to moderate shade; deep shade will result in few and/or poor flowers, and full sun will burn the tender foliage.

These plants demand well-draining soil, especially in winter. Puddling will ensure their failure, but in summer, damp conditions are important. Amend

WIT & WISDOM

• *Almost every* A. *x* arendsii *hybrid can be traced to German nurseryman George Arends (1862–1952).*

• *Astilbe can be confused with goatsbeard* (Aruncus dioicus), *aka bride's feathers, a shrub that is native to North America and bears white flower plumes over fernlike foliage in early summer.*

---

the soil to increase fertility, especially in clay types, with compost or aged manure (astilbes are heavy feeders); add perlite and coarse sand to improve drainage. They prefer a soil pH of slightly acidic to neutral.

When started from seeds, astilbes can be difficult to germinate, and resulting plants tend to be short-lived. Division is recommended.

Plant purchased plants in spring or fall about 1 to 3 feet apart, depending on the type. If setting bare-root plants, dig holes that are twice as wide as the plants' roots and 4 to 6 inches deep. Allow for the crown to be 1 to 2 inches below the soil surface. Fan the roots slightly, while pointing them downward. Cover with soil and press firmly.

Water well and keep consistently moist (not soaked).

CARE

Check that astilbes are moist. If rain does not occur, water deeply, regularly; do not sprinkle frequently.

VOICES OF EXPERIENCE

I have had a row of astilbe growing on the east side of my house for a decade, between my sidewalk and the foundation. It is in a sandy soil. I thought that I had lost them last summer during an extremely hot summer drought in SW Ontario, Canada. They died right back, and I had only one with any leaves on it. Surprisingly, they came back this spring as if nothing happened. I don't think these flowers are difficult to grow at all if they are in the right place.

–*EJB, on Almanac.com*

I planted 12 to 18 astilbes, 3 varieties, in early April. A couple did not come up. However, the rest did and some are already in bloom 6 weeks later. I would say they are very easy to grow: filtered morning and afternoon sun. No special watering needs but may require some extra watering this summer.

–*Vicky, on Almanac.com*

I live in Fairbanks, Alaska, rated Zones 2 to 3, and my astilbes do very well. I put ground cover and leaves over them in the fall, and they return every year.

–*Janet, on Almanac.com*

RECOMMENDED VARIETIES

Popular hybrids include . . .

- *Astilbe* x *arendsii* 'Fanal': dark crimson flowers; about 1¹/₂ feet tall

- *A.* x *arendsii* 'Irrlicht': elegant white flowers; up to 2 feet tall

- *A.* x *arendsii* 'Venus': bright pink flowers; up to 3 feet tall

Fertilize twice a year: Apply a balanced organic compound in spring and a high-nitrogen fertilizer in fall.

Astilbes spread quickly, forming broad clumps with crowns that rise above the soil. Cover the crowns with compost-rich soil or lift and replant.

Divide overgrown clumps every 3 or 4 years in spring. Replant the divisions immediately or put them in pots to be planted in early summer.

After the bloom period, clip off any spent flower stems. The foliage will hold visual appeal until fall.

After the first frost, the leaves may yellow. Trim them, if desired. Fresh growth will return in spring.

DISEASES/PESTS *(see pages 190–200)*

Astilbe tends to be rabbit- and deer-resistant. *Diseases:* leaf spot, bacterial; leaf spot, fungal; mildew, powdery; viruses; wilt, Fusarium. *Pests:* nematodes, foliar; nematodes, root-knot; tarnished plant bugs.

HARVEST

Cut astilbe flowers and leaves for arrangements or flowers for drying. Note: Removing flower heads will not promote continued flowering. Vase life is 4 to 12 days.

BEE BALM

Monarda spp.

THE SCARLET BEE-BALM BLAZES
. . . BENEATH THE SULTRY AUGUST SUN, DOWN SHINING BRIGHT AND CLEAR.
–"Remembering" (1893), by Dorothy H. Barron

A perennial favorite native to North America and member of the mint family, bee balm (*Monarda* spp.), aka wild bergamot, displays red, pink, purple, or white blooms in mid- to late summer—and bears fragrant foliage. In the garden, its most frequent visitors are hummingbirds, bees, butterflies, and moths, which have the long tongues required to reach the tubular flowers' nectar. The seed heads attract birds in fall and winter.

PLANTING
Plant bee balm in spring or fall in full sunshine or partial shade.

Provide rich, well-draining soil with a neutral pH. Amend with compost or aged manure, if necessary.

Give careful thought to placement: Without good air circulation, the leaves can develop powdery mildew. (Reduce watering if this appears.) Space plants 18 to 24 inches apart: Mature bee balm plants reach 2 to 4 feet in height, making them excellent background plants.

Water thoroughly.

CARE

Keep soil evenly moist throughout the growing season.

Add mulch to preserve moisture and control weeds.

Avoid fertilizer in general; apply only a sprinkling of a balanced product in spring, if desired. An excess can promote powdery mildew and/or rampant succulent growth.

Deadhead faded blooms to encourage rebloom in late summer.

After the first fall frost, leave seed heads for the birds or cut stems back to about 2 inches above the soil.

Divide every 2 to 3 years to ensure its vigor. (Clumps tend to die out from the center.)

In spring, make small divisions of newer roots of established plants and replant.

DISEASES/PESTS *(see pages 190–200)*
Diseases: blight, southern; leaf spot, fungal; mildew, powdery; rust. *Pests:* aphids; spider mites; stalk borers; thrips.

HARVEST
Cut flowers for arrangements when they are just opening. Vase life is 7 days.

RECOMMENDED VARIETIES

Monarda didyma: bright red flowers; 3 to 4 feet tall.

M. didyma varieties that are resistant to powdery mildew include 'Marshall's Delight' (bright pink), 'Jacob Cline' (deep red), and 'Raspberry Wine' (dark red).

M. fistulosa: lavender-pink blooms, in late summer; tolerant of dry soils; commonly called "wild bergamot"

M. pringlei: immune to powdery mildew; reaches 18 inches tall. 'Petite Wonder' and 'Petite Delight' are pink varieties.

WIT & WISDOM

- *Native Americans and early colonists used bee balm leaves and flowers in medicinal salves and drinks.*

- *The Native American word for a river in New York became part of the name of a bee balm drink: Oswego tea.*

- *Although called "wild bergamot," this plant is not used in "bergamot" (Earl Grey) tea, which is made from the rind of the bergamot orange.*

BLACK-EYED SUSAN

Rudbeckia hirta and other species

I KNOW A PLAIN OLD-FASHIONED FARMHOUSE DOWN A PRETTY LITTLE LANE
WHERE YELLOW DAISIES MAKE A PATHWAY TO THE FIELDS OF GOLDEN GRAIN.
THERE A LITTLE GIRL IS WAITING WHERE I FOUND HER YEARS AGO;
SOMETHING TELLS ME THAT I'M WELCOME WHERE THE BLACK-EYED SUSANS GROW.
–*"Where Black-Eyed Susans Grow," by Dave Radford, Canadian lyricist (1884–1968)*

The "black eye" of this popular wildflower refers to the dark brown center of its daisylike flower head. A member of the aster family, Asteraceae, and native to eastern North America, it has become naturalized in Zones 3 to 9.

Black-eyed Susan, aka Gloriosa daisy, blooms from June to September, often blanketing open fields with its golden-yellow beauty. Butterflies, bees, and other insects are attracted to the flowers.

These are outstanding cut flowers that also do well in borders or containers.

PLANTING

Black-eyed Susan thrives in full sunshine. It tolerates partial sun, but it will not bloom as reliably.

It prefers rich, well-draining soil, although plants will tolerate low fertility.

If direct-seeding, plant in moist, well-draining, warm (70° to 75°F) soil. Cover lightly with soil; sunlight is required for germination. Indoors, sow seeds 8 to 10 weeks before the last frost. Germination takes 7 to 10 days.

Set seeds and plants close to deter spreading or farther apart for a border and to prevent the spread of disease.

Black-eyed Susan spreads by self-seeding (after the first year) and underground rhizomes; this can result in it overtaking other nearby flowers.

CARE

Check plants regularly to see if they need watering; avoid letting them dry out but also avoid excess moisture on the leaves, as it can encourage disease (provide plants with proper spacing).

Remove dead plant material in the

RECOMMENDED VARIETIES

Black-eyed Susans grow 1 to 3 feet tall or more; dwarfs reach no more than 1 foot. Plants can spread 12 to 18 inches.

Varieties can be annual, biennial, or perennial.

Rudbeckia hirta is a biennial, or short-lived perennial. It produces showy flowers and self-seeds abundantly. Some of its many hybrids include . . .

• 'Autumn Colors': yellow, orange, red, and brown flowers; 18- to 24-inch stems

• 'Becky Mixed': lemon-yellow, golden-yellow, dark red, and reddish-brown flowers; 10- to 16-inch stems

• 'Prairie Sun': All-America Selections winner; 4- to 6-inch bright orange flowers that fade to yellow at the tips; 28- to 32-inch stems

• 'Sonora': large, golden flowers with big, chocolate-brown centers; 12- to 16-inch stems

• 'Toto Gold': dwarf type; classic yellow flowers with black centers; 12- to 16-inch stems; ideal for containers

spring to reduce the risk of infection.

Divide every 3 to 4 years to ensure healthy plants and to prevent excessive spreading.

Remove faded/dead flowers to prolong blooming and minimize self-seeding.

Cutting back black-eyed Susan after flowering may result in a second, smaller bloom in late fall.

Leave some dried seed heads on the plants in the fall to attract birds.

To prevent underground spread, dig up rhizomes, making certain to remove the entire piece of root. Even a small section of rhizome can produce another plant.

DISEASES/PESTS *(see pages 190–200)*
Black-eyed Susan is deer-resistant. *Diseases:* aster yellows; blight, Botrytis; blight, southern; leaf spot, angular; leaf spot, fungal; mildew, downy; mildew, powdery; rust; smut, white; wilt, Verticillium. *Pests:* aphids; nematodes, foliar; slugs/snails.

HARVEST
Cut flowers for display just before buds completely open. Use large blooms as centerpieces and smaller ones as accents. Change the water every day to keep them fresh. Vase life is 8 to 10 days.

WIT & WISDOM

- *Black-eyed Susan symbolizes justice.*
- *The genus name* Rudbeckia *honors Swedish scientists Olaus Rudbeck (1630–1702) and his son, Olof Rudbeck (1660–1740).*
- *The species name* hirta *means "hairy" and refers to the short bristles that cover the leaves.*

BLEEDING HEART

Dicentra spp.

ONCE TWO HEARTS FIND EACH OTHER, NO ONE SHOULD GET BETWEEN THEM—
OTHERWISE, ONE BLEEDING HEART WILL REMAIN.

–Author unknown

The old-fashioned bleeding heart has long been a favorite perennial of the shady flower garden; it was once called the finest hardy plant of the 19th century. Soon thereafter, though, it became considered to be as "common as a wallpaper pattern."

Today, it is back in favor because it is easy to grow and nothing surpasses its fascinating form: graceful, arching, 3-foot stems adorned with dangling pink (or white) flower hearts that appear to be dripping (hence its most common name).

PLANTING

Plant bleeding heart in spring after the threat of frost has passed. It is hardy in Zones 2 to 9.

Choose a site in partial or light shade; it can thrive in full sun in northern regions, if given adequate moisture.

Bleeding heart requires fertile and well-draining yet moderately moist soil, with a neutral to slightly alkaline pH. Add compost or aged manure before planting to improve fertility.

Water to soak the soil after planting.

WIT & WISDOM

- *This early-spring bloomer is also known as lady's locket, lady's heart, and lyre flower.*
- *D. spectabilis is native to Japan, Korea, and northeastern China.*

Spread mulch to keep moisture in and weeds out.

CARE

In spring, apply a thin layer of compost, followed by mulch, to help retain moisture and deter weeds.

Keep soil moist but not soggy. Water if rainfall is less than 1 inch per week. The plant tolerates drought and is fire-resistant.

Bleeding heart blooms in spring and finishes its growing cycle when warm weather sets in. The flowers fade and the leaves die back. The plant goes dormant in late spring/early summer. Cut back leaves and stems when they begin to yellow and wither away.

Bleeding heart does not like to be moved. It will thrive for years without being divided or replanted. If transplanting is necessary, do it as soon as the first leaves poke out of the soil in early spring.

Propagate by division in early spring just before growth starts or by root cuttings in autumn. Bleeding heart also self-seeds prodigiously.

DISEASES/PESTS *(see pages 190–200)*
Bleeding heart is rabbit- and deer-resistant. *Diseases:* aster yellows; blight, southern; leaf spot, fungal; mildew, powdery; viruses; wilt, Fusarium; wilt, Verticillium. *Pest:* aphids.

HARVEST

Entire stems of bleeding heart can be used as cut flowers. Vase life is up to 2 weeks.

A PRESSING MATTER

The bleeding heart is lovely as a pressed flower. Pick flowers early in the morning but after the dew has dried. Put them between between two sheets of paper and place this bundle between the pages of a thick book. After a couple of weeks, open to find perfectly flat, papery hearts.

RECOMMENDED VARIETIES

There are more than 20 species of *Dicentra*, plus many hybrids . . .

- *Dicentra spectabilis* 'Gold Heart': chartreuse foliage

- *D. spectabilis* 'Alba': white flowers

- *D. spectabilis* 'Valentine': white-tip cherry-red blooms on burgundy stems

- *D. eximia* 'Zestful': native to North America; "fringed" (fern-leaf) foliage, with pale pink flowers; 12 to 18 inches tall

- *D. cucullaria* (aka "Dutchman's breeches"): native to eastern U.S.; fragrant, yellow-tip white flowers resembling pantaloons; 4 to 12 inches tall

CANNA

Canna x *generalis*

**I DECIDED THAT IF I COULD PAINT THAT FLOWER IN A HUGE SCALE,
YOU COULD NOT IGNORE ITS BEAUTY.**
–Georgia O'Keeffe, American painter (1887–1986), speaking of her work titled Red Canna

Cannas are spectacular summer bulbs: Paddle-shape leaves wrap in ruffles around stems tapering to refined buds that open into eye-catching flowers of red, orange, yellow, and pink from late spring or early summer to first frost. When most flowers can't take the heat of late July and early August, cannas thrive.

Cannas can be both focal points and stylish accents. Use them to bring structure as a tall border or to add depth to narrow spaces. Center them in large patio pots and surround them with bright annuals. Cannas bring a tropical touch to water features, and they thrive in boggy areas. Indoors, display them in large containers near brightly lit windows.

Cannas are commonly referred to as "bulbs," although they are not true bulbs; they multiply beneath the soil from a rhizome.

PLANTING

Cannas can not tolerate cold temperatures. Soil must be 60°F or warmer. In short-season areas, start cannas in pots indoors or in a greenhouse.

The plants will tolerate partial shade but require at least 4 hours of direct sunlight. They need fertile, moist soil. Before planting, loosen the soil to a depth of 12 to 15 inches, then mix in 2 to 4 inches of compost.

Dig a hole 2 to 3 inches deep and set the rhizome in it, with the "eyes"

RECOMMENDED VARIETIES

Giant cannas can reach up to 8 feet—for example, 'Musifolia', with 3-foot-long red-vein leaves and red blooms. Here are some other exemplars . . .

• Tropicanna: tangerine, irislike blooms; exotic bronze foliage; 4 to 6 feet tall

• 'Los Angeles': large, deep pink florets; 4 to 5 feet tall

Dwarf cannas stand 2 to 4 feet tall:

• 'Picasso': bright yellow flowers with deep red spots; 2 to 3 feet tall

• 'Wyoming': lush orange flowers; dark burgundy stems; 3 to 4 feet tall

WIT & WISDOM

• *These perennials are sometimes called "canna lilies,"*
but they are unrelated to true lilies.
• *The name "canna" comes from the Greek word* kanna, *meaning "reed" or reedlike plant.*
• *Cannas' bright flowers attract hummingbirds.*
• *During the Victorian era, gardeners so loved cannas that they grew them from seed, but this isn't easy: The germination rate is low, and the seeds need to be filed or given an acid bath to break down their hard coat.*

(bumps or nodes from which growth sprouts) pointed up. Cover with 1 to 2 inches of soil. Tamp firmly.

Space rhizomes 1 to 4 feet apart. If possible, position plants out of strong wind; their large, soft leaves are vulnerable to damage.

Water thoroughly, then withhold water—for as long as 3 weeks—and watch for signs of growth. Cannas are slow to sprout. Once sprouted, water at least once a week by slowly soaking the area around the roots.

CARE

If rainfall is less than 1 inch per week, water. Provide a good soaking every other day during the hottest weeks of summer. Water freely in dry spells.

Maintain a thin layer of mulch to help retain moisture.

Stake tall varieties, if necessary.

Where soil is fertile, fertilizer is optional. If desired, apply a 5-10-5 or 10-10-10 fertilizer in spring and twice during the growing season. Fish emulsion fertilizer, a little higher in nitrogen, is a beneficial organic alternative. (Higher-nitrogen fertilizers tend to increase canna height.) Rose or tomato food products are also suitable.

As flowers fade, deadhead to promote continued flowering. After it has been deadheaded several times and with flowers no longer forthcoming, cut the flower stem back to the foliage.

DISEASES/PESTS *(see pages 190–200)*
Canna is seldom bothered by deer. *Diseases:* aster yellows; blight, Botrytis;

TO GAUGE SOIL TEMPERATURE

Dig a 2-inch-deep hole and push an old-fashioned mercury thermometer into the soil. Or apply phenology: Plant when tomatoes are set out or when lily-of-the-valley is in full bloom.

leaf spot, fungal; rot, bacterial bud; rust; viruses. *Pests:* canna leaf rollers; nematodes, root-knot; slugs/snails; spider mites.

STORING FOR WINTER

Bring cannas grown in pots into a garage or basement for winter. Keep them dry until spring's nighttime temperatures are consistently above 50°F, typically after the tulips have bloomed in northern areas. Only then move them outside for the summer.

In northern areas that experience harsh winter conditions, it is necessary to dig up (lift) in-ground cannas in the fall and bring them inside for the winter. Generally, this means Zone 6 or colder, although Zone 7 may also occasionally experience canna-killing winter temperatures. In Zones 8 and warmer, cannas can be left in the ground year-round.

After the first fall frost kills the foliage but before a hard freeze occurs, cut in-ground plants back to 4 inches. (It is not essential for canna foliage to be frosted prior to digging, but this is recommended.)

Plunge a shovel or garden fork into the soil about 1 foot away from the stem (to avoid damaging the rhizome). With

VOICES OF EXPERIENCE

Cannas were in my dad's homeplace before he was born. When his family moved away, they left them. Fifty years later, his older sister went back and brought some home and planted them. The house was gone; the whole community was gone. My dad passed away 2 years ago; he was 95. I transplanted the cannas again after he died. They are over 100 years old.

–*Johnny, on Almanac.com*

I have lived in various desert cities, and now in the high desert in New Mexico. I rely on cannas as a sure thing. They are tropical, but they thrive everywhere I plant them. Last year, I bought a bag of three or four cannas. They love the hot, full sun! I'm not used to freezes, and apparently my cannas are not either: The first hard frost did them in. I just cut them down to the ground and covered the sprawling masses of (still visible) tubers with big rocks. This year, they are thriving again! I have divided those original three or four bulbs multiple times, put some in pots, put others in various spots around my yard, and all do well. I have no shade, so all are in full, hot sun.

–*Patty, on Almanac.com*

your hands, gently loosen the soil and lift out the clump. Shake off the dirt and cut off the foliage. Divide clumps into three to five rhizomes, each with eyes.

Cure the rhizomes in the sun or in a garage or closet for a few days to toughen them up and help them to resist rot.

Wrap each rhizome in newspapers or a paper bag, along with a small amount of dry growing medium such as peat moss, to absorb moisture and prevent rot. Rhizomes should not touch each other.

Store cannas over the winter in a dry place where the temperature will not drop below 40°F (often, this is an attic or basement).

Check the rhizomes a couple of times over the winter to make sure that they don't dry out. Mist with a bit of water, as needed. If you find rot, trim it away or discard the entire rhizome. (It is common that not all survive the winter.)

When replanting, make sure that each divided piece has at least one eye; from it, new leaves will grow. Plant 4 to 5 inches deep and 1 to 4 feet apart. Blooms should appear in 10 to 12 weeks.

CHRYSANTHEMUM

Chrysanthemum x *morifolium*

WHY DON'T YOU GET A HAIRCUT? YOU LOOK LIKE A CHRYSANTHEMUM.
–P. G. Wodehouse, English writer (1881–1975)

Chrysanthemums, aka "mums," the quintessential autumn flower, celebrate the season in jewel colors: yellow, lavender, pink, purple, red, bronze, orange, and white. Each bloom consists of tiny flowers called florets. Bloom forms range in size from pincushion petite to giant spiders, and there are hundreds from which to chose.

PLANTING

Mums are hardy perennials best planted in early spring. They generally grow to a width and height of 1 to 3 feet. Set them 18 to 36 inches apart, depending on their expected size at maturity. Mums need good air circulation.

Start mums indoors from seed 6 to 8 weeks before the last spring frost date.

Select a planting site in full sun, away from trees and big shrubs but dark at night, or shade the plants every night from light sources such as street and security lights. Bloom time is determined by day length (12 hours or less), and buds start forming then.

Plants that receive light at night will be slow to bud.

Mums require rich, well-draining soil. They do not like standing water and will quickly rot if left too wet. Prepare by adding aged manure or compost to the soil (mums are heavy feeders).

Plant the mum in the ground at the same depth that it was grown at in the pot.

Water and keep it evenly moist.

CARE

Fertilize monthly by sprinkling a balanced fertilizer (10-10-10) around the plant.

Spread mulch to conserve soil moisture and minimize weeds.

Soak the soil deeply when watering. Avoid watering the leaves.

Pinch back stems to create a bushier plant: When new shoots are 3 to 4 inches tall, pinch off the top, leaving two or three leaves on the shoot. Continue pinching every 2 to 3 weeks until mid-July, when flower buds develop. On the West Coast, stop pinching in early July; in the South, stop in early August.

Stop fertilizing when flower buds emerge.

For big flowers, pinch off all buds except the largest and strongest on each stem. Remove secondary buds farther down the stem as they develop, too. Switch to a high-nitrogen fertilizer after buds have set. If flower size does not matter, stop fertilizing in mid-August.

After the ground has frozen, spread 4 to 6 inches of mulch around the plant.

Do not cut back mums in fall. The dead growth insulates the roots. Cut off the dead stems and leaves when you see the first green shoots in spring.

OVERWINTERING

In extremely cold areas, overwinter plants in a basement or dark, cold closet. Pot up plants after the first frost in the fall, capturing as many of the roots as possible. Leave the foliage on the plants until spring.

Water well and keep the roots damp. Check pots weekly.

In spring, gradually introduce the plants to light. Set them out after the last killing frost.

DIVISION

Every 2 or 3 years, divide a mum when new growth appears in spring. Use a knife to cut out the old central portion of the plant. Discard it. Cut the

WIT & WISDOM

- *The chrysanthemum was first cultivated in China as a flowering herb in the 15th century B.C.*
- *The name "chrysanthemum" comes from the Greek words* chrys, *meaning "golden," and* anthemion, *meaning "flower."*
- *It's said that a single chrysanthemum petal placed in the bottom of a glass of wine enhances the imbiber's longevity.*

remaining portion into sections that each have several shoots and good roots. Replant these sections.

DOUBLE TIME

Southerners enjoy the colorful displays of blooming mums twice yearly because the equal days and nights of temperate weather that spur mums to bloom arrive in spring and fall. Northerners must be satisfied with one show, in autumn.

PRETTY, JUST NOT PERENNIAL

Treat mums sold in garden centers in autumn as annuals; do not try to over-winter them. They are not bred to be hardy. If put in the ground, many won't make it through a cold winter.

DISEASES/PESTS *(see pages 190–200)*

Diseases: aster yellows; blight, Ascochyta ray; crown gall; leaf spot, bacterial; leaf spot, fungal; mildew, powdery; rot, Pythium root and stem; rot, Rhizoctonia root and stem; viruses; wilt, Fusarium; wilt, Verticillium. *Pests:* aphids; nematodes, foliar; spider mites.

HARVEST

Cut flowers for arrangements when they are nearly or fully open. Vase life is 7 to 10 days.

RECOMMENDED VARIETIES

Mums belong to one of 13 classes based on flower form and petal shape:

1. Irregular Incurve—giant blooms, e.g., 'Bola de Oro' (gold)

2. Reflex—very large to medium blooms, e.g., 'Pretty Polly' (purple, with pink reverses)

3. Regular Incurve—ball-shape, e.g., 'George Couchman' (bronze)

4. Decorative—flattened, e.g., 'Coral Charm' (salmon)

5. Intermediate Incurve—more open than other incurves, e.g., 'St. Tropez' (crimson, with bronze reverse)

6. Pompom—balls, e.g., 'Kevin Mandarin' (deep orange)

7. Single and Semidouble—concave/convex, e.g., 'Domingo' (crimson, with yellow center)

8. Anemone—single, e.g., 'Daybreak' (apricot, with yellow center)

9. Spoon—single/daisy with tipped ends, e.g., 'Kimie' (yellow, with green center)

10. Quill—tubular florets, e.g., 'King's Delight' (true pink)

11. Spider—varying florets, e.g., 'Lava' (yellow, with red tips)

12. Brush or Thistle—upright florets, e.g., 'Wisp of Pink' (yellow center)

13. Unclassified or Exotic—irregular, e.g., 'Lone Star' (pure white)

Extra-hardy Mums
These will survive in frigid climates: 'Betty Lou' Maxi Mum, 'Burnt Copper', 'Centerpiece', 'Grape Glow', 'Lemonsota', 'Maroon Pride', 'Mellow Moon', 'Minnautumn', 'Minnpink', 'Minnruby', 'Minnwhite', 'Minnyellow', 'Rose Blush', 'Sesqui Centennial Sun', 'Snowscape'

CLEMATIS

Clematis spp.

So many beginning gardeners plunk a plant in the ground, water it once or twice, and then walk away. Varieties of clematis are capable of tremendous growth, but they need plenty of water right away if they are to thrive and live **50** years or longer.

—Dan Long, nurseryman, Athens, Georgia

Clematis, the "Queen of the Vines," may be best known for its large-flowering, purple, star-shape blooms on twining vines—but did you know that there are more than 300 species and hundreds of hybrids of this plant, with flowers in the form of saucers, bells, tubes, tulips, open bells, doubles, and semidoubles? Small-flowering varieties produce an abundance of blossoms that last longer than larger ones. Many varieties are scented. Some are vines, while others are shrub types. Some species bloom in spring; others, in mid- to late summer. Most clematises are hardy in Zones 4 to 8 and native to North America.

Clematises appreciate a trellis, post, or stationary structure to climb; without something, the vine will sprawl, including over ground. Hummingbirds, bees, and butterflies love their elegant blooms.

WIT & WISDOM

- *The name "clematis" comes from the ancient Greek* klematis, *for a climbing vine.*
- *Clematis belongs to the buttercup family (*Ranunculaceae*).*
- *Wild clematises* (Clematis virginiana), *aka old man's beard, virgin's bower, and devil's darning needles, can grow 20 feet in 1 year.*
- *Centuries ago, Europeans used clematis vines to make baskets and fish traps.*

PLANTING

Most clematis varieties need at least 6 hours of full sun; however, the sensitive roots can not take the heat—they require a site that is, or can be, shaded and cool. Mulch, low-growing plants, and ground cover can provide relief.

Plant potted clematises anytime after the last spring frost and before fall's first one.

Clematises require loose, well-draining soil, with a neutral pH. Prior to planting, mix in compost or aged manure, if necessary, plus a few handfuls of bonemeal.

Dig a planting hole two to three times the width of the root ball and a few inches deeper. Place the plant in the hole with the crown 4 to 6 inches below the soil surface. This will encourage branching and stem development underground.

Fill in with soil, water thoroughly, and mulch to keep the roots cool and minimize weeds.

Place the climbing structure, if using.

CARE

Keep the soil moist during the first year by watering weekly. Do not let the soil dry out.

In colder regions, add extra mulch around the plant in late fall to protect the roots.

In spring, fertilize with a liquid seaweed or fish emulsion. In subsequent years, fertilize with a balanced/all-purpose (5-10-5) fertilizer.

Each spring, spread compost around the plant (away from the stems).

In spring, prune dead wood back, cutting above new, emerging buds.

Remove any stems that are 4 or more years old.

DISEASES/PESTS *(see pages 190–200)*
Diseases: leaf spot, fungal; mildew, powdery; rust; viruses; wilt, clematis. *Pests:* aphids; black vine weevils; earwigs; nematodes, root-knot; scale insects; slugs/snails; spider mites.

HARVEST
Clematises can make excellent cut flowers, although vining types can be challenging because of their short stems. Shrubby or herbaceous types for cut flowers include *C. hexapetala, C. recta, C. heracleifolia,* and *C. integrifolia.*

PRUNING
Clematises belong to one of three groups, based on flower size and bloom time.

Group 1: flowers appear in early to midspring on last year's growth; minimal pruning needed, only after flowering, if desired; examples include *C. armandii, C. alpine, C. cirrhosa, C. macropetala,* and *C. montana.*

Group 2: double and semidouble flowers; may bloom twice: in May/June on last year's wood and later in the year on new shoots; prune after spring flowers fade; remove dead wood in late winter; examples include hybrids 'Miss Bateman', 'Lady Londesborough', 'Nelly Moser', 'Henryi', 'Marie Boisselot', and 'Elsa Spath'.

Group 3: large, showy blooms in summer and autumn on current year's growth; prune severely in late winter/early spring, leaving two pairs of buds on each stem; common varieties are *C. viticella, C. recta,* and *C. x jackmanii.*

RECOMMENDED VARIETIES

Clematis armandii: the most fragrant species; clusters of large, star-shape, vanilla-scented white flowers in spring; needs sturdy support

C. 'Lincoln Star': large, deep pink blooms in late spring and late summer; 8 to 10 feet tall

C. 'Elsa Spath': profuse, large, single, blue-purple flowers; early and late summer; 8 to 12 feet tall

C. viticella 'Betty Corning': light purple, bell-like flowers; dies back to ground in winter, then climbs up to 10 feet each spring; needs sturdy support

C. heracleifolia: shrub form; small, blue, hyacinth-like flowers in late summer; dies back almost to ground in winter; gets about 4 feet tall and wide

C. tangutica: profuse, bright yellow, bell-shape flowers from midsummer to late fall, with showy, silky seed heads; grows up to 3 feet a year; needs sturdy support

C. 'Sweet Summer Love': profuse, fragrant, small, reddish-purple, star-shape flowers from July to October; grows to 12 feet tall; disease-resistant; very hardy

COLUMBINE

Aquilegia spp.

SKIRTING THE ROCKS AT THE FOREST EDGE
WITH A RUNNING FLAME FROM LEDGE TO LEDGE,
OR SWAYING DEEPER IN SHADOWY GLOOMS,
A SMOLDERING FIRE IN HER DUSKY BLOOMS;
BRONZED AND MOLDED BY WIND AND SUN,
MADDENING, GLADDENING EVERY ONE
WITH A GYPSY BEAUTY FULL AND FINE,—
A HEALTH TO THE CRIMSON COLUMBINE!

–Elaine Goodale Eastman, American poet (1863–1953)

The perennial columbine *(Aquilegia),* aka granny's bonnet, displays bell-shape, spurred flowers ranging in color from light pastels to bright reds, yellows, oranges, purples, and bicolors from midspring to early summer. Once started, columbine propagates for years and, although perennial, increases rapidly by self-seeding. The flowers attract butterflies, bees, moths, and hummingbirds! Although delicate in appearance, columbine is hardy, resilient, and drought-tolerant.

PLANTING

Columbine grows in sun or light shade.

Prepare the bed with average, well-draining soil.

Sow seeds indoors 8 to 10 weeks before

WIT & WISDOM

- *Columbine's Latin name,* Aquilegia, *is derived from the Latin word for "eagle,"* aquila. *The flowers' long spurs resemble the claws of an eagle.*
- *Native Americans used crushed seeds as a love charm and for medicinal purposes.*

the last spring frost or direct-sow in the fall or after the last spring frost: Press the seed into the soil but do not cover it.

Thin to the strongest plants.

If setting a mature plant into a container, create a hole twice the diameter of the "old" pot. Set the top of the root ball level with the soil surface. Fill in with soil, then tamp gently and water.

Outdoors, space mature plants 1 to 2 feet apart, depending on the variety.

Water thoroughly.

CARE

Avoid overwatering.

Deadhead faded flowers; new buds will develop along the stems. The bloom season can thus be extended by as long as 6 weeks, into midsummer.

Cut foliage to the ground in fall.

Before the ground freezes, mulch to protect plants.

DISEASES/PESTS *(see pages 190–200)*

Columbine is deer-resistant. *Diseases:* blight, southern; leaf spots, fungal; mildew, powdery; rust. *Pests:* leaf miners; nematodes, root-knot.

HARVEST

Cut flowers for arrangements when they are just opening. Vase life is 5 to 7 days.

RECOMMENDED VARIETIES

Among the more than 70 species of columbine, these are favorites . . .

- **Native eastern red columbine** *(Aquilegia canadensis):* pale pink to blood-red and pink/yellow flowers that point upward
- **'Corbett':** pale yellow flowers; resistant to leaf miner; dwarf variety, 1 to 1½ feet tall
- **'Little Lanterns':** red and yellow, bell-shape flowers; resistant to leaf miner; compact, 10 inches tall
- **'William Guiness' European columbine** *(A. vulgaris):* dark purple flowers with white on sepals; bushy, 24 to 30 inches tall

The Swan series includes bicolor, midsize (16- to 22-inch) hybrids excellent for cutting when half-open . . .

- **'Swan Pink and Yellow':** coral/cream/yellow flowers
- **'Swan Red and White':** red and white flowers

CONEFLOWER

Echinacea spp.

THE ORANGE CONE-FLOWERS PURPLE-BOSSED ARE THERE,
THE MEADOW'S BOLD-EYED GYPSIES DEEP OF HUE,
AND SLENDER HAWKWEED TALL AND SOFTLY FAIR,
AND ROSY TOPS OF FLEABANE VEILED WITH DEW.
–Archibald Lampman, Canadian poet (1861–99)

Coneflowers, aka echinacea, are tough upright perennials in the daisy family (Asteraceae) native to the eastern and central United States, extending from Colorado south to Texas and north to the Great Lakes. These fast growers reach 2 to 4 feet in height, flower from midsummer through fall frost, and self-sow prolifically. The central cone of the flower attracts butterflies and bees. After bloom, the seed heads attract songbirds. Coneflowers love heat and are trouble-free once established in a traditional garden or wildflower meadow.

The purple species *(E. purpurea)* is most common, but up to nine naturally occurring echinacea can be found in purple shades or yellow *(E. paradoxa)*. Hybrids present more colors and sizes but also caveats: Many are sterile (they do not produce viable seed) and lack genetic diversity.

PLANTING

Plant coneflowers when small, with blooms on the way, in spring or early summer. Seeds can be started indoors 8 to 10 weeks before the last spring frost or outdoors when the soil has warmed to at least 65°F. (Seed-sown plants are not likely to bloom for 2 to 3 years.)

Coneflowers prefer full sun and well-draining soil. Loosen soil to a depth of 12 to 15 inches and mix in compost or aged manure. (These plants will tolerate poor soil, but results may vary.)

If planting from a pot, dig a hole about twice the pot's diameter. Set the plant so that the root ball is level with the soil surface. Fill in to the top of the root ball. Space plants 1 to 3 feet apart, depending on size at maturity.

Water thoroughly.

Spread thin layers of compost, then mulch, on the soil surface to help to keep plants moist and prevent weeds.

CARE

Coneflowers are drought-tolerant, but new plants need water occasionally and more often if the spring season is especially dry.

VOICES OF EXPERIENCE

Just wanted to report that goldfinches will spend a very long time on flower seed heads. We have purple coneflowers planted outside our bedroom window at the Chesapeake Bay and in the fall I start my day by checking to see if there are any goldfinches eating outside my bedroom window. Great way to start the day.   *–Diana, on Almanac.com*

My coneflowers self-seed regularly, and where I had only one, now there are multiple places in the flower bed with lovely blooms that attract butterflies and bees. In fact, I have taken the seedpods and spread the seeds around manually to encourage more plants. Love these flowers, as they are hardy, long-lasting, and very sturdy.   *–Pat, on Almanac.com*

RECOMMENDED VARIETIES

These are native, unless noted . . .

- 'Robert Bloom' *(Echinacea purpurea)*: crimson petals; prominent, dark orange centers
- 'Finale White' *(E. purpurea)*: cream petals, greenish-brown centers
- Narrow-leaf coneflower *(E. angustifolia)*: similar to *E. purpurea*
- Pale purple coneflower *(E. pallida)*: native to Ontario
- Sanguine purple coneflower *(E. sanguinea)*: *sanguinea*, Latin for "blood," refers to streaks in petal color; southernmost species
- Smooth purple coneflower *(E. laevigata)*: narrow, drooping, pale-pink petals; endangered
- Tennessee coneflower *(E. tennesseensis)*: upturned mauve petals, greenish-pink centers
- Topeka purple coneflower *(E. atrorubens)*: deep pink short petals; rare
- Wavy leaf coneflower *(E. simulata)*: yellow pollen distinguishes it from *E. pallida* (white pollen)
- Yellow coneflower *(E. paradoxa)*, aka Ozark coneflower: yellow petals
- 'Cleopatra' *(E. hybrid)*: yellow petals, copper-green centers

Natives in ground seldom need fertilizer.

To delay blooming until fall (and compact growth), cut back stems 1 foot when plants come into bloom. For staggered bloom heights and times, cut only a few stems.

To prolong the bloom period, deadhead when flowers fade. Cut back stems to a leaf near a bud. Deadheading in late season prohibits self-seeding and bird-feeding.

Beneficial, wasplike soldier beetles may appear in August. They feed on insect eggs and larvae and pollinate plants. Do not harm them.

In late fall, lightly spread mulch in colder regions.

Cut the stems back to soil level when they wither or after frost. To promote

WIT & WISDOM

- *The genus name* Echinacea *comes from the Latin word* echinus, *for hedgehog, a reference to the often prickly centers, a feature that deters deer.*
- *Plains Native Americans used purple coneflower* (E. purpurea) *as their primary medicine (they steeped roots and other parts as tea to treat colds) and introduced it to European settlers.*

self-seeding, cut back in late winter.

Divide or transplant coneflowers in spring or fall.

IN POTS

Use 2- or 3-gallon (or larger) pots, with drainage holes. Spread crushed gravel in the bottom of the pots for drainage.

Fill the pot halfway with potting mix. Tamp down. Plant the root ball an inch below the rim of the container, spreading out the roots. Add soil slowly until it is even with the top of root ball, tamping lightly. Water deeply.

Keep pots in partial shade for 2 to 3 days, then place in full morning sun and partial afternoon shade.

Always water deeply at soil level when the soil is dry to the touch. Water on leaves can cause fungal disease.

Fertilize every couple of weeks with a water-soluble 10-10-10 product.

Deadhead just below the base of the flower for continued bloom.

To overwinter, prune plants to soil level when plant growth slows in fall. Move to a cool (40° to 50°F) area, with low to moderate indirect light. Water lightly when the soil is dry. When new growth appears in spring, move to a brighter, warmer (60° to 70°F) area.

Every 3 to 4 years, in spring after new growth has started, divide and repot echinacea plants.

DISEASES/PESTS *(see pages 190–200)* Coneflower is deer-resistant. *Diseases:* aster yellows; blight, Botrytis; leaf spot, bacterial; leaf spot, fungal; mildew, powdery; smut, white. *Pests:* aphids, black vine weevils; Japanese beetles; leaf miners; nematodes, foliar.

HARVEST

Cut flowers for arrangements when petals are expanding. Vase life is 5 to 7 days.

COREOPSIS

Coreopsis spp.

SMALL SERVICE IS TRUE SERVICE WHILE IT LASTS;
OF FRIENDS, HOWEVER HUMBLE, SCORN NOT ONE:
THE DAISY, BY THE SHADOW THAT IT CASTS,
PROTECTS THE LINGERING DEW-DROP FROM THE SUN.
–William Wordsworth, English poet (1770–1850)

Coreopsis varieties produce daisylike yellow, red, orange, pink, maroon, and violet flowers that bloom from summer to fall. Bees and butterflies love its nectar, and small birds, such as goldfinches, love its seeds.

This easy-to-grow plant makes few demands: It tolerates heat, humidity, and drought and, when cut, adds cheer to a bouquet. Plant in masses for striking visual effect; it's well suited to beds, borders, and containers. Varieties include annuals that tend to form clumps, be short-lived, and self-sow; perennials, with rhizomatous roots; and hybrids that put energy into making colorful blooms.

PLANTING

Coreopsis requires full sun and good drainage. It tolerates poor soil but not clay. Add compost and/or sand to improve drainage before planting.

Sow seeds directly outdoors after the last spring frost or start seeds indoors 8 to 10 weeks before the last spring frost. Do not cover seeds; they need light for germination. Keep indoor seeds warm and moist.

Set transplants 12 to 18 inches apart. Water until plants are established.

CARE

Water during dry spells.

Fertilizer may cause spindly plants

WIT & WISDOM

• *The name "coreopsis" stems from the Greek* koris, *for "bedbug," and* opsis, *meaning "resembling," because the seeds look like little bedbugs. The common name, tickseed, comes from the seeds' resemblance to ticks.*

• *Early Native Americans steeped coreopsis flowers and roots into teas.*

• *The flowers can be used for yellow and red dyes.*

with few flowers. Apply 10-10-10 lightly in spring, if desired.

Deadhead for continuous bloom, removing the spent flower and its stalk.

In mid- to late summer, when flowers fade, shear off one-quarter to one-half of growth to encourage reblooming.

After a couple of fall frosts, cut perennials back to 6 to 8 inches. Remove plant debris; spread a layer of compost, then a layer of mulch, around—not on—the crown.

Annual varieties can be dug up and discarded after a few frosts. Divide perennials every 3 to 4 years in spring or early fall.

DISEASES/PESTS *(see pages 190–200)*

Coreopsis is deer-resistant. *Diseases:* aster yellows; blight, Botrytis; blight, southern; leaf spot, fungal; mildew, downy; mildew, powdery; rot, Rhizoctonia root and stem; rust; wilt, Verticillium. *Pests:* aphids; slugs/snails.

HARVEST

Cut flowers for arrangements when they are fully open. Vase life is 7 to 10 days.

RECOMMENDED VARIETIES

Coreopsis verticillata 'Zagreb': golden yellow; 12 to 18 inches tall; hardy in Zones 4 to 9

C. auriculata 'Snowberry': white flowers with burgundy centers; 24 to 30 inches tall; hardy in Zones 3 to 8

C. auriculata 'Nana': yellow flowers; 2 to 4 inches tall; hardy in Zones 4 to 9

C. grandiflora 'SunKiss': large yellow flowers with burgundy centers; 12 to 14 inches tall; ideal for cutting; hardy in Zones 4 to 9

Annual native *C. tinctoria* (aka plains coreopsis and calliopsis): yellow-red flowers with dark-red centers; 2 to 4 feet tall; hardy in Zones 2 to 11

Hybrid *C.* 'Pinwheel': pinwheel-shape yellow flowers with orange centers; hardy in Zones 5 to 9

Hybrid *C.* 'Razzle Dazzle': Large, violet-purple blooms with white tips; hardy in Zones 5 to 9

DAHLIA

Dahlia spp.

**THE DAHLIA YOU BROUGHT TO OUR ISLE
YOUR PRAISES FOREVER SHALL SPEAK
'MID GARDENS AS SWEET AS YOUR SMILE,
AND COLOURS AS BRIGHT AS YOUR CHEEK.**
*–Henry Richard Vassall-Fox, 3rd Baron Holland,
English aristocrat (1773–1840), to his wife*

Dahlias are gorgeous flowers that bloom from midsummer through autumn. *Dahlia* is a genus of tuberous plants that are members of the Asteraceae family. They bloom in a rainbow of colors and in sizes ranging from petite 2-inch pompoms to giant 15-inch "dinner plates." Most varieties reach 4 to 5 feet tall.

Dahlias inspire awe and good cheer. Growing vegetables? Put a row of dahlias for cutting on the border (where they will not shade your edibles).

PLANTING

Dahlias thrive in 6 to 8 hours of direct sun, especially morning sunlight, and they benefit from protection from wind. Consider their size at maturity:

■ Plant large dahlias and those grown solely for cut flowers in a dedicated plot where they will be free from competition from other plants. Set the tubers in rows spaced 3 feet apart.

■ Plant medium- to low-height dahlias among other summer flowers. Set them 2 feet apart.

■ Plant the smallest bedding dahlias, grown from seed, 9 to 12 inches apart.

Prepare a dahlia bed to have rich, well-draining soil, with a pH level of 6.0 to 7.5. Amend heavy (clay) soil with sand or aged manure to lighten and loosen the soil texture for better drainage.

Dahlias will not tolerate cold soil. Plant when the soil reaches 60°F and any danger of frost has passed (e.g., a few days after tomatoes are planted). Dig a 6- to 8-inch-deep hole. Set a tuber into it, with the growing points, or "eyes," facing up. (Do not break or cut individual dahlia tubers as you would potatoes.) Cover with 2 to 3 inches of soil (some say that 1 inch is adequate). As the stem sprouts, fill in with soil until it is at ground level.

RECOMMENDED VARIETIES

There are about 60,000 named varieties and 18 official flower forms, including anemone, cactus, collarette, peony, stellar, and waterlily. The American Dahlia Society recognizes 15 different colors and color combinations. Here are some popular choices . . .

• 'Bishop of Llandaff': small, scarlet, intense flowers; handsome, dark-burgundy foliage; 3 feet tall

• 'Miss Rose Fletcher': 6-inch globes of long, quilled, shell-pink petals; 4 feet tall

• 'Bonne Esperance', aka 'Good Hope': 1½-inch, rosy-pink flowers; reminiscent of Victorian bedding dahlias; dwarf, at 1 foot tall

• 'Kidd's Climax': 10-inch "dinnerplate" flowers with pink petals suffused with gold; 3½ feet tall

• 'Jersey's Beauty': 4- to 6-inch pink flowers in fall; 4 to 6 feet tall

Do not water the tubers right after planting; this encourages rot. Wait until the sprouts have appeared above the soil, then water.

Do not spread mulch. Dahlias prefer sun on their roots.

Tall, large-flower cultivars require support. Place 5- to 6-foot stakes around plants and tie stems to them as the plants grow.

Dahlias begin blooming about 8 weeks after planting.

IN CONTAINERS

Medium- to dwarf-size dahlias do well in containers that have drainage and are big enough to support the plant at maturity (generally, a 12x12-inch container will suffice). Use a soilless mix and co-polymer moisture-retaining crystals, per the package's guidance. Follow the depth requirements. Cover the tuber with a few inches of soil/crystal mix. Spray water on the tuber, if necessary, until growth starts. Do not water if the soil is damp 1 inch below the surface. Fertilize through summer as directed. Add soil if roots become exposed.

CARE

When dahlias are established, water two or three times a week and more in hot, dry climates.

Be prepared to tend to plants before

VOICES OF EXPERIENCE

I had planted some dahlias last summer that were so beautiful, so I dug up the tubers and stored them in a bag of moss. Well, I accidentally threw them out, but I must not have dug up all the tubers, 'cause I now have a great big dahlia growing. It hasn't bloomed yet, but it's getting ready! I am shocked, given the harsh winter that we had here in northwest Ohio.

–Barbara, on Almanac.com

I live in British Columbia, where the ground freezes and the dahlia tubers need to be dug and stored. Unlike what is advised here and in other places, I dig up the ball whole, place it in a bag that can breathe, store it in a cool place (40° to 50°F) until spring, and plant. I have been doing this for more than 35 years without any adverse effects. I don't see any rot, and it keeps the bulbs from shriveling.

–Pat, on Almanac.com

Last spring while shopping, I discovered a pile of tubers and roots looking desolate on a shelf. My gut told me that they were dahlias. The employees were clueless, as there was no bag or instructions. They gave them to me for free!

Once planted, I pretty much ignored them until the shoots made me wonder. I asked friends, "Does this look like a weed to you?" I almost dug it up but was patient. I was rewarded with brilliant, dinnerplate, golden dahlias!

–Brian, on Almanac.com

TO PROPAGATE "BEDDING DAHLIA" SEEDS

Start seeds 4 to 6 weeks before the last frost. In a 70° to 85°F environment, set seeds in moist, soiless compost in containers with holes; sift or dust the seeds with 1/10 of an inch of damp medium. Allow 10 to 14 days for germination.

or after rain, when open blooms, especially large ones, tend to fill up with water or take a beating from the wind.

Dahlias benefit from a low-nitrogen liquid fertilizer such as 5-10-10 or 10-20-20. Fertilize after sprouting and then every 3 to 4 weeks from midsummer until early autumn. Do not overfertilize, especially with nitrogen, or you risk small/no blooms, weak tubers, or rot.

When plants are about 1 foot tall, pinch out 3 to 4 inches of the center branch to encourage bushier plants and increase stem count and stem length.

For large flowers, try disbudding: Remove the two smaller buds next to the central one in a flower cluster. The plant will put all of its energy into fewer but considerably larger flowers.

Bedding dahlias need no staking or disbudding; simply pinch out the center shoot just above the third set of leaves to encourage bushiness. For more blooms, deadhead as flowers fade.

DISEASES/PESTS *(see pages 190–200)*
Diseases: blight, Botrytis; blight, southern; crown gall; mildew, powdery; rot, Phytophthora crown and root; rot, Pythium root and stem; rot, Rhizoctonia root and stem; smut, white; viruses; wilt, Fusarium; wilt, Verticillium. *Pests:* aphids; cucumber beetles and earwigs (both eat petals but do not hurt the plants); nematodes, foliar; nematodes, root-knot; slugs/snails (bait 2 weeks after planting and continue throughout season); spider mites.

HARVEST

The more you cut dahlias, the more they'll bloom! For a bouquet, cut stems in the morning before the heat of the day and put them into a bucket of cool water. Remove stems' bottom leaves and place the flowers into water in a vase. Place the vase in a cool spot away from

direct sun and check the water daily. Vase life is about 7 days.

STORING FOR WINTER

Dahlias are hardy to Zone 8. In this and higher-number/warmer zones, dahlias can be cut back and their tubers left in the ground through winter; cover with several inches of dry mulch.

Some Zone 7 growers claim that dahlias will survive winter in the ground if the weather isn't too severe—but this is risky: They will not survive freezing temperatures.

Gardeners north of Zone 8 are advised to lift and store the tuberous roots during winter.

Dahlia foliage blackens with the first frost. Take it as a warning to begin digging up (lifting) dahlias; complete the task before a hard frost.

Cut off blackened foliage, leaving 2 to 4 inches of top growth. Carefully dig around tubers with a pitchfork or shovel; avoid damaging them. Lift the clump and gently shake off the soil. Cut off rotten tubers. Leave the clumps outside in the sun upside down to dry naturally. Pack them in loose, fluffy material (e.g., vermiculite, dry sand). Store in a well-ventilated, frost-free space: 40° to 45°F is ideal; 35° to 50°F is acceptable.

READYING FOR SUMMER

In spring, separate healthy tubers from the parent clump and discard wrinkled or rotten ones. Plan to plant the survivors. Each tuber must have at least one "eye" or a piece of the crown attached or it will not develop into a blooming plant. The eyes are little pink bumps at the base of the stem.

WIT & WISDOM

• *In the 16th century, dahlias grew wild on some Mexican hillsides.*
There, they were "discovered" by the Spanish.

• *The dahlia was named for Swedish botanist Anders Dahl, born on March 17, 1751.*

• *Both dahlia flowers and tubers are edible.*
The tubers taste like a cross between a potato and a radish.

DELPHINIUM

Delphinium spp.

THE DORMOUSE LOOKED OUT, AND HE SAID WITH A SIGH:
"I SUPPOSE ALL THESE PEOPLE KNOW BETTER THAN I.
IT WAS SILLY, PERHAPS, BUT I DID LIKE THE VIEW
OF GERANIUMS (RED) AND DELPHINIUMS (BLUE)."
–*"The Dormouse and the Doctor," by A. A. Milne,*
English poet and dramatist (1882–1956)

Delphinium is a genus consisting of more than 300 species; some are annuals, some are biennials, and some are perennials. Some grow easily from seed, and some do not. Their showy spikes of colorful summer flowers in gorgeous shades of blue, pink, white, and purple are popular in cottage-style and cutting gardens. These butterfly and hummingbird magnets always capture attention, in part because they demand specific conditions.

PLANTING

Delphiniums prefer moist, cool summers; they do not fare well in hot, dry weather or sudden wind or rain, which can knock them down. Except for the dwarf perennials, most delphiniums need staking.

Plant delphiniums in spring. Choose a spot in full sun to light shade, with shelter from strong winds.

Delphiniums require fertile, well-draining, neutral to slightly alkaline soil with a pH of 6.0 to 7.5. Prior to planting, loosen the garden soil and mix in 2 to 4 inches of compost or aged manure. Do a soil test and, if necessary, broadcast and turn in lime, wood ashes, or a mixture of the two.

Dig a hole twice the diameter of the plant's container. Make sure that the top of the root ball is level with the surface soil. Fill in with soil. Water thoroughly.

In mild climates, seeds can be sown directly in mid- to late summer. Sprinkle on prepared bed, cover with ⅛ inch of soil, and keep evenly moist. Thin seedlings to 18 inches apart when plants have three sets of leaves.

To start indoors, sow ⅛ inch deep in moist, 70° to 75°F soil 6 to 8 weeks (annuals) or 10 to 12 weeks (perennials) before the last spring frost. As seedlings emerge, provide artificial or full sunlight. When at least two pairs of true leaves appear, transplant to 3- to 4-inch pots and continue care. Harden off before planting outdoors.

CARE

Install sturdy stake supports no later than midspring or when plants reach 12 inches in height.

Do not allow soil to dry out but avoid puddling. Water plants in summer if rainfall is less than 1 inch per week.

Apply a balanced liquid fertilizer every 2 to 3 weeks.

For ideal flower spikes, thin side shoots at 3 inches high, leaving two to four

RECOMMENDED VARIETIES

Delphiniums are hardy in Zones 3 to 7.

Most of the delphiniums that exist today are not wild; they are the result of hybridization since the 19th century. Dwarf-, medium-size, and tall (6 feet and up) delphinium hybrids are available . . .

• Belladonna Group: native to North America; easier to grow and longer-lived than varieties in the Elatum Group; upright, loose, and branching; secondary flower spikes extend bloom period into autumn; 3 to 4 feet tall. 'Blue Donna' has clear blue flowers.

• Elatum Group: flowers in shades of violet, blue, pink, and/or white; short-lived plants that require attention; tallest spikes can reach to 6 feet or more. 'Aurora Deep Purple' has purple flowers with white centers.

• Pacific Hybrids: 3-inch violet, blue, and pink flowers; short-lived; tolerate warm/hot climates as annuals; giant (3- to 6-foot) heirlooms and dwarf hybrids. 'King Arthur', 5 to 6 feet tall, has plum flowers with white centers.

WIT & WISDOM

- *Delphinium seeds and seedlings are poisonous. If ingested, they can cause nausea, twitching muscles, paralysis, and even death.*
- *The centers of delphinium flowers are called "bees."*
- *The name "delphinium" comes from the Greek word* delphis, *which means "dolphin." The closed flower buds were said to resemble a dolphin's nose.*
- *The plants were called "larkspur" by English Tudors (1485–1603) because the shape of the flower's petals resembles a lark's claw.*

---

shoots on young plants and five to seven shoots on mature, well-established ones.

Deadhead by cutting spent flower spikes back to small, flowering, side shoots.

When the bloom period is finished, cut flower stalks to the ground; new, though smaller, flower stalks will develop. The flowers will survive the coming cold days and even light frosts.

Every 3 to 4 years, divide plants in spring: Remove and replant the new little plants growing around the outside of the clump. Discard the hard old heart.

DISEASES/PESTS (*see pages 190–200*)
Diseases: aster yellows; blight, Botrytis; blight, southern; leaf spot, bacterial; leaf spot, fungal; mildew, downy; mildew, powdery; mold, Sclerotinia white; rot, Phytophthora crown and root; rot, Pythium root and stem; rot, Rhizoctonia root and stem; rust; viruses; smut, white; wilt, Fusarium; wilt, Verticillium. *Pests:* cyclamen mites; nematodes, foliar; nematodes, root-knot; slugs/snails.

HARVEST

Cut flowers for arrangements when at least one bud is showing color and one bud is starting to open. Vase life is 6 to 8 days.

A VOICE OF EXPERIENCE

Don't get discouraged about growing delphiniums from seed. Use fresh seeds. I put my seeds in egg cartons and put them in the fridge using damp seed mix. I have good success. They sprout in the fridge. After most have sprouted, put them under a bright light. Normal to cool room temp. Start 10 weeks before last frost date.

–Linda, on Almanac.com

DIANTHUS

Dianthus spp.

**HOT JULY BRINGS COOLING SHOWERS,
APRICOTS, AND GILLYFLOWERS [DIANTHUS].**
–Sara Coleridge, English writer (1802–52)

Ancient Greek botanist Theophrastus (c. 371–c. 287 B.C.) gave the *Dianthus* genus its name: "divine flower" (*dios* + *anthos*). Ever since, gardeners have been smitten with these plants' charms: beguiling fragrance, many colors (white, pink, lavender, yellow, red), long bloom period (from spring sometimes until first fall frost), and prolific productivity.

Dianthus varieties range from creeping ground covers perfect for rock gardens to 24-inch (or longer) flowering stems suitable for cutting. Also known as "pinks" for the pinking-sheared-looking jagged edges of their five-petal blooms, dianthuses bring cheer to sunny borders or containers on the deck or patio.

WIT & WISDOM

- *In Tudor and, later, Edwardian times, dianthus had several names: gillyflower, pheasant's ear, and sops-in-wine. It is also known as cottage pink and clove pink.*
- *Dianthus flower petals are edible; remove and discard the bitter petal base before using.*

PLANTING

Dianthuses demand full sun (they fail to thrive in shade) and well-draining soil (standing water will rot the roots). Improve the soil drainage, if necessary (e.g., add sand to heavy clay soil).

Set transplants so that the crown is level with the soil surface. Space plants 6 to 12 inches apart, depending on variety. Water lightly.

If sowing seeds, start them indoors 10 to 12 weeks before the last spring frost. Press seeds lightly into moist potting medium. Cover lightly and keep moist. Apply bottom heat. Place seed trays in a sun-drenched window when seedlings break through the soil. Annuals germinate in about 10 days, perennials in 3 weeks. Harden off and transplant seedlings when they have four sets of leaves or when roots are well developed and there is no danger of frost.

Direct-seed outdoors in early spring when a light frost is still possible. Seeds need light to germinate, so cover lightly.

CARE

Avoid mulch, especially close to the stem; good air circulation is needed to avoid crown rot.

Water only when the soil is dry and be careful not to overwater.

Fertilize a few times during the growing season with a balanced fertilizer (equal amounts of nitrogen, phosphorus, and potassium) or a phosphate-rich tomato fertilizer.

Deadhead faded flowers, removing the stems, too, for more blooms.

Shear plants back after flowering in late summer to encourage a second set of flowers later in the season.

Many varieties self-seed if blossoms are not removed.

At season's end, leave evergreen foliage for fall and winter interest or cut stems back to 1 to 2 inches above the soil surface.

Divide established plants every 2 to 3 years in early spring or after flowering.

DISEASES/PESTS *(see pages 190–200)*
Dianthus is deer-resistant. *Diseases:* aster yellows; blight, Botrytis; leaf spot, bacterial; leaf spot, fungal; rot, Pythium root and stem; rot, Rhizoctonia root and stem; rust; viruses; wilt, bacterial; wilt, Fusarium. *Pests:* aphids; grasshoppers; slugs/snails; sow bugs.

HARVEST
Cut flowers for arrangements when they are just opening. Vase life is 7 to 21 days, depending on variety.

RECOMMENDED VARIETIES

The *Dianthus* family contains over 300 species and hundreds of hybrid varieties. According to the North American Dianthus Society, these are the best varieties for home gardens . . .

• Hardy rock garden pinks, which include alpine pinks *(Dianthus alpinus)* and cheddar pinks *(D. gratianopolitanus)* and their hybrids: strongly scented, small flowers on 2- to 6-inch-tall plants; grassy, gray-green leaves; hardy in Zones 3 to 9

• Cottage pinks *(D. plumarius):* clove-scented, lilac-pink flowers; grasslike foliage; deadhead 12 to 15 inches for rebloom in fall; hardy in Zones 3 to 9

• China pinks *(D. chinensis):* lightly scented flowers on 6- to 10-inch-tall stalks over 3- to 4-inch-high mounds; hardy perennials in Zones 7 to 10, yet considered annuals

• Clusterheads, e.g., sweet William *(D. barbatus):* clusters of single or double white, pink, red, or salmon flowers on 12- to 24-inch-tall stems; annual, biennial, or short-lived perennial; hardy in Zones 3 to 9

• Carnations *(D. caryophyllus),* aka the florist's flower: multipetal blooms on 12- to 24-inch-tall stems; curly, blue-green foliage; hardy in Zones 5 to 8. Choose hardy perennial border carnations (aka wild carnations) over frost-tender perpetuals that require a greenhouse.

Miscellaneous fragrant species hardy in Zones 3 to 8 include the sand pink *(D. arenarius),* with 6- to 10-inch-tall, deeply fringed, white blossoms; Noe's pink *(D. petraeus* ssp. *noeanus),* an alpine species with white flowers; 'Grenadin Yellow' *(D. caryophyllus),* with 16- to 20-inch-tall, creamy yellow blooms; and Superb pink *(D. superbus),* aka fringed pink, with feathery, deeply cut petals.

FOXGLOVE

Digitalis purpurea

THE FOXGLOVE, WITH ITS STATELY BELLS
OF PURPLE, SHALL ADORN THY DELLS.
–David Macbeth Moir, Scottish writer (1798–1851)

Foxglove's tall stalks bear stunning, speckle-throated, tubular blossoms. Common foxglove is a biennial: In its first year, the plant forms a rosette and foliage; in the second, it blooms from late spring to midsummer and then dies. Be aware that foxglove self-seeds prolifically. For continuous blooms, plant it for 2 consecutive years. Or, look for varieties that flower in Year 1. Bees and hummingbirds love the tubular flowers of foxglove, and its tall stalks make stunning cut flowers.

TAKE CARE AND BEWARE

All parts of foxglove are poisonous to people and livestock. Depending on the species, ingestion of *Digitalis* can induce symptoms ranging from nausea to cardiac arrhythmia. Nonetheless, compounds from the plant have sometimes been used in heart medications.

PLANTING

Foxglove grows best in full sun, with light afternoon shade. Because stalk height is typically 3 to 5 feet, it is best suited to the back of a flower bed.

Foxglove prefers a moist, well-draining bed that is high in organic matter, with a slightly acidic to neutral pH. Prepare soil by mixing in a 3- to 4-inch layer of compost or aged manure.

To set seeds, sow outside in containers

There are many foxglove cultivars and a few hybrids commonly available. Here are a few of our favorites . . .

- 'Alba': pure-white flowers; sturdy, 4-foot stalks

- 'Apricot Beauty': apricot-pink flowers with spotted interiors; 3 to 4 feet tall

- Camelot series: horizontally held lavender, rose, and white blooms; blooms from seed the first year; 3-foot stalks

- 'Candy Mountain': large, upturned, rose-to-purple flowers; biennial that blooms in the first year; strong, 4-foot stalks

- 'Foxy' mix: white, cream, purple, and rose flowers; blooms reliably from seed the first year; up to 3 feet tall

seedlings accordingly); the foliage spread can be 1 to 3 feet.

If planting a potted plant, dig the hole twice the diameter of the container. Set the top of the root ball level with the soil surface. Fill in around the root ball and tamp the soil. Water thoroughly.

CARE

Keep soil moist.

Add a thin layer of compost around the plant each spring.

Stake tall varieties.

Cut the center flower stalk back after flowering to allow additional flower stalks to develop later in the season.

Leave the flower stalk on the plant if you want it to reseed, as well as to attract birds to the garden in the fall.

DISEASES/PESTS (see pages 190–200)

Foxglove is rabbit- and deer-resistant. *Diseases:* anthracnose; blight, southern; leaf spot, fungal; mildew, powdery; rot, Phytophthora crown and root; rot, Pythium root and stem; rot, Rhizoctonia root and stem; wilt, Verticillium. *Pests:* aphids; Japanese beetles; mealy bugs; thrips.

in late spring or direct-sow in late summer.

Seeds need light to germinate; do not cover. (If desired, plant seedlings into the garden bed in early fall so that they can establish the root system before cold weather arrives.)

Space plants 1 to 2 feet apart (or thin

HARVEST

Cut stems for arrangements when lower flowers are just opening. Vase life is 10 to 14 days.

WIT & WISDOM

- Digitalis *comes from the Latin word for "finger"* (digitus), *which here alludes to the shape of the flower.* Purpurea *refers to the flower color, often purple.*

- *A single foxglove plant can produce 1 to 2 million seeds.*

- *Foxglove was often grown in cottage gardens in the Middle Ages.*

HOLLYHOCK

Alcea spp.

FLOWERS HAVE AN EXPRESSION OF COUNTENANCE AS MUCH AS MEN
OR ANIMALS. SOME SEEM TO SMILE; SOME HAVE A SAD EXPRESSION; SOME
ARE PENSIVE AND DIFFIDENT; OTHERS AGAIN ARE PLAIN, HONEST,
AND UPRIGHT, LIKE THE BROAD-FACED SUNFLOWER AND THE HOLLYHOCK.
—Henry Ward Beecher, American clergyman (1813–87)

Hollyhocks are old-time favorites, classic cottage garden flowers traditionally grown up against a building or fence. Most of the old-fashioned types *(Alcea rosea)* are biennial: They produce foliage in the first year, then flower and self-seed before dying in the second. Once established, the plants perform like perennials, setting seed year after year. Some newer varieties are considered perennial—they will bloom the first year and keep coming back year after year.

Hollyhocks grow 3 to 8 feet tall on a single stem, with single or double flowers that bloom from the bottom up. Butterflies, bees, and hummingbirds love the colorful blooms. Although hollyhocks originated in Asia, lore suggests that their name may have originated during the "holy" religious Crusades (1095–1291), when anti-inflammatory salve from the plants was used to heal horses' legs, or hocks.

PLANTING

Hollyhocks thrive in partial sunlight and are not fussy about soil, but they produce the best results in full sun and rich, well-draining, but moisture-retaining soil. Mix in compost, aged manure, or leaf mold prior to planting. Select a location

RECOMMENDED VARIETIES

Alcea rosea 'Radiant Rose': large, pink, single flowers in the first year when started early; 5 to 6 feet tall; a true perennial; hardy to Zone 3

Summer Carnival series: showy, long-lasting, double flowers in the first year from seed; pink, red, yellow, or white; 4 to 5 feet tall

'Powder Puffs' mix: dense, 3- to 4-inch double flowers in shades of pink, red, white, yellow, and purple; 6 to 8 feet tall; hardy; reseeds vigorously

'Spring Celebrities', 'Queeny', 'Majorette' mixes: double blooms in bright colors; about 3 feet tall; perfect for smaller gardens or containers

sheltered from the wind.

Sow groups of two or three seeds 2 to 3 feet apart, depending on fully grown plants' size at maturity, in early spring after the last frost or beginning in August until 2 months before the first fall frost. Press seeds into the soil and cover lightly with soil; sunlight aids in

WIT & WISDOM

• *Dahlias were often grown in front of hollyhocks to hide their "shins."*

• *Sometimes used to hide outhouses, hollyhocks were called "outhouse flowers."*

• *All parts of the hollyhock are edible; use petals in salad or as garnish.*

• *Hollyhocks are in the mallow (Malvaceae) family and cousins of okra, cotton, and hibiscus.*

germination. Or, start seeds indoors 8 to 10 weeks before the last spring frost. (Sprouts emerge in 10 to 14 days.) Transplant outdoors when they are a few inches high.

When transplanting seedlings or mature potted plants, minimize disturbance to the roots.

For a stunning display, plant in groups of 8 to 12 plants along a fence or wall (in which case, staking is seldom needed).

Water well.

CARE

Fertilize one or two times in season with a 10-10-10 or soluble fertilizer.

Stake, if not grown against a backing.

Soak the soil around the plants regularly.

Remove faded flowers.

If collecting seeds, after petals fall, look for brown seedpods that contain flat, blackish seeds.

Cut plants to the ground at the end of the season.

Clean up and discard all plant debris in fall to minimize or avoid rust or remove infected plants completely and start new ones in a different location.

DISEASES/PESTS *(see pages 190–200)*
Diseases: anthracnose; blight, southern; leaf spot, fungal; rust. *Pests:* Japanese beetles; leafhoppers; nematodes, root-knot; spider mites.

HARVEST

Remove faded flowers to allow buds higher on the tall stem to open.

Cut stems for arrangements when one-third of the florets are open. Vase life is 7 to 10 days.

Add hollyhocks to a bouquet with bellflowers, phlox, baby's breath, and roses.

HYDRANGEA

Hydrangea spp.

A DEAD HYDRANGEA IS AS INTRICATE AND LOVELY AS ONE IN BLOOM.
—Toni Morrison, American writer (1931–2019)

With immense flower heads, hydrangeas flaunt an old-fashioned charm in summertime. These flowering shrubs are low-maintenance, and proper care will keep them blooming.

Hydrangeas are ideal for a range of garden sites, and varieties abound (every year, it seems, breeders present more options!)—so many that gardeners' expectations of bloom size and color are boundless. To know how your hydrangea will perform, pay attention to the types.

PLANTING

Plant in spring after the last frost and before the heat of summer arrives or in fall before the first frost.

Generally, hydrangeas prefer partial sun, with full sun in the morning and some mid-afternoon shade. This is especially true for the bigleaf hydrangea *(Hydrangea macrophylla)*, which is prone to wilting.

Most hydrangeas thrive in fertile, well-draining soil. Add compost or aged manure to enrich poor soil.

Space hydrangeas from 3 to 10 feet

apart, depending on type.

Dig a hole as deep as the root ball and two to three times as wide. Set the plant in the hole and half-fill it with soil. Water thoroughly. When the water is absorbed, fill in with soil and water thoroughly again.

CARE

In the 2 years after planting and during any drought, provide plenty of water. If possible, water in the morning to prepare hydrangeas for the heat of the day and to avoid disease. Generally, water at a rate of 1 inch per week throughout the growing season. Deep soaks three times a week (with a soaker hose or the like that keeps moisture off flowers and leaves) encourage root growth more than frequent sprinkles. All varieties benefit from consistent moisture, but bigleaf and smooth hydrangeas require more water. Leaves wilt and flowering will be hampered if the soil is too dry.

Spread mulch around the base of plants to keep the soil moist and cool.

Hydrangeas in rich soil seldom need fertilizer: Too much encourages leafy growth over blooms. However, each variety has specific needs. For example, smooth hydrangeas need fertilization only in late winter. Oakleaf and panicle varieties do best with applications in April and June. Bigleaf hydrangeas can benefit from light fertilization in March, May, and June. To determine soil fertility, do a soil test and check the variety.

In fall, cover plants from the ground up with at least 18 inches of bark mulch, leaves (not maple), pine needles, or straw. If possible, wrap the plants with snow fencing or chicken wire and loosely fill the cages with mulch, covering the entire plant.

Old, established hydrangeas can be divided and transplanted in early spring. Use a shovel or knife to split the root clump.

HOW TO CHANGE THE COLOR OF HYDRANGEA FLOWERS

Hydrangea flowers' colors can be changed, but not instantly. Color correction takes weeks or more, and not every cultivar is changeable: White flowers are not affected by soil pH, the condition that imparts the blue and pink hues. Some bigleaf hydrangeas— especially mophead and lacecap types—

WIT & WISDOM

• *The name "hydrangea" is derived from the Greek* hydor, *meaning "water," and* angeion, *meaning "vessel," both referring to the plant's seedpods, which look like small water jugs.*

and mountain hydrangea *(H. serrata)* cultivars change color based on the soil pH.

Acidic soils with a pH of less than 5.5 produce blue flowers; soils with a pH greater than 6.0 produce pink flowers. Do a soil test to determine the existing pH and amend as indicated to change it.

A plant should be at least 2 years old before undergoing a pH change; this will give it time to recover from the shock

of its original planting. Also note that it's easier to change blue flowers to pink than pink to blue.

PRUNING

Pruning is confusing and depends on the hydrangea variety. (The most common garden hydrangea shrub is the bigleaf variety.) If you know which type you have, you can figure out the pruning technique to employ.

"OLD WOOD" VARIETIES

Bigleaf *(H. macrophylla)*, oakleaf *(H. quercifolia)*, mountain *(H. serrata)*, and climbing *(H. anomala* ssp. *petiolaris)* hydrangea varieties bloom on the previous season's stems (aka "old wood"). Prune after the flowers fade in summer.

If flower buds form in the late summer and bloom in the following season, avoid pruning after August 1.

Cut away dead wood only in the fall or very early spring. To prune, cut one or two of the oldest stems down to the base to encourage branching and fullness.

If the plant is old, neglected, or damaged, prune all of the stems down to the base. The plant will not flower in the upcoming season, but it will be rejuvenated for future years.

Avoid deadheading mophead varieties. Leave the faded flowers on the bush. Then, in early spring, cut them back to the first healthy pair of buds.

Deadhead the lacecap varieties: Cut to the second pair of leaves below the flower head.

H. macrophylla (and *H. serrata*) varieties in Zones 4 and 5 should not be pruned unless absolutely necessary, and then only immediately after blooming.

Dead stems can be removed in the spring.

"NEW WOOD" VARIETIES

Panicle *(H. paniculata)* and smooth *(H. arborescens)* varieties bloom on the current season's stems ("new wood"). Prune before flower buds form.

Prune in the late winter, when the

RECOMMENDED VARIETIES

There are two main groups of hydrangeas . . .

Plants that bloom on old growth (last year's stems)
These hydrangeas set flower buds in fall and are suited to Zone 8 or warmer; they are hardy to Zones 4 and 5 but in cool climate zones will risk frost damage. This, and untimely pruning, can result in inconsistent flowering or no flowering.

• Bigleaf hydrangeas *(H. macrophylla):* 'All Summer Beauty' (mophead) bears dark blue flowers; in near-neutral pH soil, these turn pink. If buds are winter-killed, new ones will form in spring and bloom. 'Nikko Blue' (mophead) is vigorous, with large, rounded, blue flowers. 'Color Fantasy' (mophead) has reddish- or deep purple flowers. 'Blue Wave' (lacecap) produces rich blue–to-mauve or lilac blue–to-pink flowers.

• Climbing hydrangeas *(H. anomala* ssp. *petiolaris)*: 'Firefly' boasts variegated foliage.

• Mountain hydrangeas *(H. serrata):* 'Bluebird' and 'Diadem' are early bloomers. In acidic soil, 'Preziosa' flowers bear shades of blue, mauve, violet, and green.

• Oakleaf hydrangeas *(H. quercifolia):* Expect exceptional fall color from 'Snow Queen', 'Snow Flake', and 'Alice'.

Plants that bloom on new growth (this year's stems)
These hydrangeas form flower buds in early summer, flower reliably each year, and require no special care.

• Panicle hydrangeas *(H. paniculata):* 'Grandiflora' and 'PeeGee' are large, old-fashioned, floppy varieties; 'Tardiva', 'White Moth', and 'Pee Wee' are suited to small gardens; 'Limelight' produces cool-green flowers and grows 6 to 8 feet tall.

• Smooth hydrangeas *(H. arborescens):* 'Grandiflora' and 'Annabelle' produce large (14-inch) blooms in late summer.

plant is dormant. If the buds are killed during winter, the plant will produce new buds in spring; these will bloom. In general, prune only dead branches and do not prune to "shape" the bush.

PROPAGATING

Rooting cuttings: Find a new branch on a well-established hydrangea—a branch that has not flowered and bears three or more pairs of leaves. (New growth will appear lighter in color than old, and the branch will not be as rigid.)

Cut 5 to 6 inches from the tip of the branch. Discard the bottom piece.

If the tip cutting has at least two pairs of leaves, remove the lowest pair of leaves flush to the stem, or at the node.

If the remaining leaves are large, cut them in half, removing the tip half.

Dust the cutting's end with rooting hormone and, if desired, an antifungal plant powder. This will encourage rooting and discourage rotting.

Fill a small pot with moistened potting mix. Plant the cutting, sinking it up to the first pair of remaining leaves. Water lightly to eliminate any air gaps around the stem. Cover the pot and cutting loosely with a plastic bag (to maintain humidity). If necessary, use chop- or kebab sticks to prop up the bag so that it does not touch the leaves; if it touches the leaves, they might rot. Place in a warm area, sheltered from direct sunlight and wind. Water when the top layer of soil is dry.

After a week or so, gently pull on the cutting. If you feel resistance, roots have formed. If there is no resistance, check for rotting.

Layering: For bigleaf hydrangeas, in summer, dig a trench next to the plant, near a branch that easily reaches beyond the trench. Where the branch contacts the soil, remove an inch of the outer bark all around it. Bury the bared portion, pinning it with a florist's pin or a gentle weight, leaving 6 to 12 inches of the end of the branch tip uncovered. Water regularly. In early spring, the branch should be ready to remove from the mother plant and transplant.

DISEASES/PESTS (see pages 190–200)
Protect against disease and pests by choosing resistant cultivars. Pests are rare but can appear when plants become stressed. Proper care is the best defense. *Diseases:* blight, Botrytis; blight, southern; leaf spot, bacterial; leaf spot, fungal; mildew, powdery; rot, Armillaria root; rot, Phytophthora crown and root; rot, Pythium root and stem; rot, Rhizoctonia root and stem; rust; viruses. *Pests:* aphids; nematodes, foliar; nematodes, root-knot; nematodes, stem and bulb; spider mites.

HARVEST
Cutting fresh flowers: Cut fully mature hydrangea flowers in the morning after you have watered the plant.

Immediately place fresh stems in cold water to prevent wilting. Recut the woody stems at a slant under water. Remove the lower leaves on the stems. Arrange them in a vase and place in a cool location, out of direct sunlight.

Check the water level and quality daily. Change the water, if it becomes cloudy. Mist the blooms with water.

Soak wilting blooms in cool water for 10 to 15 minutes to revive them.

Drying flowers: Cut flower heads when the blooms have matured to a papery consistency. Remove the leaves from the stems and hang the stems upside down in a warm, dry, dark, airy room.

When completely dry (usually in a couple of weeks), store or display in a dry location out of direct sunlight.

Use dried hydrangea flowers to create a wreath or other decor for the home.

A VOICE OF EXPERIENCE
I have a florist's hydrangea that was given to me by a garden center right after Mother's Day about 12 years ago. I planted it, and, after being moved three times, it finally found its home in an area that gets about 3 hours of morning sun. It has lived in this spot for 9 years now and has lovely blue blooms every year. It's a rather compact bush, growing only to about 3 to 3½ feet. This is a tough little bush!
–Donna, on Almanac.com

IRIS

Iris spp.

THOU ART THE IRIS, FAIR AMONG THE FAIREST,
WHO, ARMED WITH GOLDEN ROD
AND WINGED WITH THE CELESTIAL AZURE, BEAREST
THE MESSAGE OF SOME GOD.
–Henry Wadsworth Longfellow, American poet (1807–82)

Tall, beautiful, colorful iris is named after the Greek goddess who rode rainbows. The genus *Iris* embraces more than 250 species. Despite its divine origins, this eye-catching bloomer is rugged, reliable, and easy to grow.

The most familiar irises are the tall (28 or more inches) bearded *Iris germanica.* Their distinctive six-petal flowers have three outer hanging petals ("falls") and three inner upright petals ("standards"). Irises may be a "bearded" or crested ("beardless") type. Bearded iris is so named for the soft hairs along the center of the falls. The hairs on crested iris, such as Siberian, form a comb or ridge.

Most irises flower in spring to early summer. Some—mostly bearded hybrids—are remontant, meaning that they flower a second time later in summer. The Siberian iris bloom period tends to follow that of bearded irises.

Irises attract butterflies and humming-birds and make lovely cut flowers.

WIT & WISDOM

- *Irises are called the "poor man's orchids."*
- *The iris is depicted in the French royal standard* fleur-de-lis. *It is the emblem of New Orleans, Louisiana, and Florence, Italy, and the state flower of Tennessee.*
- *Orris root, taken from the dried roots of* I. germanica, *is used as a scent fixative in perfumes.*

PLANTING

Plant most irises in late summer to early fall, when nighttime temperatures hold between 40° and 50°F. Plant the tall bearded varieties later in fall; they go dormant in early to midsummer. Plant bare rhizomes or irises in a container earlier—as soon as it is convenient; don't wait for a perfect time.

Irises bloom best in full sun. They can tolerate as little as half a day of sun, but this is not ideal. Without sufficient sunlight, they will not bloom. Similarly, bearded irises must not be shaded out by other plants; many do best in a special bed by themselves.

Provide well-draining, fertile, neutral to slightly acidic soil. Loosen soil to a depth of 12 to 15 inches, then mix in compost or aged manure. Good drainage is critical: Irises prefer "wet feet, but dry knees." They will not tolerate wet soil in winter.

Plant bare-root rhizomes (the thick stems) horizontally, with the top exposed and only the roots underground. In areas with hot summers, set the rhizome just below the soil surface: Dig a hole 10 inches in diameter and 4 inches deep. Make a ridge of soil down the middle and place the rhizome on the ridge, spreading the roots down both sides. Fill in the hole and firm it gently, leaving part of the rhizome and the foliage uncovered. Plant singly or in groups of three, 1 to 2 feet apart, depending on the fully grown plant's size.

Soak Siberian iris rhizomes in water

A VOICE OF EXPERIENCE

I received a nice bag of irises from a friend. These irises are sentimental because they came out of my mom's garden years ago, went to him, then to me. My mom was a Master Gardener and a perennials expert. When both she and my dad passed, we took 80 specimens from her garden and planted them at our house. Because she preceded my dad in death, her irises were mostly gone. Getting these irises back, via a friend of hers, is very special. I'll keep them as you directed on Almanac.com, in a bag with a few holes for air circulation in the garage or some other place that is cool, dark, and dry—and plant them this coming spring.

–Larry, on Almanac.com

overnight before planting, then set them 1 inch deep (2 inches, if the soil is sandy), 2 feet apart. Over a period of years, they will form clumps; divide when blooms get smaller and vigor declines.

Do not spread mulch; it may encourage rot.

Water thoroughly.

CARE

Fertilize in early spring, scratching an all-purpose fertilizer around the plants. Avoid high-nitrogen fertilizers. Reblooming irises perform best if fertilized again after the first wave of flowering is finished.

Iris borer overwinters as eggs in spent leaves. Signs include vertical streaks in the leaves. If apparent, look for the pests and squash them! If you see rot in the rhizome, dig it up and remove the affected parts.

Do not overwater; too much moisture can cause rot. Water consistently and deeply, especially during drought.

Keep rhizomes exposed. Bearded iris rhizomes need some sun and air. If covered with soil or crowded by other plants, they'll rot.

Stake, if necessary.

Deadhead (remove spent blooms) consistently. Bearded irises flower sequentially on buds along the stems.

After the bloom period, cut stems down at the base to discourage rhizome rot. Do not trim foliage; it prepares the plant for next year's growth. Cut brown tips from foliage, if desired.

After a hard frost in the fall, cut the foliage back hard and remove and discard any foliage that appears spotted or yellowed, including borer eggs.

Cover rhizomes with 1 to 2 inches of sand, topped with a layer of evergreen boughs, after the ground freezes.

RECOMMENDED VARIETIES

Tall, bearded, *Iris germanica* varieties come in flamboyant colors. They are generally planted only in fall.

Rebloomers (remontant) . . .
- 'Immortality': fragrant white flowers; hardy to Zone 4
- 'Feed Back': fragrant dark purple flowers; Zones 4 to 9
- 'Earl of Essex': white flowers, with purple edging; Zones 3 to 10
- 'Jennifer Rebecca': mauve pink flowers; Zones 4 to 9

Siberian iris, *I. sibirica,* offers a range of colors and is pest- and disease-free.
- 'Blueberry Fair': ruffled blue flowers; Zones 3 to 8
- 'Fond Kiss': white flowers with pink flush; Zones 3 to 8

Japanese iris, *I. ensata,* bears huge, flat blooms; these heavy feeders thrive on moisture during the growing season and do well around ponds; move to drier ground for fall and winter.
- 'Coho': pink flowers with golden flush; Zones 4 to 9
- 'Variegata': dark purple-reddish flowers; Zones 4 to 9

Remove when forsythias bloom in the following spring.

DIVIDING

When irises become overcrowded (usually every 2 to 5 years), the rhizomes lose vitality and stop blooming. The best time to divide is after flowering, usually in midsummer.

Trim the foliage back to 6 inches. Carefully dig up (lift) the clumps. The original rhizome (the "mother") will have produced several offshoots. Separate these from the mother and discard the mother. Inspect the rhizomes for rot or disease and remove and discard infected parts or entire unhealthy rhizomes.

Plant the freshly unearthed rhizomes in a new bed or replant them where they were after adding new soil.

DISEASES/PESTS *(see pages 190–200)*

Iris is deer-resistant and drought-tolerant. *Diseases:* blight, southern; blight, Botrytis; ink spot; leaf spot, bacterial; leaf spot, fungal; leaf spot, iris; rot, bacterial soft; viruses. *Pests:* aphids; iris borers; iris weevils; nematodes, foliar; nematodes, root-knot; nematodes, stem and bulb; slugs/snails; thrips; verbena bud moths; whiteflies.

HARVEST

Cut flowers for arrangements when they are just showing color. Vase life is 3 to 7 days.

JASMINE

Jasminum spp.

IF THERE WERE AS GREAT A SCARCITY OF SOIL AS OF JEWELS OR PRECIOUS
METALS, THERE WOULD NOT BE A PRINCE WHO WOULD NOT SPEND
A BUSHEL OF DIAMONDS AND RUBIES AND A CARTLOAD OF GOLD JUST TO
HAVE ENOUGH EARTH TO PLANT A JASMINE IN A LITTLE POT.
–Galileo Galilei, Italian astronomer (1564–1642)

A favorite for centuries, the sweetly scented jasmine flower can fill a room or a garden with its heady scent. Although jasmine is a southern vine usually grown on support outdoors, some varieties thrive as houseplants. Jasmine can be pruned as a shrub near the house or a walk so that its intense fragrance can be enjoyed by passersby as well as the hummingbirds and butterflies that are drawn to the flowers.

The genus *Jasminum* contains more than 200 vines and shrubs.

PLANTING

All summer-flowering jasmines prefer full sun; winter or early spring bloomers do fine in partial shade.

Jasmines have few soil requirements: They like moderately fertile, loamy, sandy, and moisture-retaining yet well-draining soil with a moderately acidic, alkaline, or neutral pH.

Most *Jasminum* species are semitropical vines, best planted in spring after the danger of frost is past.

Plant in-ground anytime from June to November. Dig only so deep that the plant crown is level with the soil surface. Container plants are best planted in the fall.

If grown as a vine, provide support—for example, an arbor or trellis. As a shrub, jasmine needs frequent pruning, as it can get lanky and semi-vining.

If growing jasmine as a shrub border, set plants at least 8 feet apart.

AS A HOUSEPLANT

Plant jasmine in potting mix that contains porous material so that it drains well. Soil should be moist but not soggy. Provide a trellis or support.

Humidity is important. Set the plant pot on a tray of pebbles or gravel; add water to the top of the stones. Run a humidifier, if possible.

Water only when the top inch of potting mix is dry to the touch.

Place soon-to-bloom jasmine in a

RECOMMENDED VARIETIES

Common jasmine *(Jasminum officinale)*, aka poet's jasmine or true jasmine: clusters of very fragrant, pure-white flowers from early summer to autumn; fast-growing (1 to 2 feet per year, up to 20 feet), twining, deciduous vine; requires pergola, fence, or large trellis; native to Asia; hardy in Zones 7 to 10

J. officinale 'Argenteovariegatum': pink buds open to powerfully fragrant white flowers; blooms through August; cream-white variegation on leaves; adaptable from full sun to dappled shade; deer-resistant; hardy in Zones 7 to 10

Winter jasmine *(J. nudiflorum)*: unscented yellow flowers appear in winter or early spring before its leaves unfold; use to cascade over retaining walls or as bank cover (it spreads by rooting stems that touch the soil); a favorite of hummingbirds; hardy in Zones 6 to 10

J. polyanthum: the most common indoor variety; white flowers waft a sweet aroma, especially in the evening

Star jasmine, aka Confederate jasmine *(Trachelospermum jasminoides)*: not a true jasmine, although similar in appearance; highly scented, phloxlike flowers bloom on twining stems in spring and summer; native to China; hardy in Zones 8 to 10

Carolina yellow jasmine *(Gelsemium sempervirens)*, aka Carolina jessamine: not a true jasmine; fragrant, bright yellow blooms in late winter to early spring on stems up to 20 feet long; native across the U.S. Southeast and in Central America; hardy in Zones 7 to 10

WIT & WISDOM

- *In Hawaii, jasmine and ginger blossoms are often used in the floral garlands worn on Lei Day, May 1.*
- *J. officinale's essential oil, known as the "King of Oils," has been used to aid the quality of sleep, reduce anxiety, and reduce depression.*

partly sunny spot. After it blooms, place near a south-facing window.

Provide fertilizer that is rich in potassium and phosphorus two times per year. During the spring and summer growing seasons, feed it a balanced liquid fertilizer every 2 to 4 weeks.

Indoors, jasmine needs to stay cool, with well-circulated air. Maintain the temperature at between 60° and 75°F.

Keep jasmine under control with proper pruning, especially at the beginning of spring. Remember, jasmine is a climbing vine!

Repot in springtime. Prune the roots when moving to fresh soil, as needed.

CARE

Tie the vine's stems to the support.

Water once per week, increasing frequency or volume during dry periods.

Deadhead blooms after flowering.

Snip or pinch vine stem tips to stimulate bushier lateral growth.

If the vine is grown as a ground cover, trim the upward-twining stems. (Additional plants can be propagated from stem cuttings.)

Water less in fall. In winter and spring months, keep the plant slightly dry.

Prune out thin, old shoots after flowering to shape the plant.

DISEASES/PESTS *(see pages 190–200)*

Common jasmine is relatively disease- and pest-free. Winter jasmine can be affected by spider mites. If this happens, cut the plant to the ground after blooming and discard the infested plant material. Feed the crowns to stimulate new growth. Yellowish leaves indicate the need for fertilizer. With houseplants, look out for mealybugs (white, cottony masses under leaves and on stems). To remove, use a cotton swab dipped in alcohol.

A VOICE OF EXPERIENCE

I keep mine in a large pot next to the house. A drip line waters it daily. In the winter, I tent it with thick, clear plastic to keep it from freezing. It does fine that way and doesn't lose all of its leaves. I live in the Seattle area, and it gets down to the 20s in the winter. In southern Oregon, my jasmine grew nicely against the house, and tenting wasn't necessary. Tenting is easy and is just a precaution if you're concerned. I have lost a jasmine to the cold prior to tenting them in the winter.

–Stephanie, on Almanac.com

LAVENDER

Lavandula angustifolia

LAVENDER'S BLUE, DILLY DILLY, LAVENDER'S GREEN,
WHEN I AM KING, DILLY DILLY, YOU SHALL BE QUEEN.
—Old English folk rhyme

Prized for its fragrance, medicinal properties, and beautiful, bluish-purple color, *Lavandula angustifolia,* or English lavender, is a valued plant across the world. In warm areas, such as its native region around the Mediterranean Sea, the gray-to-green foliage of this bushy perennial plant stays evergreen throughout the year—and it thrives in some of the toughest of garden conditions. Plus, it often blooms twice in one season.

Called "English" because it proliferates in the English climate, lavender's main requirements are lots of sun and good drainage; it is not fussy about soil, and its presence lures bees and butterflies. Plant lavender along a walkway or near a seating area.

PLANTING

Lavender is best planted as a young specimen in spring when the soil is warming. If planting in fall, use larger,

A VOICE OF EXPERIENCE

My lavender was so prolific that at the end of the year, I used long stem cuttings in the fireplace. They gave off a lovely scent and almost completely covered the smell of burning wood in the house. It also helped with a "quick start" to light the fire. From now on, I will be using the end-of-the-year long cuttings in the fireplace. I use some of the earlier cuttings that dry naturally in the kitchen and bedrooms. Why put such fragrance in the composter?
    –*JC, on Almanac.com*

HOW TO ROOT SOFT CUTTINGS

Take a softwood cutting of several inches of stems with no flower buds immediately following the plant's bloom. Remove foliage from the bottom half of each stem and insert each into sterile potting soil or horticultural vermiculite. Rooting hormone is not necessary, but moisture is: Water well and mist regularly. Allow 3 weeks for roots to appear.

more established plants to ensure survival through winter.

Lavender makes only one demand of soil: It must drain well. Standing water and wet to moist areas could encourage root rot. Amend compacted or clay soil with compost or aged manure to improve drainage.

Growing lavender from seed is not easy (germination can take up to 3 months). It's more efficient to buy small plants from a garden nursery or root a cutting from a mature plant.

Place lavender plants 2 to 3 feet apart to allow for a typical mature height of 1 to 3 feet.

Spread mulch (or rock or pea gravel) to help minimize weeds. Keep mulch away from the plant's base, however, to prevent excess moisture and root rot.

CARE

Water once or twice a week until plants are established. Water mature plants every 2 to 3 weeks until buds form, then once or twice weekly until harvest. (Yellowing leaves are a sign of overwatering.)

In colder areas, plants may need winter protection. Cover with evergreen boughs or straw to block freezing winds and temperatures. Or, simplify things by growing lavender in a pot and keeping it outdoors in summer and indoors in winter. While it's indoors, place the pot in a south-facing window with as much light as possible. Water sparingly, as the plant will be dormant at this time.

PRUNING

In warm climates, prune in autumn.

In cool climates, prune established plants in spring when green leaves start to emerge from the base. Remove about one-third of the top to keep the plant from becoming leggy and bare at the base, but do not cut back into old wood, as it will not regrow.

If you do not harvest stems, keep plants tidy by snipping off stems when flowers fade.

WIT & WISDOM

• *Ancient Egyptians used lavender in the embalming process. They wrapped the dead in shrouds that had been soaked in lavender water.*

• *In A.D. 77, ancient Romans were documented to have used lavender to repel insects and soothe insect bites.*

• *The herb is also known for its calming effects. Lavender oil is used to naturally induce sleep.*

Leave the foliage over the winter to protect new growth from frosts.

DISEASES/PESTS *(see pages 190–200)*
Diseases: leaf spot, bacterial; rot, Phytophthora crown and root; rot, Pythium root and stem: rot, Rhizoctonia root and stem; viruses; wilt, Fusarium. *Pests:* aphids; nematodes, root-knot; thrips; whiteflies.

HARVEST

Lavender is a wonderful herb for drying. Harvest flowering stems while in bloom in the morning hours when the oils are the most concentrated.

Snip off stems when about half of the flower buds have opened, cutting the stems as long as possible.

Gather stems into bundles and secure them with rubber bands. Dry the bundles of lavender by hanging them in a sheltered, cool, dark place with good air circulation.

After a few weeks, the flowers will have dried fully and can be shaken gently from the stems into a lidded jar. Store the flowers in a cool, dark place.

LAVENDER IN THE HOME

Use lavender in sachets to keep linen and clothing smelling sweet and to repel moths.

If you suffer from insomnia, insert a sachet into a pillow/pillowcase so that the scent can help you to drift off to a restful slumber.

Although edible, lavender is little used in recipes. It's occasionally included as a constituent of *herbes de Provence* mixes, and leaves can be chopped and added sparingly to some sauces or used in shortbread biscuits.

RECOMMENDED VARIETIES

English lavender (*Lavandula angustifolia*), the most common, is hardy to Zone 5. Hundreds of varieties exist in many colors (white, pink, blue violet, and many shades of purple) and sizes.

- 'Hidcote': deep purple flowers; silver-gray foliage; compact form
- 'Munstead': violet-blue flowers; dark green foliage; compact form
- 'Miss Katherine': deep pink flowers; aromatic foliage; mounding form

Lavandins (*L. x intermedia*)—a hybrid of English and Portuguese lavender (*L. latifolia*)—are generally larger plants that bloom one time, later in summer.

- 'Phenomenal': vigorous variety highly tolerant of heat and humidity; resistant to common root and foliar diseases; long flower spikes
- 'Provence': vigorous, long-stem variety; very fragrant

Spanish lavender (*L. stoechas*) and French, or fringed, lavender (*L. dentata*) are typically only winter-hardy in Zones 7 to 9.

LILAC

Syringa spp.

**NOTHING IS MORE WISTFUL THAN THE SCENT OF LILAC,
NOR MORE ROBUST THAN ITS WOODY STALK, FOR WE MUST REMEMBER
THAT IT IS A TREE AS WELL AS A FLOWER.**
–Stevie Smith, English poet (1902–71)

Lilacs, said to symbolize the joy of youth and associated with spring's awakening, are hardy, easy to grow, and low-maintenance. Although they can reach heights of 5 to 15 feet (or more), depending on the variety, the ideal lilac shrub produces flowers at eye level—all the better to enjoy their sweet, haunting fragrance.

The common lilac, *Syringa vulgaris, is* native to southeastern Europe and blooms in the northern U.S. for about 2 weeks in late May. However, early-, mid-, and late-season lilac varieties can ensure steady blooms for a longer period of time.

Aromatic lilac flowers are attractive to butterflies and wonderful for cutting.

PLANTING
Plant lilacs in spring or fall, although fall is preferred.

For strong blooms, lilacs require full

WIT & WISDOM

- *Poet Walt Whitman (1819–92) wrote "When Lilacs Last in the Dooryard Bloom'd" to honor Abraham Lincoln after his assassination.*
- *The lilac belongs to the olive family, Oleaceae.*

sun for at least 6 hours; given less, they will not flower well.

Lilacs thrive in fertile, rich, neutral to alkaline soil (at a pH near 7.0). If soil is in poor condition, mix in compost or aged manure. Choose or prepare a site that drains well. Poor drainage or pooling water can cause "wet feet," potentially leading to root rot, stunted growth, and/or failure to flower.

Transplant stock from a nursery may be in a container or balled and burlapped (aka "B and B"). Prepare a hole that will put the plant's base 2 to 3 inches deeper than it grew in the nursery. If the plant is container-grown, spread out the roots as you settle it into the ground; if it's balled and wrapped in burlap, gently remove the covering and any rope before planting. Work in topsoil around the roots. Water, then fill in the hole with more topsoil, leaving a slight depression around the stem(s); alternatively, create a ring of soil around each plant that will capture water so that it will be absorbed and not run off.

RECOMMENDED VARIETIES

For early flowers, try *Syringa* x *hyacinthiflora* hybrids; they bloom 7 to 10 days before *S. vulgaris.*

The most common and fragrant lilacs are of the *S. vulgaris* variety:

- 'Charles Joly': double magenta flowers; an early bloomer

- 'Monge', with dark reddish-purple flowers, and 'Firmament', with blue flowers: midseason bloomers

- 'Primrose': huge, fragrant yellow flower trusses; blooms in late spring

S. x *prestoniae* hybrids 'Miss Canada', with reddish-pink flowers, and 'Donald Wyman', with pink-purple flowers: late bloomers

Uncommon types/varieties include . . .

- *S.* x 'Penda' Bloomerang Purple: flowers in spring, pauses, then flowers again from midsummer through fall

- Although common lilacs love cold weather, a few thrive as far south as Zone 8, including cutleaf hybrid *S.* x *laciniata*, with fragrant, pale lavender flowers, and *S. pubescens* ssp. *patula* 'Miss Kim', with pale, lilac-blue blooms that fade to white.

If you purchase a bare-root specimen or a friend gives you a sucker (offshoot) of lilac root, plant it in the spring with the same care and consideration due a mature shrub. Dig a hole, backfill it with enriched soil, and put the sucker into it. Then water and wait. In 4 or 5 years, you'll be rewarded with fragrant blossoms.

Space multiple lilac bushes 5 to 15 feet apart, depending on the variety.

CARE

Each spring, apply a layer of compost to the soil, followed by mulch to retain moisture and control weeds.

Water in summer, if rainfall is less than 1 inch per week.

When the bloom period has passed, prune the bush to shape it. Spread lime and well-rotted/aged manure on the soil surface.

Limit fertilizer to a handful of balanced product (10-10-10) in early spring. Lilacs will not bloom if they are overfertilized.

PRUNING

Lilacs bloom on old wood, so it's critical to prune in the spring right after the flowers fade. If you prune later, in summer, you risk removing the following year's buds. Note: If over a few years your lilac flower clusters are getting smaller, it's time to prune!

Every year, after bloom, cut out any dead wood and remove the oldest canes down to the ground. Remove the small suckers. Cut back weak branches

---

SOIL DRAINAGE TEST

Test soil drainage by digging a hole 8 inches in diameter and 12 inches deep. Fill it with water; if it does not drain within an hour, choose another spot.

---

to a strong shoot. Cut back tall canes to eye height.

The ideal lilac shrub has about 10 canes. If your lilac is old and in really bad shape, remove one-third of the oldest canes (down to the ground) in Year 1, half of the remaining old wood in Year 2, and the rest of the old wood in Year 3. Another option for old lilacs is to chop the whole thing back to about 8 to 12 inches tall. This sounds drastic, but lilacs are very hardy.

Note that severe pruning results in the loss of blooms for 1 to 3 years. For these reasons, a wise pruning program aims to give the bushes annual attention.

GOOD SUCKER SENSE

Gertrude Jekyll, the 19th-century no-nonsense English horticulturist (1843–1932), advocated a strenuous exercise: "When taking away suckers . . . it is better to tear them out than to cut them off. A cut, however close, leaves a base from

which they may always spring again, but if pulled or wrenched out, they bring away with them the swollen base."

DISEASES/PESTS *(see pages 190–200)*

Diseases: blight, Botrytis; blight, lilac bacterial; crown gall; leaf spot, fungal; mildew, powdery (although unsightly, does no serious harm to plant); rot, Phytophthora crown and root; wilt, Verticillium. *Pests:* lilac borers; mealy bugs; scale insects; slugs/snails; thrips.

HARVEST

Lilac flowers are edible, but flavor varies among cultivars from no flavor to "green" and lemony flavor. Gather insect- and disease-free blooms early in the day. Avoid any that are unopened or past their peak. Wash the flowers gently in cool water. Pat them dry and refrigerate until ready to use.

EDIBLE ORNAMENTALS

Make candied lilac flowerets for a special cake decoration: Separate the individual flowers. Using tweezers, dip each one into a beaten egg white, reconstituted egg white powder, or packaged egg whites. Then dip the flower in finely granulated sugar. Set it aside to dry before placing it on a cake.

FORCING

To force a winter bouquet from cut lilac branches, bruise the cut ends and set them in water. Spritz the branches frequently with water. Keep them in a cool place until they bloom, then move to a warmer area for display.

LILY

Lilium spp.

THE ROSE IS THE FLOWER AND HANDMAIDEN OF LOVE—
THE LILY, HER FAIR ASSOCIATE, IS THE EMBLEM OF BEAUTY AND PURITY.
–Dorothea Dix, American activist (1802–87)

Everyone loves lilies! Grown from bulbs, lilies are perennials that require minimal care if they are planted in the right place. By carefully blending early-, mid-, and late-season varieties, you can make sure that their magnificent blooms add elegance to your garden from spring through first frost. Most lilies do well in containers and look spectacular in a vase.

These lily species and their hybrids provide endless options:

Asiatic lilies are the shortest type of lily (about 2 to 3 feet tall) but bear lots of buds and flowers in many hues. Most are unscented and bloom in early summer.

Easter lilies are typically forced into bloom around Easter (March or April). These are generally hardy to Zone 5 (and to Zone 4 if given 1 to 2 feet of mulch in autumn for winter protection).

Oriental lilies, with a famously strong fragrance and large flowers, tend to grow slowly.

Trumpet lilies, similar to orientals,

WIT & WISDOM

- *Many plants have "lily" in their name, but most are not "true lilies." Peace lilies, canna lilies, water lilies, lily-of-the-valley, and calla lilies are not true lilies.*
- *Daylilies* (Hemerocallis *spp.*), *which have many leaves that grow from a crown, are also not true lilies.*
- *True lilies are of the genus* Lilium *and have only one stem or shoot that grows from an onionlike bulb.*

produce many blooms with a sweet scent. The eponymous flowers tend to be smaller and tighter than the others.

Other lilies include **tiger lilies** and native **Turk's cap lilies,** as well as hybrids like **Orienpet** (Oriental + Trumpet) and **LA lilies** (Easter + Asiatic).

PLANTING

In most regions, plant lily bulbs in fall, a few weeks before winter's freezing temperatures. In areas with particularly harsh winters, plant in spring, as soon as the threat of frost has passed.

Container-grown lily plants can be planted anytime during early summer.

Buy bare bulbs close to planting time. Because lily bulbs don't go dormant, they will deteriorate over time, so don't buy bulbs in fall to plant in spring.

Select a site in full sun with well-draining soil. Water trapped beneath a bulb's overlapping scales may cause rot. Most popular varieties prefer acidic to neutral soil, but some (e.g., the Madonna lily) tolerate alkaline soils. Test and amend soil as directed to ensure proper pH.

Lilies need 6 to 8 hours of direct sunlight per day. In shade, the stems will lean toward the sunlight or become

spindly and fall over.

Loosen the soil to a depth of 12 to 15 inches. This encourages the stem to send out roots to help stabilize the plant and perhaps eliminate the need for staking. Deep planting keeps bulbs cool when temperatures soar. Mix in leaf mold or well-rotted organic matter to encourage good drainage.

For each bulb, dig a hole three times as deep as its height. Place the bulb in it, pointy side up. Fill with soil and tamp gently. (Got critters? Bury the bulbs in wire cages to protect them from getting eaten.)

Space bulbs about 8 to 18 inches apart, depending on the variety (the "rule" is at a distance equal to three times the bulb's diameter). For visual appeal, plant lilies in groups of three to five if space allows; crowding leads to poor circulation and gray mold in a cool, wet spring or summer.

Water thoroughly.

CARE

Each spring, apply a thin layer of compost, followed by a 2-inch layer of moist—but not wet—mulch.

During active growth, water generously, especially if rainfall is less than 1 inch per week.

Apply high-potassium liquid fertilizer

RECOMMENDED VARIETIES

Stagger lily bloom times for the most enjoyment.

Asiatic lilies are a favorite of floral arrangers and hardy in Zones 4 to 9.

• 'Patricia's Pride': white flowers brushed with deep purple; about 32 inches tall; blooms in early to midsummer

• 'Gran Paradiso': large (4- to 5-inch) red flowers; 3 to 4 feet tall; hardy in Zones 3 to 8; blooms in early to midsummer

Trumpet lilies produce many blooms with a heady, sweet fragrance and are hardy in Zones 5 to 9.

• 'Album', aka regal lily: white flowers; up to 6 feet tall; blooms in midsummer

• 'Yellow Planet': extra-large, buttery yellow flowers; 4 feet tall; blooms in mid- to late summer

Oriental hybrids bloom when Asiatic lilies are beginning to fade. Tiny 2-foot-tall to towering 8-foot stems bear masses of huge white, pink, red, or bicolor blooms that are wonderful as cut flowers. Their intoxicating, spicy fragrance intensifies after dark.

• 'Black Beauty': dark red, 5-inch, funnel-shape flowers; 5 to 6 feet tall; blooms in mid- to late summer

• 'Casa Blanca': white flowers; 3 to 4 feet tall; blooms in mid- to late summer

• 'Stargazer': large, deep pink, white-edge flowers; 2 to 3 feet tall; blooms in mid- to late summer

Native lilies provide a range of options; here are a few . . .

• Turk's cap lily: densely spotted orange flowers; 4 to 7 feet tall; blooms in midsummer

• Canada lily: yellow to orange-red flowers; 3 to 8 feet tall; blooms in late spring to midsummer

• Wood lily: North America's most wide-ranging lily; orange, pink-to-red flowers; 1 to 3 feet tall; blooms in July and August

every 2 weeks from planting until 6 weeks after flowering.

Stake tall lilies.

Lilies bloom only once per season; remove faded flowers so that the plants don't waste energy making seeds.

After blooms fade, cut off the stem. Do not remove leaves until they have turned brown in fall. They help to provide nourishment to the bulb for the next season's blooms.

Cut down dead stalks in late fall or early spring.

Before winter, add 4 to 6 inches of mulch; this delays the ground freeze and allows roots to keep growing. Leave the mulch until spring's last hard frost has passed.

In regions that do not get snow cover, keep the soil moist in winter.

When lily shoots grow through the mulch in the spring, start to remove the mulch gradually.

Divide lilies every 3 to 4 years in spring as new growth begins. Dig up the plants and divide the clumps. Replant the bulbs, amending the site's soil as needed.

SAVING THE EASTER LILY

These stunning seasonal potted blooms can be enjoyed in the garden for years. Allow the flowers to fade and remove each in its turn. Set the pot in the sun and treat it as a houseplant, fertilizing when watering, until the leaves yellow. In mid-May, remove the bulb from its pot and plant it outdoors in a protected but sunny spot. New growth will soon emerge. Typically, during the first outdoor season, Easter lilies bloom in late September. In ensuing years, they will reach a height of about 3 feet.

DISEASES/PESTS *(see pages 190–200)*

Diseases: blight, Botrytis (fire); rot, Fusarium basal; viruses. *Pests:* aphids; deer; groundhogs; lily leaf beetles; nematodes, foliar; nematodes, stem and bulb; rabbits; slugs/snails; voles.

HARVEST

Cut stems for arrangements when the first, lowermost bud shows full color but has not yet opened. Vase life is 10 to 14 days.

LILY-OF-THE-VALLEY

Convallaria majalis

SWEETEST OF THE FLOWERS A-BLOOMING
IN THE FRAGRANT VERNAL DAYS
IS THE LILY-OF-THE-VALLEY
WITH ITS SOFT, RETIRING WAYS.

–*"The Lily-of-the-Valley," by Paul Laurence Dunbar, American poet (1872–1906)*

Lily-of-the-valley—aka May bells, Mary's tears, and Our Lady's tears—is a woodland plant but not a lily; it belongs to the asparagus family. It produces tiny, fragrant, bell-shape white or pink flowers that can be cut for arrangements. This low-growing (6 to 12 inches tall), spreading perennial comes up in late spring and blooms for about 3 weeks. The genus *Convallaria* includes a single species, *C. majalis,* which is among the most useful ground covers for shade.

TAKE CARE AND BEWARE

Lily-of-the-valley is an aggressive spreader.

All parts of the plant, including the berries, are poisonous to people and animals.

PLANTING

Plant in spring or fall. Lily-of-the-valley thrives in a site that gets partial or full shade and has fertile, well-draining soil. It struggles in hot, dry climates. Before planting, mix a couple of inches of compost or aged manure into the soil, if necessary.

Lily-of-the-valley can also be planted in a pot and placed in a shady spot.

The plant grows from rhizomes (underground, rootlike stems), which produce upright pointed buds, aka pips. Place each rhizome into a shallow hole, spreading the roots. Cover with soil.

Space rhizomes about 6 inches apart. Water thoroughly.

CARE

Side-dress with compost when new growth appears in the spring.

Keep the soil evenly moist; do not let plants dry out.

After the bloom period, do not remove the foliage. It will turn golden, and orange berries will appear in fall.

Mulch with aged manure or compost in late fall.

Divide when dormant in early spring or in fall by digging up (lifting) clumps and separating the rhizomes. Replant the rhizomes as directed.

RECOMMENDED VARIETIES

Convallaria majalis var. *rosea* has pink flowers; these are less fragrant than the white varieties.

C. majalis 'Albostriata': white flowers and variegated (white-stripe) leaves

C. majalis 'Bordeaux': produces large white flowers on long stalks

C. majalis 'Fernwood's Golden Slippers': golden-green leaves in early spring

DISEASES/PESTS (see pages 190–200)

Diseases: anthracnose; blight, Botrytis; blight, southern; leaf spot, fungal; rust. *Pests:* aphids; black vine weevils; lily leaf beetles; nematodes, foliar; slugs/snails; spider mites.

HARVEST

Cut a stem for arrangements when one-quarter of the buds on it are open. Vase life is up to 7 days.

FORCING

Dig up a few plants in the fall. Plant in a container, bring it indoors, and place it in a bright spot. Blooms should appear during the winter months.

WIT & WISDOM

• *In the language of flowers, lily-of-the-valley symbolizes sweetness, purity, and pure love.*

• *It is the birth flower for May.*

• *According to folklore, lily-of-the-valley protects gardens from evil spirits.*

LUPINE

Lupinus spp.

AH, LUPINE, WITH SILVERY LEAVES
AND BLOSSOMS BLUE AS THE SKIES,
I KNOW A MAID LIKE THEE,
AND BLUE, TOO, ARE HER EYES.
–Arlo Bates, American poet (1850–1918)

Lupines, renowned for their 1- to 4-foot-tall colorful spikes, were once thought to steal nutrients from the soil—hence their genus name, *Lupinus*, which is Latin for "wolf." However, lupines are in the pea family and as nitrogen-fixers can actually improve soil. *Lupinus* includes about 280 species, many native to North America. They thrive both in the wild and in gardens from California to Maine. One of the most famous, the Texas bluebonnet, carpets fields and roadsides every April. Yellow-flower Carolina lupine *(Thermopsis villosa)*, aka southern lupine, is a "false" variety yet nonetheless a native perennial and one of the easiest "lupines" to grow.

Lupine foliage is gray-green, with silvery hairs; the flowers resemble pea flowers. The seedpod looks like a hairy pea pod and contains up to 12 seeds.

PLANTING

Plant in cool temperatures; lupine can not tolerate heat, humidity, or drought.

Select and prepare a spot in full sun or light shade.

Lupines prefer moist, sandy, well-draining, slightly acidic soil, although they will grow in heavier soils. Before planting, loosen soil to a depth of about 1 to 1½ feet to accommodate the long taproots. Avoid overly rich soil, especially manure; it rots the plant's crown. Lupine also dislikes lime.

Sow seeds directly in early spring or fall. Soak them in a bowl of warm water

WIT & WISDOM
• *Lupine flowers symbolize happiness and imagination.*
• *Many species are poisonous to livestock.*
• *Bees, butterflies, and hummingbirds are attracted to lupines.*

RECOMMENDED VARIETIES

Lupines usually bear blue, white, pink, or yellow flowers. The original blue is the hardiest.

• Garden lupine *(Lupinus polyphyllus)*, aka big-leaved lupine: blue, pink, and purple flowers; native to much of western North America; prefers moist environments

• Wild lupine *(L. perennis)*, aka sundial lupine: blue and purple flowers; native in eastern North America; hosts the endangered Karner blue butterfly

• Texas bluebonnet *(L. texensis)*: dark blue flowers with white markings; found in central and north Texas; the easiest of the species to cultivate

• Russell hybrid lupines *(L. polyphyllus)*: introduced to England from North America in the 1820s; crossed with other species by English horticulturist George Russell (1857–1951) to produce reliable hybrids; include Russell mix; the most common perennial lupines.

• *L. polyphyllus* 'Minarette': a Russell strain; multicolor dwarf hybrids; up to 20 inches tall

• Lupine Woodfield hybrids: built on Russell hybrids stock; deeper shades and bicolor blooms

for up to 48 hours before planting.

If starting seedlings indoors, transplant them at 4 to 6 weeks, before they develop the long taproot; they will have a better chance of survival. Prepare a hole ½ inch deeper than the seedling pot and twice as wide. Space seedlings about 1 foot apart. Because of the long taproot, lupines do not transplant well.

CARE

Avoid fertilizing; if necessary, apply an acidifying agent to maintain slightly acidic pH in the soil.

Stake tall varieties as needed.

To promote more blooms, deadhead flowers as they begin to produce seed.

Harvest and save seeds when the pods turn yellow and the seeds rattle inside.

Avoid pruning dead flower stalks in fall; wait until spring.

Add mulch around plants for winter protection.

DISEASES/PESTS *(see pages 190–200)*

Lupine is deer-resistant. *Diseases:* anthracnose; blight, Botrytis; blight, southern; brown spot; leaf spots, fungal; mildew, downy; mildew, powdery; rot, Phytophthora crown and root; rot, Rhizoctonia root and stem; rust; viruses; wilt, Fusarium. *Pests:* aphids; slugs/snails; thrips.

HARVEST

Cut stems for arrangements when most buds are open. Vase life is up to 7 days.

PEONY

Paeonia spp.

THE FATTEST AND MOST SCRUMPTIOUS OF ALL FLOWERS, A RARE
FUSION OF FLUFF AND MAJESTY, THE PEONY IS NOW COMING INTO BLOOM.
–Henry Mitchell, American writer (1923–93)

In the 1930s and '40s, plant catalogs listed only three peony choices: white, crimson, and rose pink. Today, thousands of varieties are available.

Peonies have lovely foliage and are easy to grow, magnificent as cut flowers, and hardy anywhere you need an overcoat (they require a cold period for bud formation—a frustration to some southern gardeners). Once settled in the garden, they can be content for generations. Some have been known to thrive for a century!

PLANTING

Peonies do not respond well to transplanting, so choose a site carefully. The plants thrive in 6 to 8 hours per day of full sun, but they can manage with less. In southern states, provide some shade. Everywhere, avoid close proximity to trees. Space peonies 3 to 4 feet apart to allow for good air circulation. Stagnant, humid air can lead to disease.

The time to plant bare-root tubers with three to five "eyes" (buds) or move mature dormant peonies in most of the U.S. and Canada is late September or October; do it later in Zones 7 and 8. Plants should be settled into place about 6 weeks before the ground freezes. Planting in spring is fine, but the growth of spring-planted peonies tends to lag behind that of those planted later in the year.

For each tuber, dig a hole about 2 feet deep and 2 feet wide. Peonies prefer

RECOMMENDED VARIETIES

For a successive display, plant several varieties. Choose from six types . . .

- **Anemone** (an advanced Japanese form)—'Laura Dessert': cream/pale lemon to white; strong fragrance; early-season
- **Single** (one row of petals)—'Sparkling Star': deep pink; early- to midseason
- **Japanese** (decorative centers)—'Carrara': white, with soft yellow centers; fragrant; midseason
- **Semidouble** (five or more guard petals and prominent centers)—'Pink Hawaiian Coral': pink to coral rose form; slight fragrance; early-season
- **Double** (large petals, needs support)—'Candy Stripe': white, with red streaks; slight fragrance; mid- to late-season
- **Bomb** (large, like a scoop of petals)—'Angel Cheeks': soft pink; slight fragrance; midseason

Consider, too, the **Itoh peony:** Named after its developer, Japanese botanist Dr. Toichi Itoh (d. 1956), this flower is a cross between a herbaceous (bush) peony and a tree peony. Its large single, semidouble, and double blooms appear later in season and last longer than traditional peonies.

WIT & WISDOM

• *After at least 2,000 years of cultivation and breeding in China, the ornamental peony was introduced to Europe and America in about 1800.*

• *Two peony species are native to North America. Brown's, aka western, peony ranges from California to Montana, and the California peony is found along the Pacific coast of that state.*

• *When peonies blossom, it is safe to plant heat-loving melons, such as cantaloupes.*

• *Marco Polo described peony blossoms as "roses as big as cabbages."*

---

rich, moist, yet well-draining soil with a neutral pH. Mix plenty of compost or aged manure into the soil from the hole. If the soil is heavy clay or very sandy, increase the amendment. Add about 1 cup of bonemeal.

About 2 inches below the soil surface, create a soil mound in the hole. Set the tuber on it with the eyes facing upward. (In southern states, plant early-blooming varieties on a mound about 1 inch below the soil surface.)

Fill the hole, taking care not to bury the root deeper than 2 inches. Tamp the soil gently.

If planting a container-grown peony, cover it no deeper than it grew in the pot.

Water thoroughly.

CARE

Peonies thrive on benign neglect. Allow a few years for the plants to become established, bloom, and grow. Division every few years is not necessary.

Fertilizer is seldom needed. If soil is poor, mix in bonemeal, compost, or well-rotted manure in early summer, after the flowers have bloomed and been deadheaded—but only every few years.

Protect plants from strong winds

and themselves; large blooms can be top-heavy. Consider using three-legged metal peony rings or wire tomato cages that allow the plant to grow through the center.

Deadhead blossoms as soon as they begin to fade, cutting to a strong leaf.

In fall, cut the foliage to the ground to avoid any overwintering diseases. Cover tuber sites with mulch but do not smother them. Where winters are severe, mulch loosely with pine needles or

A VOICE OF EXPERIENCE

I deadhead only the flowers that have not produced a seedpod. I have been growing peonies from seed for 30 years and now have mixed colors that I did not originally have. A labor of love, as it may take years (!!!) before they flower. I second the "Do not disturb the roots" idea, as we had to dig out two beds due to a huge invasion of creeping bellflower. They are just starting to flower again after several years.

–Tara, on Almanac.com

shredded bark prior to the plant's first winter. Remove mulch in spring.

HOW TO USE

Peonies stand tall when lining walkways or as a low hedge. They bloom from late spring through early summer, depending on location and type and/or bloom period (early-, mid-, or late-season).

After flowering, the bushy clump of glossy green leaves lasts all summer, before turning purplish-red or gold in fall.

DISEASES/PESTS *(see pages 190–200)*

Peony tends to be hardy and is rabbit- and deer-resistant. *Diseases:* blight, Botrytis; crown gall; leaf blotch; leaf spots, fungal; mildew, powdery; mold, Sclerotinia white; rot, Phytophthora crown and root; viruses; wilt,

Verticillium. *Pests:* aphids; Japanese beetles; nematodes, foliar; nematodes, root-knot; scale insects.

GOT ANTS?

Ants crawl on peony buds because they are attracted to the sugary droplets on the outside of flower buds and/or to the honeydew produced by aphids and scale insects. Ants eat the peony's nectar in exchange for attacking bud-eating pests. Learn to love the ants—they keep peonies safe!

HARVEST

Cut stems for arrangements when buds are puffy and colored. Vase life is 5 to 10 days.

Peony petals are edible. Add to summer salads or use as garnish for lemonade and ice tea.

RHODODENDRON

Rhododendron spp.

I HAVE SPOKEN TO PLANTS MYSELF, AND IF PRESSED FOR CONCLUSIONS
WOULD HAVE TO SAY THAT THOSE I THREATENED DID BETTER THAN THOSE
I—WELL, I WOULDN'T SAY PRAYED OVER, BUT PLEADED WITH, CAJOLED.
A RHODODENDRON THAT HADN'T BLOOMED FOR 6 YEARS WAS FLATLY TOLD
THAT IT WOULD BE REMOVED THE FOLLOWING YEAR IF THERE WERE
NO FLOWERS. NEED I SAY THAT IT HAS BLOOMED PROFUSELY EVER SINCE?
–Eleanor Perényi, American garden writer (1918–2009)

Rhododendrons and azaleas are both from the genus *Rhododendron.*

Each welcomes spring with spectacular clusters of often fragrant tubular-, funnel-, or bell-shape blooms in shades of pink, red, white, yellow, and purple.

With more than a thousand species, there is a specimen for just about every landscape, from low-growing ground cover azaleas to rhododendrons that can reach 25 feet in height.

These shrubs prefer climates with adequate rainfall and summers that are moist.

The two main azalea groups, evergreen and deciduous (varieties that drop their leaves in the fall), can be found throughout North America, everywhere from the frosty Canadian prairies to tropical Florida climes.

The rhododendron types are fussier, preferring temperate climates (Zones 5 to 8). Most require a chilling to develop strong flower buds.

PLANTING

When choosing a variety, note the flower period. Early varieties can blossom in March and late ones in July or even the fall.

In hot climates, buy plants in 3-gallon pots. Smaller plants, with fewer roots, struggle in heat.

If spring brings temperatures above 90°F, avoid white-flowering azaleas. Their thin petals drop off in the heat.

Buy plants with deep green (not yellow) and open (not wilted) foliage. Avoid bone-dry plants. Push a finger into the container's soil to check that it has been well watered.

Plant in spring or early fall.

Most large-leaf varieties require dappled shade; avoid deep shade or full sun. A sunny spot that receives a few hours of shade is perfect.

In cold or temperate regions (Zones 3 to 6), plant in full sun (6 hours per day, minimum) to improve flowering and avoid mildew and on the sheltered side of a windbreak. If subjected to cold, dry winds, the leaves and buds dry out and die.

In warm or hot regions (Zones 7 to 11), plant in afternoon shade. In tropical zones, azaleas will bloom in full shade.

Azaleas and rhododendrons have shallow root systems. Soil should be rich, moisture-retaining yet well-draining, and acidic (a pH of 4.5 to 6.0). Amend as needed with compost or aged manure. Test the soil for proper pH and amend as advised.

Dig a hole as deep as the root ball and twice as wide. Space plants 2 to 6 feet apart, depending on estimated size at maturity.

Set plants so that top roots are at soil level or slightly below—and no deeper, or the roots will rot.

Half-fill the hole with soil, then water it well to settle the soil. Fill in with remaining soil, water, and spread mulch to prevent the plant from drying out.

CARE

Mulch in spring with 2 to 5 inches of pine bark chips or pine needles to protect shallow roots and retain moisture. Dry conditions reduce flower bud formation.

Avoid a so-called "mulch volcano," which is mulch piled heavily around a shrub's trunk. This can encourage rot. Leave a few inches around the trunk free of mulch.

Fertilize sparingly and only when flower buds swell in early spring. Heavy applications of fertilizer will burn plants.

Water in summer if rainfall is less

WIT & WISDOM

• The name "rhododendron" comes from the Greek rhodo, for "rose," and dendron, meaning "tree."

• The American Rhododendron Society provides information on more than 2,000 rhododendrons and azaleas. Annually, the society names several the Rhododendron of the Year as the best-performing plants for different regions.

than 1 inch per week.

After flowering, deadhead where it's practical, carefully: Next year's buds are under the old heads. This will promote vegetative growth, not seed production.

Where winters are severe, wrap evergreen rhododendrons with burlap in fall and apply extra mulch around the base.

Azaleas and rhododendrons transplant most successfully during the cool temperatures of fall or early spring, when in dormancy, but they may be transplanted at any time during the growing season.

PRUNING

If necessary to reduce height, prune after flowering in spring. Otherwise, remove dead, damaged, or diseased branches at any time. On young and old plants, snap off spent flower stalks by bending them over until they break away from their stems. Be careful not to damage growth buds at the base of each flower stalk.

DISEASES/PESTS (see pages 190–200)

Diseases: blight, Ovulinia petal; bud blast; canker and dieback, Botryosphaeria; leaf gall, azalea; leaf spot, algal; leaf spot, fungal; mildew, powdery; rot, Phytophthora crown and root; rust. *Pests:* aphids, black vine weevils, caterpillars, lacebugs, leafhoppers, scale insects, whiteflies.

HARVEST

Cut branches once the buds have just opened. Change the water every few days and give the stems a fresh cut at the same time. Vase life is about 7 days.

RECOMMENDED VARIETIES

The more than 1,000 species in the *Rhododendron* genus vary greatly. Here are a handful of options:

• 'Purple Gem': small, pale-purple flowers; dwarf (2-foot) rhododendron; early midseason; Zones 5 to 8

• 'Blue Diamond': violet-blue flowers; dwarf (3-foot) evergreen rhododendron; early midseason; Zones 7 to 9

• 'Hydon Dawn': pale pink flowers; low-growing rhododendron; tolerates full sun; late midseason; Zones 7 to 9

• 'Nova Zembla': bright red flowers; 5- to 10-foot evergreen rhododendron; midseason; Zones 5 to 8

• 'Cecile': dark salmon-pink blooms; grows to 7 feet tall; vigorous azalea; midseason to late midseason; Zones 5 to 8

• 'Rosy Lights': deep purple-pink flowers; grows to 6 feet tall; extra-cold-hardy azalea; late midseason; Zones 3 to 8

ROSE

Rosa spp.

LOVELIEST OF LOVELY THINGS ARE THEY,
ON EARTH, THAT SOONEST PASS AWAY.
THE ROSE THAT LIVES ITS LITTLE HOUR
IS PRIZED BEYOND THE SCULPTURED FLOWER.
—William Cullen Bryant, American poet (1794–1878)

For thousands of years, the rose has been a symbol of beauty, love, and passion, and it remains so today. Growing roses can be demanding or carefree.

Roses are shrubs of many forms, available for every bloom season and in a range of colors. Knowing rose classifications helps in understanding their growth habit, climate preferences, and general requirements.

- **Species, or wild, roses** grew wild for thousands of years and have been adopted into modern gardens. Adaptable to any climate, they are climbers or bushy shrubs that bloom from spring to early summer. Most have single blossoms.

■ **Old, or "old-fashioned" (aka "heirloom"), roses** are those introduced prior to 1867. There are hundreds of varieties of these lush, invariably fragrant roses. Hardiness varies, but they exist for both warm and mild climates.

■ **Modern hybrid roses,** introduced after 1867, are sturdy, long-blooming, hardy, and disease-resistant. Bred for color, shape, size, and fragrance, some bear flowers in clusters; others, on single stems. Most are remontant.

BLOOM HABITS

Some classes of roses bloom only once a year in spring, but flowers can cover plants for more than a month.

Remontant roses bloom a second time in a season, generally 50 to 60 days after the first flush of flowers.

RECOMMENDED VARIETIES

These three are considered to be the easiest roses to grow:

• Knock Out shrub roses: continuous blooms; high disease resistance; require no spraying, dusting, pruning, deadheading; hardy to Zone 5

• Flower Carpet ground cover roses: continuous blooms; require no deadheading; drought-tolerant once established; minimal pruning; hardy in Zones 4 to 11

• David Austin climbers (to 6 feet), including 'Gertrude Jekyll': continuous pink blooms; strong fragrance; hardy in Zones 4 to 11

Rugosa roses include 5-foot-tall/-wide shrub 'Jens Munk': pink blooms in June through August; disease-resistant; hardy to Zone 2

"Bests" are highly subjective. These roses tend to be crowd-pleasers, but choose a rose that pleases you . . .

• Best pink rose—'New Dawn' (the first U.S.-patented plant): blush-pink hybrid climber (15+ feet); sweet fragrance; disease-resistant; good cut flower; hardy in Zones 5 to 9

• Best red rose—'Don Juan': hybrid climber (up to 12 feet); sweet fragrance; good cut flower; spiny stems; hardy in Zones 6 to 9

• Best white rose—'Iceberg': hybrid climber (up to 12 feet); honey scent; disease-resistant; heat-/humidity-tolerant; good cut flower; hardy in Zones 4 to 9

• Best yellow rose—'Sunsprite' (aka 'KORresia'): 3-foot bush floribunda hybrid; fragrant; disease-resistant; good cut flower; hardy in Zones 5 to 9

• Best rose for fragrance—'Pink Peace': vigorous hybrid bush; sweet scent; large (6-inch), continuous double blooms; good cut flower; hardy in Zones 5 to 10

PLANTING

Roses are purchased as either "bare-root" or container-grown.

Bare-root roses are usually shipped in spring when plants are fully dormant. Check that the packing material is moist and store in a cool, dark place until ready to plant—in early spring or late fall.

Plant container-grown roses by late spring or early summer for best results, although they can be planted at almost any time. When fall planting, be sure that the rose is in the ground for at least 6 weeks before the ground freezes so that roots can start growing.

Roses require 5 to 6 hours of full sun per day; they bloom in proportion to their exposure to sunlight: More sunlight begets more flowers. Morning sun is especially important because it dries any dew on the leaves; this helps to prevent diseases. Roses planted in partial sun will weaken gradually.

In the upper half of the United States and northward, choose a site in full sun year-round. In southern areas, choose a spot with some afternoon shade to protect blossoms from the scorching sun.

Roses like loose, slightly sandy, loamy, well-draining soil. Loose soil facilitates good drainage. Rose roots in heavy clay can become waterlogged. Amend soil with compost or aged manure, if necessary. Roses prefer a near-neutral pH range; 6.5 is just about right. Test the soil and amend as needed.

When planting more than one rose, the distance between plants should be about two-thirds of their height at maturity. Old garden roses need more space; miniature roses, less.

When planting bare-root roses . . .
■ Soak bare-root roses in a bucket of warm water for 8 to 12 hours before planting.
■ Dig a big hole about 15 to 18 inches wide. Mound soil in the center of the hole. Place the roots over the mound. Add soil to hold the plant in place and add some water to firm the soil around the roots. Fill the hole, firm the soil, and water well.

When planting potted roses . . .
■ Dig a hole the depth of the rose pot and 15 to 18 inches wide. Remove the plant from the pot, loosen the soil from the roots, place in the center of the hole, and spread the roots. In mild winter areas, the graft union (knobby area) on the stem should be level with or just above the soil surface; in cold winter areas (north of Zone 6), the graft union should be about 4 inches below the soil surface. Fill in with soil, water well, and firm the soil. Scatter and scratch in slow-release fertilizer formulated for roses around the plant.
■ When planting in autumn, heavily mulch the plant to keep the soil from freezing and do not fertilize.

CARE

Water diligently but not to excess. Do not let roses sit in water. Soak the root zone at least twice a week in dry summer weather. Avoid frequent shallow sprinklings; these will not reach the deeper roots and may encourage fungus. In autumn, reduce the amount of water but do not allow roses to dry out completely.

Feed roses monthly from April through July with a balanced granular fertilizer (5-10-5 or 5-10-10). Allow ¾ to 1 cup for each bush. Sprinkle it around the drip line, not against the stem. In May and June, add a tablespoon of Epsom salts; the magnesium sulfate will encourage new growth. Stop fertilizing 6 weeks before the first frost.

Deadhead regularly. Start after the first flush of flowers and continue through summer to encourage more blooms. Stop deadheading 3 to 4 weeks before the first hard frost so as not to encourage new growth that may be damaged by the cold.

Continue watering during dry fall weather.

After a few frosts but before the ground freezes, apply a 2- to 4-inch layer of mulch around roses, up to about 1 inch from the stem.

PRUNING

Wear gloves when pruning. Prune in spring and summer. Do not prune roses in fall. This will encourage new growth, which could incur winter damage. Simply cut off any dead or diseased canes.

In spring, prune roses before growth begins. Always cut to a live bud pointing away from the center of the shrub to encourage outward growth.

In early spring, remove diseased, broken, or dead branches. After the bloom period, prune selectively to shape plants and control growth.

Remove winter-killed branches or damaged wood on climbing and rambling roses but defer an annual pruning until after the peak of bloom. Climbers and ramblers tend to bloom on old wood, and side branches tend to flower more heavily than central leaders.

Cut back old canes by about 30 to 40 percent on repeat-flowering hybrid and floribunda roses; these generally bloom on "new wood" (the current season's growth).

Remove crossing canes and spindly growth. Destroy all old or diseased plant material.

Clear away any trimmed debris from around the base of rosebushes; it can harbor disease and insects.

OVERWINTERING

Container roses acquired in late summer or fall can be overwintered above ground.

■ **In northern zones,** expose the plant to the first deep freeze (this helps with dormancy). Put it in a dark, unheated room, basement, or garage. Water occasionally, only enough to moisten the soil. Bring the plant outdoors when it shows signs of coming back to life. Plant when the soil warms.

■ **In tropical climate areas** (where it's never below 20°F), container roses can

---

NATURE'S TIMING

Phenology suggests pruning roses at about the time that forsythias bloom.

WIT & WISDOM

• *The cultivation of roses began about 5,000 years ago in China.*

• *In 17th-century Europe, roses were considered legal tender for purchases.*

• *The rose is the U.S. national flower and is honored by
the annual Rose Parade on New Year's Day.*

FIVE ROSE TIPS THAT REALLY WORK

• To avert deer, plant lavender at the base of rosebushes. They are attracted by rose scent, and lavender muddies the rose aroma.

• To acidify the soil slightly, scatter used coffee grounds and tea leaves around rosebushes.

• Feed roses a banana peel; it contains calcium, sulfur, magnesium, and phosphates. Lay a strip of peel at the base of each bush or chop up the peel, let it sit for 2 weeks in a sealed jar of water, and pour the mixture under each bush. Or, bury a black, mushy banana next to each bush.

• To make flower colors more intense, scratch 2 tablespoons of Epsom salts into the soil around a rosebush.

• Fertilize with rabbit food; it contains alfalfa meal, which supplies a growth stimulant, nitrogen, and trace elements. Scratch ½ cup of pellets into the soil around a rosebush, then water well.

remain outdoors. Water regularly to keep roots alive.

PROPAGATION BY POTATO

To root a rose cutting, insert it into a potato, then plant both as one.

GROWING UP?

Climbing roses do not climb—they just grow taller. Climbers must be tied or trained against a support. They produce more flowers when grown horizontally rather than vertically.

DISEASES/PESTS (see pages 190–200)

Horticultural oil and insecticidal soap can help to control mildew and insects. *Diseases:* anthracnose; black spot; blight, Botrytis; crown gall; leaf spot, fungal; mildew, downy; mildew, powdery; rot, Armillaria root; rot, Phytophthora crown and root; rust; viruses. *Pests:* aphids; Japanese beetles; nematodes, root-knot; rose stem girdlers; spider mites; stalk borers; thrips.

HARVEST

Cut roses in early morning. Choose buds with outer petals already open. When inside, strip off lower leaves and recut the stems. Change water in vase every couple of days and recut the stems at the same time. Vase life is up to 12 days.

SALVIA

Salvia spp.

IN THESE TIMES OF FASHIONABLE RAGES
LET US HONOR ENDURING SAGES.
KNOWN TO CURE, TO MEND, TO EASE;
COMPANIONS TO COOKS; SPLENDID TEAS,
HUNDREDS OF SPECIES OUR WORLD ADORN,
RICHLY DIVERSE IN FLOWER AND FORM.
HAIL TO SALVIA, THAT SCENTED SALVATION,
WORTHY OF STUDY AND OUR ADMIRATION.
–Andrew M. Doty, poet and educator, Stanford University

Perennial salvias (aka "sage") appear as spikes of colorful, densely packed tubular flowers atop square stems with velvety leaves. Planted in spring and blooming from summer to autumn, they are foundation plants in the midsummer garden border. Aromatic and colorful, salvias are suited for cutting and display, and they are beloved equally by bees, butterflies, and hummingbirds. Plus, they are heat- and drought-tolerant!

PLANTING

Salvias look best when planted in groupings of three or more. Space plants 1 to 3 feet apart, depending on the variety.

All salvias thrive in full sun (a south-facing location is ideal) and well-draining soil. Many varieties (typically, those with light-color flowers) do well in partial shade, but flowering will be reduced.

Loosen soil to a depth of 12 inches,

RECOMMENDED VARIETIES

Part of the mint family (Lamiaceae), the genus *Salvia* includes about 960 species; many of the tender perennials are grown as annuals in cold regions. Depending on the variety, plants can be 18 inches to 5 feet tall, but many are suitable for containers, too.

These common salvias are usually grown as annuals; they may be grown as perennials in warmer regions . . .

• Pineapple sage *(Salvia elegans)*: Mexico/Guatemala native; bright red, edible flowers in late summer; leaves emit a fruity fragrance when crushed; up to 4 feet tall; hardy in Zones 8 and up

• Scarlet or Texas sage *(S. coccinea)*: bright red flowers; hardy in Zones 9 and higher; 1 to 3 feet tall

• Scarlet bedding sage *(S. splendens)*: Brazilian native; flowers can be red, purple, orange, lavender, yellow, or white; heart-shape leaves; up to 2 feet tall

These salvias are usually grown as perennials . . .

• Autumn sage *(S. greggii)*: blooms from spring to frost in a rainbow of colors; disease-free and drought-tolerant; 2- to 3-foot-tall mounding form

• Hybrid sage *(S. x superba)*: ideal for cold areas; rosy purple blooms in late spring to early summer; rebloom to fall if faded flowers are cut back; 1 to 2 feet tall; 'Rose Queen' bears pink flowers

• Pitcher sage *(S. azurea var. grandiflora)*, aka "blue sage": aromatic foliage; large, sky-blue flowers in late fall; 3- to 5-foot clumping form

• Peruvian sage *(S. discolor)*: native to Peru; leaves are gray-green on the top, with white undersides; dark purple flowers; spreading, floppy form; 1 to 3 feet tall

removing any large stones or roots. Mix in a 3-inch layer of compost.

Dig a hole twice the diameter of the plant's container. When placing the plant in the ground, ensure that the top of the root ball is level with the surface soil. Carefully fill in around the plant and firm the soil gently.

Water thoroughly.

Plant salvia by seed outdoors after all danger of frost has passed in the spring.

If planting in a container, add some grit to the compost to improve drainage.

CARE

In spring, apply a 2-inch layer of both compost and mulch to retain moisture and control weeds.

Water plants in summer if rainfall is less than 1 inch per week. Avoid excessive summer irrigation.

Feed container plantings in spring. Plants grown in a garden bed do not need feeding.

To encourage continuous blooms, deadhead spent flowers periodically.

At season's end, leave flowers on

take soft stem cuttings that are about 3 to 5 inches long. Remove the lower leaves and trim each cutting just below a node (a node is where a leaf emerges from a stem).

Insert cuttings into a pot of prewatered compost. Cover with a clear plastic bag; avoid letting the bag touch the foliage.

Place cuttings in a spot with indirect light. Cuttings should be ready to pot in soil in 3 weeks.

plants to encourage reseeding (and to feed the birds). Some plants develop woody lower stems with age; prune as desired.

After the first killing frost, cut stems back to 1 to 2 inches above the soil line.

PROPAGATING SALVIA

Some salvias self-propagate, so you may find seedlings in your landscape.

Divide perennial salvias every few years in spring before new growth begins: Lift the root ball, divide it into clumps, and replant each one.

Salvia stem cuttings can be taken in the spring. Before flower buds develop,

DISEASES/PESTS *(see pages 190–200)*

The pungent odor of salvia leaves acts as a repellent to garden pests, including rabbits and deer. *Diseases:* blight, Botrytis; leaf spot, fungal; mildew, downy; mildew, powdery; rot, Pythium root and stem; rust. *Pests:* aphids; nematodes, foliar; spider mites; whiteflies.

HARVEST

Cut stems when about half of the flowers have started to open. Gather early in the morning. Vase life is 5 to 7 days.

For dried use, pick stems at midday. Air-dry by tying stems together with a rubber band and hanging them upside down in a cool, dry place.

WIT & WISDOM

• *The name "salvia" comes from the Latin word* salvere, *which means "to heal." Salvia has been used for its herbal and medicinal qualities since ancient times.*

• *Ancient Romans believed that salvia stimulated the brain and memory; they also used it to clean their teeth.*

• *The common kitchen herb sage—*Salvia officinalis—*is a relative of the many ornamental species and has a few attractive ornamental varieties itself.*

SUNFLOWER

Helianthus annuus

EVERY FRIEND IS TO THE OTHER A SUN, AND A SUNFLOWER ALSO.
HE ATTRACTS AND FOLLOWS.
–Jean Paul Friedrich Richter, German writer (1763–1825)

Sunflowers, the annual plants with the scientific name that comes from the Greek words *helios* ("sun") and *anthos* ("flower"), say "summer" like no other plants. Their large, daisylike flowers come in many colors—yellow, red, orange, maroon, brown—but they are commonly bright yellow with brown centers. Their heavy heads fill with seeds that can be harvested to be eaten, replanted, or fed to the birds.

The largest sunflower varieties stand over 16 feet tall, while smaller varieties mature at 1 foot. Flower heads on large-seed varieties grow to more than 12 inches in diameter.

Sunflowers are heliotropic: Their flowers turn to follow the movement of the Sun from east to west and then return at night to face the east, ready to do it again. Heliotropism occurs during the early stages before the flower grows heavy with seeds.

Very few plants are as heat-tolerant, resistant to pests, and simply beautiful. Sunflowers make excellent cut flowers, and many attract bees, birds, and butterflies.

PLANTING

Sunflowers grow best with 6 to 8 hours of full, direct sunlight each day and long, hot summers to flower well. Shelter from strong winds—for example, along a fence or near a building—helps as they mature. Larger varieties may become top-heavy, and a strong wind can topple them.

Sow sunflower seeds directly into well-draining, warm (50°F or above) soil in the ground or plant smaller varieties in outdoor containers after the danger of frost has passed.

Prepare the soil by tilling about 2 feet deep. The soil should be

A VOICE OF EXPERIENCE

We garden in a very windy spot. Thanks to the wind, our sunflowers grow massive and impressive-looking trunks like trees. A very few get knocked over when the soil is wet and a hard wind comes through, but they just make up for it and grow stronger with a bend at the base. By the end of summer, the thick stems tower overhead like the canopy of a magnificent flower forest. *–Michael, on Almanac.com*

WIT & WISDOM

- *In some cultures, the sunflower is a symbol of courage.*
- *Native Americans used sunflowers for cooking, the oil for healing skin ailments, and petals and seeds for drying.*
- *In 2014, a sunflower in Germany stood 30 feet 1 inch tall, setting a world record for the tallest of its kind.*
- *Kansas is "The Sunflower State."*

somewhat alkaline (with a pH of 6.0 to 7.5). Sunflowers are heavy feeders: Add compost or aged manure or work in a slow-release granular fertilizer to 8 inches deep. The soil can not be too compact: The long taproots need to stretch out. Mix in coarse (not beach) sand or loam, if necessary.

Plant seeds 1 to 1½ inches deep about 6 inches apart in rows 30 inches apart. Allow plenty of space, especially for low-growing varieties that will branch out.

If desired, plant seeds closer together and thin to keep the strongest seedlings when the plants are 6 inches tall. Water and keep soil moist until seedlings sprout.

Most sunflower varieties are fast-growing plants, maturing in 70 to 95 days. Stagger plantings over 5 to 6 weeks to enjoying continuous blooms.

If birds scratch around for the seeds, spread netting over the planted area until seeds germinate.

CARE

While plants are small, water around the root zone, about 3 to 4 inches from the stem.

If snails or slugs are a threat, put bait around the stem.

When plants are established, water with several gallons weekly to encourage deep rooting. (Adjust accordingly if the weather is wet or dry.)

Feed sparingly; overfertilization can cause stems to break in autumn. If desired, add diluted fertilizer to the water.

Tall species and cultivars may require support, such as bamboo stakes.

DISEASES/PESTS *(see pages 190–200)*
Diseases: black stem, Phoma; blight, Botrytis; leaf spot, fungal; mildew, downy; mildew, powdery; mold, Sclerotinia white; rust; viruses; wilt, Verticillium. *Pests:* birds; slugs/snails; squirrels; sunflower moths.

RECOMMENDED VARIETIES

'Autumn Beauty': up to 7 feet tall; large (6-inch) yellow, bronze, and mahogany flowers on branching stems

'Mammoth': giant (12+ feet tall); seeds excellent for snacks or feeders

'Sunrich Gold': about 5 feet tall; single 4- to 6-inch, pollenless, yellow flower; good for arrangements

'Teddy Bear': 2 to 3 feet tall; for small spaces or containers; fluffy, gold, 5-inch flowers on branching stems; good for vases

HARVEST

Handle sunflowers gently.

Cut stems in early morning. They may wilt if cut later.

For indoor bouquets, cut the main stem just before its flower bud opens to encourage side blooms.

Strip stems of all leaves, except for those closest to the flower head. Recut bottoms of stems at a 45-degree angle.

Arrange flowers in tall containers that provide good support. Change the water every 2 to 3 days. Vase life is about 7 days at room temperature.

SAVING SEEDS

Let the flower heads dry on or off the stem until the back of the head turns brown, the foliage turns yellow, the petals wilt, and the seeds look plump and are loose.

Protect the heads from birds and squirrels by covering with light fabric (e.g., cheesecloth) secured with a rubber band. Or, cut off the flower head before it dries and hang it upside down indoors or where it is safe from critters outdoors, until the seeds are dry.

Cut the stem about 6 inches below the flower head and place the flower head on a flat, clean surface.

To remove the seeds, rub a hand over the flower's center, then pull the seeds off or dislodge them with a fork. Or, grip the sunflower head and rub it across an irregular surface such as an old washboard.

Rinse seeds before laying them out to dry for several hours or overnight.

When saving seeds to replant, store them in an airtight container in a cool, dry place until planting time.

SEED AND STEM RECYCLING

Save whole, dry flower heads and set them out in winter for the birds.

Dry thick sunflower stems and save them for winter kindling.

ROASTING SEEDS

Soak seeds overnight in salted water. Rinse and dry on a layer of paper towels. Preheat the oven to 325°F. Spread seeds in a single layer on a baking sheet. Roast for 25 to 30 minutes, stirring frequently. Remove when seeds are slightly browned. Set aside to cool. Toss with olive oil, salt, and/or spices (cayenne, chili powder, ground cinnamon, ground cloves, smoked paprika), if desired.

TULIP

Tulipa spp.

I FOUND MYSELF ACHING TO ORDER UP SACKS OF BULBS,
TO LIFT MY TROWEL, TO SLICE INTO THE EARTH, AND TUCK AWAY WHAT
AMOUNTS TO HOPE, FAITH, AND PROMISE.
–Barbara Mahany, American journalist

There's a tulip for every setting, from small "species" tulips in naturalized woodland areas to larger tulips suited to formal garden plantings as everything from beds to borders. By planting varieties with different bloom times, it's possible to have tulips blooming from early to late spring. The upright flowers may be single or double and vary in shape from simple cups, bowls, and goblets to more complex forms with three petals and three sepals. Heights range from 6 inches to 2 feet. One flower grows on each stem, with two to six broad leaves per plant. Some types are good for forcing into bloom indoors, and most are excellent for cut flowers.

PLANTING

Plant tulip bulbs in autumn 6 to 8 weeks before a hard, or ground-freezing, frost is expected. Or apply this rule of thumb: Plant bulbs when the average nighttime temperatures are in the 40°Fs. Bulbs need time to become established, but planting too early can lead to disease.

In areas with mild winters, chill bulbs

RECOMMENDED VARIETIES

'Cracker' tulip: purple, pink, and lilac petals; midseason bloomer

'Ile de France': red blooms on stems to 20 inches tall; midseason bloomer

'Marilyn': large, ruffled, candy cane–color flower; late-season bloomer

'Spring Green': creamy-white petals feathered with green; late-season bloomer

'Renown': hot pink, egg-shape flower; late-season bloomer

Wild, or "species," tulips are small in size, ranging in height from 3 to 8 inches. They are tougher than hybrids. Rock and herb gardens are ideal places to plant them. They look stunning when planted in large groupings.

• For early to midspring bloom time: *Tulipa bakeri, T. batalinii, T. humilis, T. kaufmanniana, T. turkestanica*

• For later blooming time: *T. linifolia, T. neustreuvae, T. sprengeri, T. vvedenskyi*

• For multicolor varieties: *T. biflora, T. greigii* 'Quebec', *T. praestans* 'Fusilier' and 'Unicum', *T. tarda, T. turkestanica*

• For a container: *T. kaufmanniana* 'Goudstuk'

• For (mottled) foliage: *T. greigii* (mottled or striped), *T. fosteriana* 'Juan', *T. kaufmanniana* 'Heart's Delight'

• For fragrance: *T. aucheriana, T. biflora, T. saxatilis, T. sylvestris, T. turkestanica*

• For warmer regions: Lady tulip (*T. clusiana*), Candia tulip (*T. saxatilis*), and Florentine tulip (*T. sylvestris*) overwinter in the South or mild-winter areas of the West (Zones 8 to 10) without need of a chilling period

in the refrigerator (away from food, especially fresh fruit and vegetables) for about 12 weeks or buy them pre-chilled. Plant in late November, December—or later.

Bulbs that were not planted in time should be planted as soon as possible. They are not like seeds and can not be saved.

Choose a site in full or afternoon sun, with space to set bulbs 4 to 6 inches apart. (Spacing recommendations vary widely.) Tulips generally do not like a lot of heat; in Zones 7 and 8, choose a site with shade or morning sun only. If planting tall varieties, provide shelter from strong winds.

Soil must be neutral to slightly acidic, fertile, and well-draining. Prepare the bed by loosening the soil to a depth of 12 to 15 inches, then mix in compost or aged manure. (An alternative to a dug bed is a raised bed.) Bulbs contain enough nutrients for 1 year, but perennial tulips benefit from a balanced, time-release bulb food fertilizer or bonemeal when planted in fall.

Plant bulbs at least 8 inches deep, measuring from the base. The bigger the bulb, the deeper the hole it needs.

Set bulbs with the pointy end up.

To deter mice, voles, and other rodents (if they are a problem), put thorny leaves (e.g., holly), kitty litter, or crushed gravel into the planting holes. Bulbs can also be set in buried wire cages for protection.

Cover with soil and press firmly.

Water bulbs immediately after planting; moisture will trigger growth. Water weekly, if no rain falls, until the ground freezes.

Tulips usually emerge in early to midspring. If a mild winter causes premature growth and then cold conditions return, keep calm. Tulips (and daffodils) are cold-tolerant. A late spring snow puts the plant's growth on pause and protects the foliage.

THE PERENNIAL QUESTION

Tulips are perennials, botanically speaking, but centuries of hybridization have weakened the bulb's ability to come back year after year. As a result, tulips are often treated as annuals and replanted every autumn. Weary of this? Try Triumph or Darwin hybrids. Or, go wild with native species tulips that naturalize in almost any region.

CARE

In spring, when leaves emerge, feed tulips the bulb food or bonemeal used at planting time.

Water well.

Deadhead tulips as they go by but allow the leaves to remain on the plants for about 6 weeks after flowering. The foliage helps the bulb to gather energy for the next year. When the foliage turns yellow and dies back, prune it off.

Rainy summers, irrigation systems, and wet soil are death to tulips. Wet soil leads to fungus, disease, and rotted bulbs.

Water a bulb bed only in drought. If drainage is poor, add shredded pine bark, sand, or other rough material to the soil.

Apply compost annually to provide the nutrients needed for future blooms.

Large varieties may need replanting every few years; small types usually multiply and spread on their own.

DISEASES/PESTS *(see pages 190–200)*
Diseases: blight, Botrytis (fire); rot, Fusarium basal; rot, gray bulb; viruses. *Pests:* aphids; mice; nematodes, stem and bulb; rabbits; slugs/snails; squirrels; voles.

HARVEST

Cut tulips just before the buds fully open. Leave some of the foliage behind to build up energy in the bulb for the next year's growth. Recut the stems at an angle before placing in a vase. Tulips continue to grow after being cut, and they are "phototropic," reaching towards the light. Rotate the vase daily to keep stems upright. Change the water every day, and tulips will last about 7 days in a vase.

To get a long vase life of at least a week, cut stems diagonally and wrap upper two-thirds of stems (with flowers) in a newspaper funnel. Stand in cool water up to the funnel for 1 to 2 hours, recut stems, and set in fresh water.

WIT & WISDOM
• *Tulips, and the word for them, come from the Far East: "Tulip" from the Turkish word for "turban,"* tülbent, *comes from the Persian word* dulband, *meaning "round."*
• *In 17th-century Holland, a handful of tulip bulbs was worth about $44,000.*

VIBURNUM

Viburnum spp.

A GARDEN WITHOUT VIBURNUMS IS LIKE A LIFE WITHOUT
THE PLEASURES OF MUSIC AND ART.
*–Michael Dirr, garden writer and University of Georgia
professor of horticulture (b. 1944)*

For a spring-flowering shrub with abundant benefits—fragrance, fruit, colorful foliage, pollinator appeal, and more—look no further than viburnums, but look closely. The species offers more than 150 evergreen, semi-evergreen, and deciduous woody plants from which to choose.

Also known as cranberrybush, hobblebush, arrowwood, nannyberry, or snowball bush, viburnums range in size from 2 to 20 feet tall and usually serve in the landscape as screening, hedge, or focal points. Depending on the variety, viburnum provides year-round visual interest: The cream/white or pale pink bloom clusters can be lacecap, dome, or snowball-shape, with intoxicating or light perfume (although some have no scent). In fall, the flowers—favored by bees and butterflies—give way to yellow, orange, red, pink, blue, or black fruit attractive to birds and wildlife, and foliage on plants that are not evergreen changes to glossy red, violet, or purple.

All of this, plus viburnums are easy-care: fast-growing, not fussy about soil, need little to no pruning, and seldom are troubled by diseases or pests.

PLANTING

Plant viburnums in spring or fall; if planting in summer, water well during hot and dry periods.

Viburnums thrive in full sun to partial or mostly shade, depending on the variety.

Provide moisture-retaining but well-draining, fertile soil. Add compost or aged manure, if necessary, before planting. The pH needs may vary; a pH of 5.5 to 6.5 is average. Check the variety, test the soil, and amend it as required.

Dig a hole as deep as the root ball and twice as wide. Set plants so that the top roots are at the soil level or slightly below.

Half-fill the hole with soil, then water it well to settle the soil. Fill in with remaining soil.

On the soil surface, form a rim of soil around the outer edge of the hole. Water

RECOMMENDED VARIETIES

Viburnum dentatum (aka arrowwood): scentless white lacecap flower clusters; blue-black berries; 6 to 15 feet tall, with wide, mounded form; fall leaf colors of yellow, orange, and red; hardy in Zones 2 to 8

V. lantana (aka wayfaringtree): scentless creamy white lacecap flower clusters; red to black berries; 10 to 15 feet tall and wide; green leaves turn purplish-red in fall; hardy in Zones 3 to 7

V. plicatum var. *tomentosum* (aka doublefile, Japanese snowball): scentless white flower balls; red to blue-black berries; 8 to 12 feet tall and wide; green leaves turn burgundy to purplish-red in fall; hardy in Zones 5 to 8

V. x carlcephalum (aka fragrant snowball): fragrant white flower balls; red to black berries; 6 to 10 feet tall and wide; green leaves turn reddish-maroon in fall; hardy in Zones 6 to 8

V. carlesii (aka Korean spice): very fragrant pink to white flower balls; blue-black berries; 4 to 8 feet tall and wide; green leaves turn red to burgundy in fall; hardy in Zones 4 to 7

V. setigerum (aka tea): scentless small white flower clusters; abundant bright red berries; 8 to 12 feet tall, 5 to 8 feet wide; green leaves turn purplish in fall; hardy in Zones 5 to 7

inches of pine straw or 2 to 3 inches of bark.

Fertilizer is seldom applied. In spring, apply a few shovelfuls of compost or aged manure. In autumn, feed the roots by mixing fish meal with some compost.

In early spring, prune selectively to maintain height and spread. If an overgrown shrub requires a hard pruning (shearing), do it at this time or after the bloom period.

DISEASES/PESTS *(see pages 190–200)*
Diseases: anthracnose; canker and dieback, Botryosphaeria; crown gall; leaf spot, algal; leaf spot, bacterial; leaf spot, fungal; mildew, downy; mildew, powdery; rot, Armillaria root; wilt, Verticillium. *Pests:* aphids; nematodes, root-knot; root weevils; scale insects; spider mites; thrips; whiteflies.

HARVEST
Viburnum is one among many woody ornamentals that can be cut and put in a vase. Cut thin branches when the buds are starting to open. Recut the bottom of the stem before placing in a vase. Change the water every 2 to 3 days. Vase life is about 7 days. Viburnum branches can also be forced into bloom in early spring.

inside the ring.

Space plants 4 to 10 feet apart, depending on the size at maturity.

CARE
Water with a soaking once per week if rainfall is less than 1 inch.

Once established, mulch with 4 to 6

WIT & WISDOM
- *The straight stems of arrowwood viburnum are believed to have been used as arrow shafts by Native Americans.*
- *Tea viburnum leaves were used to make tea.*
- *Dark blue at maturity, the berries of nannyberry viburnum* (V. lentago) *are edible raw or in jams and baked goods.*

WISTERIA

Wisteria spp.

IN PALE MOONLIGHT
THE WISTERIA'S SCENT
COMES FROM FAR AWAY.
—Yosa Buson, Japanese poet (1716–84)

A high-climbing, long-lived vine, wisteria blooms vigorously in spring with large, drooping clusters of lilac or bluish-purple flowers that look spectacular hanging from a pergola or archway. Wisteria flowers are also beautifully fragrant—a feast for the senses. After flowering, a brown, beanlike pod stays on the plant until winter.

However, this plant comes with caveats: It's a fast and aggressive grower, often reaching to more than 30 feet long. Its tendrils will work their way into any nook or cranny, eventually becoming quite heavy.

PLANTING

Plant wisteria in spring or fall, while the plant is dormant. It can be grown from seed, but the plant would take many years to reach the size and maturity needed to produce flowers. The purchase of established wisteria plants or starting one from a cutting is recommended.

Choose a site that gets full sun. Wisteria will grow in partial shade, but it is unlikely to flower with less than 6 hours of direct sunlight.

Provide fertile, moist but well-draining, slightly acidic soil. Add compost or aged manure, if necessary.

Plant this vine by itself; it grows quickly and can easily overtake neighboring plants or nearby structures (e.g., houses, garages, sheds).

Provide a sturdy structure for it to climb—for instance, a metal or strong wooden trellis or pergola. Mature plants can become so heavy that they break their supports, so plan with care and hefty materials.

To plant, dig a hole as deep as the root ball and two to three times as wide. Place the plant in the hole and fill in with soil around the root ball. Water well.

Space plants 10 to 15 feet apart.

CARE

In spring, apply a layer of compost and a 2-inch layer of mulch to retain moisture and control weeds.

If desired, scratch a couple of cups of bonemeal into the soil.

RECOMMENDED VARIETIES

Native Wisteria
In North America, the recommended species are those that are native to the continent.

• American wisteria (*Wisteria frutescens*) grows in Zones 5 to 9. It's native from Virginia to Texas, southeast to Florida, and north up through New York, Michigan, and Iowa. The vine grows 25 to 30 feet long, with shiny, dark-green leaves and large, drooping lilac or bluish-purple flower clusters that appear in midspring on new wood after the plant leafs out.

• Kentucky wisteria grows in Zones 4 to 9. This spring to early summer bloomer (*W. macrostachya*) is native to the southeastern U.S. and similar to American wisteria (of which it is sometimes considered a variety or subspecies). Kentucky wisteria is the quickest-blooming wisteria: It bears mildly fragrant, bluish-purple flowers in its second or third year. 'Blue Moon' is an extra-hardy (to −30°F) cultivar, with showy, silvery-blue bloom clusters.

Non-Native Wisteria
Chinese wisteria (*W. sinensis*) and Japanese wisteria (*W. floribunda*) are non-native, invasive species; we do not recommend them for North American gardens, despite the fact that they are widely available. Two common varieties of Japanese wisteria are . . .

• 'Honbeni' (syn. 'Honko'): clusters of pink flowers; late spring

• 'Alba' (syn. 'Shiro Noda'): clusters of pure-white flowers; late spring to early summer

In autumn, if desired, scratch in some rock phosphate. These amendments are believed to aid with flowering. Similar claims have been made about liquid tomato or rose fertilizer.

Water when less than 1 inch of rain falls per week.

PRUNING

Prune established wisteria in July or after flowers have faded. Cut side shoots to about 6 inches long, while retaining the climbing branches. This will create lots of short spurs all along the main vines. In late winter, prune the same side shoots, leaving two or three buds on each.

Just don't make the mistake of never pruning. Do the following at any time:

■ When pruning an established but untamed plant, be ruthless. Cut the stem several feet below the desired height; there will be an upsurge of new vegetative (not flowering) shoots in the following spring. Give it space to grow and full sun.

■ Remove suckers from the base of the plant to control spread.

■ Remove seedpods at will or leave a few for winter interest. If you bring any indoors for display/decoration, be aware that the ambient warmth of the home may cause them to explode.

FROM A VINE TO A TREE

Late winter is the time to turn a wisteria vine into a tree. Set a tall, strong post

VOICES OF EXPERIENCE

I put a wisteria in my backyard, but it didn't get enough sun and in 7 to 8 years never bloomed. However, it got comfortable with its location and eventually moved 12 feet along the fascia of my house, hitched onto a thin, tall, 25-foot poplar, and rode it vertically before attaching to a mostly dead 100-foot-tall ash. I couldn't believe it. Once it wrapped onto the ash, it grew around 6 inches every day and was 75 feet from its base. What an impressive climber. When I sold the home, the first thing that I did was to warn the new owners that the innocent-looking wisteria actually stood a chance of pulling the dead ash tree down onto the roof of the house.   *–Scott, on Almanac.com*

I have a 30-year-old wisteria that has bloomed beautifully every year since it was a tiny baby. It's now as high as the roof and as wide as the house. I love it.   *–Hazel, on Almanac.com*

Native wisterias are much better for our ecosystem because native plants support pollinators, caterpillars, birds, and wildlife that depend on native plants for food and shelter. Our native plants are just as beautiful or more beautiful than non-native plants, even the natives that are considered weeds. So, come on, everybody, let's go native!   *–Wanda, on Almanac.com*

WIT & WISDOM

• *Native wisterias produce smooth seedpods. Asian wisterias produce fuzzy seedpods.*

• *All parts of the wisteria plant contain lectin and wisterin,
which are toxic to pets, livestock, and humans. They can cause
a range of ills, from nausea and diarrhea to death, if consumed in large
amounts. Call a poison control center in case of ingestion.*

(metal, ideally) close to the main stem. Secure the stem to the post with tape or other material that will not restrict it. Remove errant side shoots as they appear. In the next year, when the stem reaches the desired height, prune it above the top of the post; the "tree's" crown will form here as branches develop. Continue to remove errant shoots. Before the first frost, prune branches to about 6 inches, with five or six large buds. Repeat each year.

NO BLOOMS?

Wisteria are notorious for taking a long time to bloom. Don't expect flowers for 2 to 3 years after planting; if the process is taking longer, try "shocking" the vine into reproduction (flowering): About a foot and a half away from the main trunk, drive a shovel 8 to 10 inches into the ground; the goal is to cut into the roots. Repeat, slicing about half of the roots. This will not hurt the plant.

Failure to flower may also be due to frigid winter temperatures that have injured the flower buds, excessive nitrogen fertilizer that has promoted foliage over flowers, and/or insufficient sunlight.

DISEASES/PESTS *(see pages 190–200)*

Diseases: crown gall; canker and dieback, Botryosphaeria; leaf spot, fungal; mildew, powdery; rot, Armillaria root; rot, Phytophthora crown and root; viruses. *Pests:* aphids; Japanese beetles; leaf miners; mealy bugs; nematodes, root-knot; scale insects.

HARVEST

Droopy wisteria blooms are spectacular in a bouquet. Gently cut a branch with just-opened flowers. Recut the branch at an angle or cut straight up the bottom of the stem to allow more water intake. Remove most of the leaves and place in a sturdy vase. Vase life is about 7 days.

HOW DOES MY GARDEN GROW?

VARIETY	SOURCE	YEAR PLANTED

HOW DOES MY GARDEN GROW?

VARIETY	SOURCE	YEAR PLANTED

INSPIRATION

EXPERT ADVICE FOR CONSTANT COLOR

Plants with an asterisk (*) are profiled in this book.

GOD'S COLORS ARE ALL FAST.
–John Greenleaf Whittier, American poet (1807–92)

Nonstop bloom is easy to create just by planting the right varieties for your location. Try some of these regional favorites, recommended by experts with experience in each area, and enjoy season-long brilliant color. Most of these perennials will bloom in the very first year and serve as a focal point or backdrop in your landscape.

THE U.S. SOUTH

Felder Rushing, a garden writer and lecturer who lives in Mississippi, has his favorite kind of long-blooming perennial—one that is easy to

TO KEEP THE COLOR COMING

Most continuously blooming plants need to be deadheaded (have faded flowers removed before they go to seed) by having their stem "pinched" or cut off just below the base of the flower. Some plants repeat flowers after a generous shearing back.

grow, dependable, and low-maintenance. "Dead people can grow these plants," he says with a laugh, explaining

that he has planted all of his favorites in a nearby old cemetery. "These plants are absolutely unkillable."

His favorite perennials to grow in the South include lantana *(Lantana camara)*, Mexican petunia *(Ruellia brittoniana)*, and salvias,* such as *Salvia carnea*. "All bloom with little or no care, without having to be deadheaded or prompted in any way. And they all happen to be fantastic butterfly and hummingbird plants," he notes. Add some small shrubs, Rushing adds, such as dwarf crape myrtle, abelia, and a

THE U.S. SOUTH

LANTANA

MEXICAN PETUNIA

'HOME RUN' SHRUB ROSE

'SWEET LAURA' PERUVIAN LILY   BLOOMERANG PURPLE LILAC   'INVINCIBELLE SPIRIT' HYDRANGEA

shrub rose* like 'Home Run', 'The Fairy', or 'Caldwell Pink', and you've got a recipe for continuous color.

THE U.S. NORTHEAST

Although Peruvian lily (*Alstroemeria*) is known mostly as a cut flower and isn't considered hardy in the North, there is a variety called 'Sweet Laura' that makes it through the cold spells. If it's not in a well-exposed place, it proceeds to bloom nonstop from mid- to late June until frost, comments William Cullina, former executive director of Coastal Maine Botanical Gardens in Boothbay, Maine (and most recently executive director of the Morris Arboretum of the University of Pennsylvania). Bloomerang Purple is a reblooming lilac* that just keeps coming back with more and more flowers all summer, he says. This small, 4- to 5-foot-tall shrub is blanketed with a smaller flower than the traditional lilac but still retains some of its nice aroma. 'Macy's Pride'

is a rose* in the Easy Elegance series with a nice, traditional, tea rose shape. "In bud, it is yellow, and it then opens to an ivory white—and what I like is that it also has great fragrance," he says. 'Twist-n-Shout' is a reblooming hydrangea* in the Endless Summer series that guarantees flowers all season long. Descended from the old favorite 'Annabelle' hydrangea* (*Hydrangea arborescens*) are white 'Incrediball', pink 'Invincibelle Spirit', and magenta 'Bella Anna', which provide long-lasting blooms on strong stems.

Cullina likes to keep color coming in his Maine garden by mixing long-blooming perennials with a few nontraditional annuals: "Not the zinnia, petunia, geranium, impatiens sorts of annuals, but some of the mint family plants, like salvia* or agastache, which look more like a perennial."

THE U.S. MIDWEST

The longest bloomer has to be yellow corydalis (*Corydalis lutea*), says Ed Lyon, former director of Allen Centennial Gardens in Madison, Wisconsin (and most recently director

---

BLUE FLOWERS FOR ANYWHERE

South: Blue anise sage* (*Salvia guaranitica*)
Northeast: 'Rozanne' hardy geranium
Midwest: 'Rooguchi' clematis*
West: 'Fama Deep Blue' scabiosa

SHADE-TOLERANT LONG-BLOOMERS

South: lilyturf (blooms even under magnolia trees)
Northeast: 'Domino' barrenwort
Midwest: 'King of Hearts' fern-leaf bleeding heart*
West: border penstemon (*Penstemon x gloxinioides* or *P. hartwegii*)

THE U.S. MIDWEST

YELLOW CORYDALIS   LESSER CALAMINT   LAVENDER

of Reiman Gardens in Iowa). "It blooms from spring until the snow crushes it, tolerates our dry shade, has lovely foliage, and brightens up dark areas," he says. Although it reseeds freely, it is not invasive in the Midwest because the little seedlings are easy to pluck out. For long bloom, Lyon also favors lesser calamint (*Calamintha nepeta* ssp. *nepeta*). From mid- to late summer, it is completely covered with delicate pale blue to white flowers that look like baby's breath. It not only tolerates poor soil but also is a bee magnet. The hardy varieties of lavender* (*Lavandula* x *intermedia*) are great for

long bloom as well, if they are planted in sandy, well-draining soil, he notes.

THE U.S. WEST
Native autumn sage* *(Salvia greggii)* gets rave reviews from John Beaudry, a landscape designer in San Diego, California. "It comes in red, white, pink, and a bicolor," he reports, "and grows really fast. It will keep reblooming from spring all the way through to December." 'The Third Harmonic' Peruvian lily is a

LEADING A COLORFUL
GARDEN LIFE? SHOW
US YOUR PICS ON
@ALMANAC

steady bloomer in this region as well, says Beaudry. "It will spread vigorously, but it is not invasive. It's also a great cut flower that will last 2 to 3 weeks in a vase." He also recommends the Little Miss series of dwarf Peruvian lilies (Zoe, Olivia, Christina, et al.), which come in a variety of colors. Beaudry says that he would not be without Mexican butterfly weed (*Asclepias curassavica):* "It's a butterfly magnet that blooms the entire summer. The butterfly larvae may devour all of the foliage, but the flowers will just keep on coming. It resows freely, and I let it."

THE U.S. WEST

AUTUMN SAGE   'THE THIRD HARMONIC' PERUVIAN LILY   MEXICAN BUTTERFLY WEED

MY COLOR INVENTORY

PLANTS THAT BLOOM	BLOOM DATE AND DURATION	NOTES

PERENNIALS FOR EVERY REGION

Plants with an asterisk (*) are profiled in this book.

My green thumb came only as a result
of the mistakes I made while learning to see
things from the plant's point of view.
–H. Fred Dale, Canadian garden writer

Looking for ideas? Want a "sure thing"? Here, at a glance, are the best bets for your region. Inquire at your local garden center to learn about new varieties developed to withstand the rigors of your climate.

	NEW ENGLAND/ UPPER GREAT LAKES	MID-ATLANTIC/ OHIO VALLEY	SOUTHEAST	MIDWEST/ GREAT PLAINS
LONGEST- BLOOMING	Musk mallow (*Malva moschata*)	Black-eyed Susan* (*Rudbeckia hirta*)	Lenten rose (*Helleborus orientalis*)	'Magnus' purple coneflower* (*Echinacea purpurea*)
BEST FOR CUTTING (long vase life)	'Purple Dome' New England aster* (*Symphyotrichum novae-angliae*)	Ox eye daisy (*Leucanthemum vulgare*)	Garden phlox (*Phlox paniculata*)	Perennial sweet pea (*Lathyrus latifolius*)
MOST BEAUTIFUL IN THE GARDEN	Garden phlox: pink, purple, and white (*Phlox paniculata*)	Butterfly weed (*Asclepias tuberosa*)	'Honorine Jobert' Japanese anemone (*Anemone x hybrida*)	Lady's mantle (*Alchemilla mollis*)
BEST FOR COLOR WHEN MASSED	Garden phlox: pink, purple, and white (*Phlox paniculata*)	Purple Mexican sage* (*Salvia leucantha*)	Swamp sunflower (*Helianthus angustifolius*)	Russian sage (*Perovskia atriplicifolia*)
EASIEST TO GROW (good choice for beginners)	Fern-leaf bleeding heart* (*Dicentra eximia*)	Black-eyed Susan* (*Rudbeckia hirta*)	Joe Pye weed (*Eutrochium purpureum*)	'Autumn Joy' sedum (*Hylotelephium*, aka *Sedum spectabile*)
SURVIVAL TRAITS OF PERENNIALS THAT FLOURISH	Cold-hardy natives that flower in a short growing season	Long taproots that survive in dry clay soil	Heat tolerance and low chill requirements	Cold-hardy with large root systems that survive drought

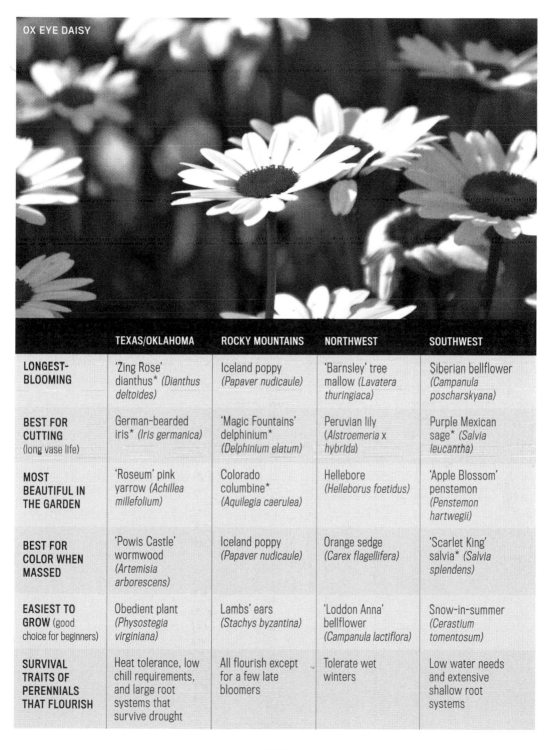

OX EYE DAISY

	TEXAS/OKLAHOMA	ROCKY MOUNTAINS	NORTHWEST	SOUTHWEST
LONGEST-BLOOMING	'Zing Rose' dianthus* (*Dianthus deltoides*)	Iceland poppy (*Papaver nudicaule*)	'Barnsley' tree mallow (*Lavatera thuringiaca*)	Siberian bellflower (*Campanula poscharskyana*)
BEST FOR CUTTING (long vase life)	German-bearded iris* (*Iris germanica*)	'Magic Fountains' delphinium* (*Delphinium elatum*)	Peruvian lily (*Alstroemeria* x *hybrida*)	Purple Mexican sage* (*Salvia leucantha*)
MOST BEAUTIFUL IN THE GARDEN	'Roseum' pink yarrow (*Achillea millefolium*)	Colorado columbine* (*Aquilegia caerulea*)	Hellebore (*Helleborus foetidus*)	'Apple Blossom' penstemon (*Penstemon hartwegii*)
BEST FOR COLOR WHEN MASSED	'Powis Castle' wormwood (*Artemisia arborescens*)	Iceland poppy (*Papaver nudicaule*)	Orange sedge (*Carex flagellifera*)	'Scarlet King' salvia* (*Salvia splendens*)
EASIEST TO GROW (good choice for beginners)	Obedient plant (*Physostegia virginiana*)	Lambs' ears (*Stachys byzantina*)	'Loddon Anna' bellflower (*Campanula lactiflora*)	Snow-in-summer (*Cerastium tomentosum*)
SURVIVAL TRAITS OF PERENNIALS THAT FLOURISH	Heat tolerance, low chill requirements, and large root systems that survive drought	All flourish except for a few late bloomers	Tolerate wet winters	Low water needs and extensive shallow root systems

TINY BULBS

Plants marked with an asterisk (*) are profiled in this book.

BULBS NEED SO LITTLE AND GIVE BACK SO MUCH.
THEY START OFF HOMELY, EVEN UGLY, AND RETURN TRANSFORMED.
–Lauren Springer Ogden, American garden writer and designer

When it seems as though winter will never lose its icy grip, an array of seldom-used bulbs push through the snow to put on a show of colorful renewal. Small bulbs not only provide winter garden color but also naturalize (spread and come back year after year)—with minimal care—for an ever-larger display. Deer, squirrels, and rabbits seldom bother with early little bulbs—all the more reason that we should!

The best little bulbs are listed here in the order in which they flower, the earliest one first. Bloom time depends on your climate and can start anytime from mid-January to the end of March.

- **Winter aconite *(Eranthis hyemalis):*** Yellow, buttercup-like blossoms, 2 to 4 inches tall. Plant in meadows or large beds, where they will naturalize into a golden carpet.
- **Snowdrop *(Galanthus nivalis):*** Dainty, 4-inch-tall, white bells show up about a week before the first crocus. Plant under or near peonies,*

shrubs, and small flowering trees; the fading flowers like the shade from emerging foliage.

- **Iris* *(Iris reticulata):*** Fragrant flowers, just 4 to 6 inches tall—an excellent choice for borders and rock gardens. Grasslike foliage may appear in late autumn before the first snowfall.
- **Crocus *(Crocus):*** From snow crocuses (the first to bloom) to giant Dutch crocuses—all just 2 to 6 inches tall —these blooms offer variety in refreshing

WINTER ACONITE

SNOWDROP

IRIS

CROCUS

STRIPED SQUILL

pastel colors. Many have strong perfumes that lure bees out of their hives in February or March.

■ **Striped squill** *(Puschkinia libanotica):* Clusters of starlike, pale blue flowers top 4- to 6-inch stems. Excellent in rock gardens, under old trees, and in shady corners.

■ **Siberian squill** *(Scilla siberica):* Delicate, nodding, blue or white bells grow in loose clusters atop 3- to 6-inch stems. Very cold-hardy; plant under shrubs or allow to naturalize in lawns and meadows.

■ **Glory-of-the-snow** *(Chionodoxa forbesii):* Each

HAS YOUR PLOT
THICKENED? SHARE
YOUR GARDEN PICS
ON 🅟 @ALMANAC

stem holds 5 to 10 pastel, starlike flowers in a spray on 6-inch plants. They tolerate partial shade and do equally well in rocky areas, meadows, and lawns.

■ **'Tête-à-Tête' daffodil** *(Narcissus tazetta* 'Tête-à-Tête'):* The first daffodil to bloom, this miniature pairs well with striped and Siberian squills. Each bulb produces multiple stems, with two or three bright yellow flowers on each. The 6-inch-tall plants thrive in rocky areas.

PLANTING

Before the ground freezes in the fall, plant early bulbs almost anywhere, except in dense shade—for example, on the north side of buildings. Provide well-draining soil; they will rot in soggy ground. Work in compost, aged manure, or shredded leaves to a depth of at least 10 inches. Plant bulbs in groups or clusters. Avoid spacing them in a single line; singles get lost in the landscape. Consider planting in lawns and meadows where they can form carpets of color or mass them along the front edge of flower beds.

SIBERIAN SQUILL

GLORY-OF-THE-SNOW

'TÊTE-À-TÊTE' DAFFODIL

MY BULB INVENTORY

NAME	DATE PLANTED	QUANTITY	LOCATION

MY BULB INVENTORY

NAME	DATE PLANTED	QUANTITY	LOCATION

9 SUMMER-FLOWERING SHRUBS

Plants marked with an asterisk (*) are profiled in this book.

THE IDEAL GARDEN IS ONE IN WHICH A COLLECTION OF TREES,
SHRUBS, AND PLANTS HAVE BEEN PROCURED AND ALLOTTED TO THE BEST
SPACE AVAILABLE AND ARE SO ARRANGED AND TENDED THAT
THEY ARE SEEN TO THEIR ADVANTAGE, EACH IN RELATION TO THE OTHER.
–Penelope Hobhouse, British garden writer (b. 1929)

Spring-blooming shrubs put on a great opening act, but summer shrubs steal the show. Their strong silhouettes add balance, mass, and scattered shade as they link trees and larger woody plants with smaller flowers, vines, and ground covers. They enhance the garden's dynamic swirl of colorful annuals and perennials. Here are some options, with their distinctive benefits.

HEAVENLY BLUE
Bluebeard, aka Blue mist
(*Caryopteris* x *clandonensis*)
Although technically a shrub, this Asian native is often treated like a perennial. Birds and butterflies love it, bees buzz it so vigorously that you can hear them clearly, and it makes a great cut flower. Bluebeard never flinches at summer heat and humidity, doesn't tempt deer, and manages with less-than-ideal rainfall. However, after 4 to 5 years, it may need replacement. Meanwhile, it's well worth having. Bluebeard forms a low, fine-texture mound of powder blue flowers in airy clusters on spreading branches. 'Kew

'SAPPHIRE SURF' BLUEBEARD

Blue' has deep violet-blue flowers, while 'Sapphire Surf' is amazing in mass plantings. Its leaves are aromatic and, on some cultivars, such as 'Worcester Gold', variegated. Cut it back in late winter or early spring for strong, dense growth.
GROWTH: 2 to 3 feet tall/wide
CONDITIONS: partial shade to full sun; well-draining, alkaline soil
HARDY: Zones 5 to 9

POWERFULLY FRAGRANT
Carolina allspice, aka Sweet-shrub or Strawberry shrub
(*Calycanthus floridus*)
Native to the Alleghenies, this uncommon but fragrant hardy shrub is an underused gem. It produces deep reddish purple-brown, strawberry/pineapple/banana–scented flowers up to 2 inches across in summer.

CAROLINA ALLSPICE

(Each plant's fragrance can vary widely; look for one in bloom and sniff before you buy.) Leathery, dark-green leaves smell of spice when crushed and become golden yellow in fall. It's a tough, low-care plant, resistant to disease and insects, that needs little pruning. It has one caveat: You must keep suckers under control to avoid naturalization.
GROWTH: 6 to 9 feet tall
CONDITIONS: partial shade (best) to full sun; rich, sandy loam
HARDY: Zones 4 to 9

SHOWY SPLENDOR
Hydrangea*
(*Hydrangea* spp.)
The queen of the late-summer garden, hydrangea stars in various species. All are extremely showy, and their long-lasting blossoms provide months of color. The top three—*H. paniculata*, *H. macrophylla*, and *H. quercifolia*—enjoy similar growing conditions.

H. paniculata is the easiest to grow. It's a rugged shrub with bold, fluffy, 8- to 12-inch-long clusters of white flowers that fade to pink and green. It blooms on buds produced in the current year. Many cultivars, such as 'Tardiva', can be successfully trained into a standard form perfect for a large container or just about any landscape spot. The flower color of bigleaf hydrangea, *H. macrophylla*, famously depends on the character of your garden soil. Blossoms are pink in neutral to slightly alkaline soil and blue in acidic soil. Then there's white 'Wedding Gown', aka 'Dancing Snow', which is unchanged by soil acidity. While most *H. macrophylla* flower on branches from the preceding year, reblooming varieties such as 'Endless Summer' flower on both old and new growth. This ensures lots of blooms throughout the summer. Oakleaf hydrangea, *H. quercifolia*, native to the U.S. Southeast, produces clusters of white flowers that turn pink. It blooms on old wood. Cut one-fourth to the ground every 2 to 3 years to reduce crowding.
GROWTH: to 5 feet tall, some varieties more compact; *H. paniculata*, to over 10 feet tall
CONDITIONS: partial shade; moist, yet well-draining soil; *H. paniculata* belongs in sun
HARDY: Zones 4 to 9

FOOLPROOF LONG-BLOOMER
Potentilla, aka Shrubby cinquefoil
(*Potentilla fruticosa*)
Bring sunshine to your garden with this compact, long-lived, water-thrifty native, one of the easiest shrubs to grow.

'FIRE LIGHT' PANICLE HYDRANGEA

It blooms from late spring through autumn, bearing a profusion of radiant, buttercup-like, yellow flowers that attract butterflies. Cultivars bloom in white, pink, peach, yellow, orange, or red on new wood. Its foliage is dark yellow-green and finely textured. Worthy cultivars are 'Primrose Beauty', 'Pink Beauty', and early- and long-blooming 'Coronation Triumph'. Use potentilla massed or as a low hedge.

GROWTH: 1 to 4 feet tall
CONDITIONS: partial shade to full sun (best); well-draining soil (native in both bogs and dry areas)
HARDY: Zones 2 to 7

'PRIMROSE BEAUTY' POTENTILLA

SIMPLY STATELY
Rose of Sharon
(Hibiscus syriacus)
This exotic beauty thrives in moderate climates. Its tropical-looking pink, lavender, or white funnel-shape blossoms revive any faltering midsummer garden. At full height, the Rose of Sharon is V-shape. But be

'MINERVA' ROSE OF SHARON

forewarned: This beauty can be invasive, shedding seed capsules that spur weedy seedlings. Remove the capsules before they mature or look for sterile hybrid varieties, such as lavender 'Minerva'; dark pink, compact 'Aphrodite'; or pure white 'Diana'. Mulch well in cooler winter regions. In winter or early spring, cut away last season's growth (for bigger blossoms).

GROWTH: 10 to 15 feet tall
CONDITIONS: partial shade to full sun; moist, well-draining, neutral to slightly alkaline soil
HARDY: Zones 5 to 8

REMARKABLE ROSE
Shrub rose*
(Rosa spp.)
No summer garden is complete without roses, and thank goodness that not all roses are finicky plants needing high

---

PLACING AND PLANTING

From a design point of view, shrubs should be planted where they can be enjoyed. For summer shrubs, this might mean near the porch, patio, or pool or in a perennial border. Choose shrubs matched to your hardiness zone and give them the sun, soil, and moisture that they prefer so that they won't need coddling.

Whether your shrubs arrive with bare roots, come balled and burlapped, or were container-grown, be sure to loosen and untangle their roots. Prepare a hole two to three times larger than the root mass, amend the soil, add fertilizer, set the plant at the same depth that it was in the container or at the nursery, and water immediately. Be protective: Shield the shrub from full sun and wind and keep watering every few days. Then mulch.

maintenance. Shrub roses are a class of hybrid roses created by the American Rose Society to include plants with a large and bushy growth habit that have eluded other categories. Informal, modern shrub roses offer beautiful blooms all summer and autumn on disease-resistant, easy-growing plants. Flower color ranges in shades of pink, red, white,

CORAL KNOCK OUT ROSE

and yellow. Almost without exception, shrub roses are tough, winter-hardy plants that can tolerate neglect and poor growing conditions. Use shrub roses as landscape plants, mass plantings, hedges, ground covers, or borders. Climbers 'Alchymist' and 'Constance Spry', both fully double bloomers (apricot/ yellow and pink, respectively), are good examples, but don't miss the Knock Out series— showy shrub roses that bloom in clusters all summer, usually followed by showy hips.
GROWTH: 6 to 20 feet tall

and wide
CONDITIONS: full sun; fertile, well-draining soil
HARDY: Zones 3 to 9, depending on type

PUFF 'N' STUFF
Smoke bush, aka Smoketree
(Cotinus coggygria)
Save some space: This one's spectacular. In summer, its puffy, pink to purple plumes are as eye-catching as cotton candy. In fall, its dark purple leaves turn shades of yellow, orange, and red to create new drama. The plumes aren't exactly flowers. The small, rather inconspicuous flowers are yellow-green and grow in groups 6 to 8 inches long; most of them remain unfertilized and grow hairs that appear as smoke. Highly drought-tolerant, it needs little pruning, except to be kept small.
GROWTH: 12 to 15 feet tall
CONDITIONS: full sun; well-draining soil
HARDY: Zones 5 to 8

'VELVET FOG' SMOKE BUSH

'DOUBLE PLAY' SPIREA

TWO-SEASON COLOR
Spirea, aka Japanese meadowsweet
(Spiraea japonica)
Easy-to-grow, summer-flowering spirea spreads slender branches into fans of dark green foliage with clusters of raspberry-rose flowers that are attractive to butterflies. If deadheaded, the bloom continues into September, sometimes followed by red or orange autumn leaf color. Varieties such as 'Goldmound' provide attractive golden or lime-green foliage. Spirea needs little pruning; thin the oldest stems to maintain vigor and reduce crowding. Cultivars such as 'Magic Carpet' and 'Double Play' are short and compact.
GROWTH: 2 to 6 feet tall, 5 to 7 feet wide
CONDITIONS: partial shade or full sun; well-draining soil
HARDY: Zones 3 to 8

'SIXTEEN CANDLES' SUMMERSWEET

OLD-FASHIONED CHARM
Summersweet, aka Sweet pepperbush
(Clethra alnifolia)
Nothing is sweeter than this native blooming in a shady spot. Its fragrant pink or white flowers in slender racemes 4 to 6 inches long have a wonderful, haunting fragrance and stand up like birthday candles against lustrous green foliage. In fall, the leaves turn to a lovely, showy gold. Summersweet spreads slowly by suckers; shape it and control sprawl by cutting weak wood to the ground in late winter or early spring. Look for compact 'Sixteen Candles', floriferous dwarf 'Hummingbird', or pink- to white-flowered 'Rosea'.
GROWTH: 3 to 8 feet tall
CONDITIONS: partial to full shade; moist, acidic soil
HARDY: Zones 3 to 9

THE PRUNING PREDICAMENT
"Americans overprune,"

John Brookes (1933–2018), a famous British gardener, once said. So, restrain yourself, prune cautiously, and step back to evaluate your work after every few cuts. Get rid of any dead wood. This is satisfying and makes it easier to spot other dull, dead branches and eliminate twiggy tangles. Unless you are reshaping a hedge, just thin shrubs to give them breathing room and exposure to light. Your goal is to allow each shrub to take its natural shape and show to its best advantage. Normal maintenance pruning on a flowering shrub must be timed to its bloom cycle.

The general rules are these:
■ Shrubs that bloom on old wood should be pruned immediately after they flower.
■ Shrubs that bear flowers on new growth should be pruned when they're dormant in late winter or in early spring.

BENEFITS OF SUMMER-FLOWERING SHRUBS					
SHRUB	SHOWY	FRAGRANT	FOR BIRDS AND BUTTERFLIES	TOLERATES SHADE	EASY TO GROW
BLUEBEARD	•	•	•	•	•
CAROLINA ALLSPICE		•		•	•
HYDRANGEA*	•			•	
POTENTILLA	•		•	•	•
ROSE OF SHARON	•		•	•	
SHRUB ROSE*	•		•		•
SMOKE BUSH	•				
SPIREA	•		•	•	•
SUMMERSWEET	•	•	•	•	

MY SHRUBS

NAME	DATE PLANTED	NOTES

FEATHER YOUR NEST

Plants marked with an asterisk (*) are profiled in this book.

POOR INDEED IS THE GARDEN IN WHICH BIRDS FIND NO HOMES.
–Rev. Abram L. Urban, writer (1849–1932)

To attract birds to your yard as residents or occasional guests, you need to extend the invitation. Start with a few of these wonderful, bird-friendly plants.

PERENNIALS
Aster* (*Aster* spp., *Symphyotrichum* spp.)
This plant's late summer to autumn, daisylike flowers develop tasty seed heads sought by cardinals, chickadees, finches, nuthatches, and many others.

Black-eyed Susan*
(*Rudbeckia fulgida, R. hirta*)
The summer to autumn flowers of black-eyed Susan leave a mass of seed heads resembling brown cones. These attract many birds, including goldfinches, pine siskins, sparrows, and other overwintering species.

Coneflower*
(*Echinacea purpurea*)
The seed heads of the purple coneflower attract the cardinal, chickadee, goldfinch, junco, siskin, and other songbirds.

Goldenrod (*Solidago* spp.)
Goldenrod's showy panicles of golden-yellow flowers appear from late summer to fall, providing food (flower seeds) and cover for birds. Its nectar-rich flowers attract insects, which are a feast for bluebirds, mockingbirds, warblers, wrens, and other insect eaters; goldfinches and other small birds relish the seed heads.

ANNUAL
Sunflower*
(*Helianthus annuus*)
Seed-heavy sunflower heads are favored by cardinals, goldfinches, woodpeckers, and others. (Avoid pollenless, seedless, cutting varieties if your goal is to attract birds.)

SHRUBS
Beautyberry (*Callicarpa* spp.)
The densely clustered white, pink, red, or purple fruit of this plant are favored by many

ASTER

BLACK-EYED SUSAN

CONEFLOWER

GOLDENROD

SUNFLOWER

'PEARL GLAM' BEAUTYBERRY

birds, including bluebirds, bobwhites, cardinals, cedar waxwings, robins, and thrushes.

Cotoneaster
(*Cotoneaster* spp.)
This shrub's arching branches provide seasonal shelter, nesting sites, and food. Its spring to summer flowers attract hummingbirds, and its colorful (yellow, black, pink, orange, or red) fall and winter berries are enjoyed by cardinals, catbirds, finches, jays, towhees, and others.

Currant (*Ribes* spp.)
More than 90 species of birds find summer shelter and nesting sites here. The red to purple-black berries are

favored by flickers, robins, sparrows, tanagers, towhees, and woodpeckers, among others. Golden-yellow spring flowers attract hummingbirds.

Elderberry (*Sambucus nigra* ssp. *canadensis*)
More than 120 bird species seek food, shelter, and nesting sites here. In early summer, large, umbel-shape heads of creamy white flower clusters attract hummingbirds as well as black-headed grosbeaks, indigo buntings, orioles, tanagers, and other migrant songbirds; late summer's crop

SHARE YOUR FLOWERY OUTLOOK WITH PICS ON **f** @THEOLDFARMERSALMANAC

of purple to black berries draws bluebirds, catbirds, orioles, robins, tanagers, thrashers, warblers, waxwings, and woodpeckers, to name a few.

Evergreen holly
(*Ilex* spp. and hybrids)
Hollies may say "Christmas" to many of us, but songbirds seek them out year-round. The dense, prickly foliage is superb protection from hawks, cats, raccoons, and other predators, as well as shelter from the weather. The red berries are packed with lipids (fat). Migrating bluebirds, tanagers, and thrushes will feast on the crop in fall. Cedar waxwings, mockingbirds, robins, and

'LITTLE DIPPER' COTONEASTER

CURRANT

ELDERBERRY

DELPHINIUM   PENSTEMON   SNAPDRAGON

SAY "HELLO" TO HUMMINGBIRDS

No matter where in North America you live, you have a good chance of hosting hummingbirds in your yard. Nectar-filled flowers will entice hummingbirds, but not just any blooms will do. Hummingbirds seek plants with deep, tubular blossoms that point up and are arranged around a stem (think columbine* or honeysuckle). Because a hummingbird usually hovers while it eats, its wings whizzing at 80 beats per second, it favors flowers that stand clear of leaves or branches (agaves, bee balm,* salvias,* penstemons).

Although a hummingbird will feast on flowers of any hue, certain colors capture its attention more than others. Red flowers attract especially well, but those of related shades (red-orange, orange, hot pink) also call to them. Studies have shown that hummingbirds also seek blue flowers, such as salvia* and delphinium* blossoms, that have the necessary shape and structure. Both native and non-native plants attract hummingbirds, as long as the blossoms have tubular flowers. Here are a few:

Annuals
Garden balsam
  (*Impatiens balsamina*)
Monkey flower (*Mimulus* spp.)
Scarlet bedding sage*
  (*Salvia splendens*)
Snapdragon
  (*Antirrhinum majus*)
Texas sage* (*S. coccinea*)

Perennials
Anise hyssop (*Agastache* spp.)
Bee balm* (*Monarda* spp.)
Brakelights (red) and
  yellow yucca (*Hesperaloe
  parviflora*)
Clematis* (*Clematis* spp.)
Columbine* (*Aquilegia* spp.)
Coneflower* (*Echinacea* spp.)
Delphinium*
  (*Delphinium* spp.)

Foxglove* (*Digitalis* spp.)
Hollyhock* (*Alcea* spp.)
Iris* (*Iris* spp.)
Jasmine* (*Jasminum* spp.)
Penstemon (*Penstemon* spp.)
Red-hot poker
  (*Kniphofia* spp.)
Salvia* (*Salvia* spp.)
Speedwell (*Veronica* spp.)
Vermillionaire firecracker
  plant (*Cuphea* hybrid)

EVERGREEN HOLLY

NORTHERN BAYBERRY

REDTWIG DOGWOOD

other winter birds will enjoy it in winter.

Northern bayberry
(*Morella pensylvanica,* formerly *Myrica pensylvanica*) Tall, evergreen bayberry provides valuable shelter to birds, plus color in a winter yard. The tiny, waxy, gray berries tempt cedar waxwings, woodpeckers, yellow-rumped warblers, and even tree swallows from fall to late winter. Snip some berried branches and poke them into a window box or doorstep urn to bring berry-eaters into view.

Redtwig dogwood
(*Cornus alba, C. sericea*)

The spring brings clusters of fuzzy white flowers and small white berries on this cousin of the flowering dogwood tree—all highly tempting to insect- and fruit-eating songbirds. In fact, the berries disappear fast when bluebirds, native sparrows, robins, thrashers, and thrushes find them.

Serviceberry (*Amelanchier* spp. and hybrids)
The abundant crop of juicy berries that follow serviceberry's white flowers bring in bluebirds, brown thrashers, cedar waxwings, gray catbirds, robins, rose-breasted gros-

beaks, and scarlet tanagers, among others.

Sumac (*Rhus* spp.)
Sumac attracts more than 95 species of birds with summer shelter and nesting sites. The deep red, fuzzy berries are sought by bluebirds, cardinals, chickadees, jays, juncos, robins, sparrows, tanagers, woodpeckers, and others.

Viburnum* (*Viburnum* spp.)
This shrub attracts bluebirds, cardinals, catbirds, chickadees, grosbeaks, redpolls, robins, towhees, waxwings, and others with fruit, shelter, and nesting sites.

SERVICEBERRY

SUMAC

VIBURNUM

HEAR THE BUZZ?

Plants with an asterisk (*) are profiled in this book.

THE HUM OF BEES IS THE VOICE OF THE GARDEN.
–Elizabeth Lawrence, American gardener, writer, and landscape architect (1904–85)

Populations of the honeybee, that all-important pollinator of fruit and vegetable crops, are declining. Factors such as habitat loss, pesticide use, and diseases have taken a toll on these heroes of the horticultural world. The story that seldom gets attention is that for home gardeners, there are plenty of native pollinators.

Roughly 4,000 species of bees are native to North America, including approximately 45 types of bumblebees. Many types of flies, certain wasps, and even butterflies and bats can act as pollinators. By attracting a diversity of these beneficial visitors, you will improve the pollination in your garden. Even better, for many gardeners (especially those allergic to bee stings), these industrious alternative pollinators seldom sting, as they are too busy gathering the pollen and nectar that they need to survive.

You can take three steps to welcome pollinators to your garden.

1. PROVIDE NECTAR- AND POLLEN-RICH PLANTS, INCLUDING NATIVES & HERBS

The native pollinators in your region have co-evolved with the native plants, so use native wildflowers to draw them to your yard. What's more, have plants in bloom all season long. For early bloom, consider clarkia, dianthus,* larkspur, lupine,* sweet alyssum, and wallflower. Midseason flowers can include bee balm,* black-eyed Susan,* coneflower,* coreopsis,* cosmos, and gaillardia. To carry the bees until frost, plant agastache, cleome, salvia,* and sunflower.*

Herbs can attract native pollinators and provide them with nourishment, too. These include borage, calendula, chamomile, holy basil (tulsi), lavender,* marjoram, mint, oregano, and rosemary. Native plants are easy to grow because they are adapted to your local climate and growing conditions and, once established, are fairly low-maintenance.

2. PROVIDE NEST SITES FOR POLLINATORS

Many native pollinators nest

MAKE A TINY HOUSE

Welcome the orchard mason bee and others with a home of their own: Bundle paper drinking straws or cardboard tubes into a waterproof container or drill a series of small horizontal holes into a block of wood. Place these nest sites at least 3 feet above the ground in a shady, protected location near fruit trees or on the side of a barn or shed. For more information, see Almanac.com/beehouse.

176

QUEEN ANNE'S LACE

as alkali, plasterer, and sweat bees dine only on open flowers like asters,* calendulas, and daisies.

■ Long-tongue bees such as bumble-, digger, leaf cutter, mason, miner, and squash bees drink from deeper, tube-shape flowers like honeysuckle, lupines,* salvias,* and snapdragons.

■ Many butterflies and moths have an extremely long, tube-like tongue called a proboscis, which is coiled when not in use, so flowers with a tubular shape attract them as well.

■ Large butterflies have long legs and need a platform on which to land. The best choices for them are flowers with multiple tiny blossoms, such as lilac,* phlox, Queen Anne's lace, and yarrow. They can get nectar from many small blossoms while perched in one place, saving energy.

underground, so have some open areas. Many others nest in cavities in trees and hollow plant stems. Bumblebees often make their homes in abandoned mouse and vole tunnels, while others prefer piles of rocks. Small bees may fly only a few hundred yards from their nest when foraging; large bees such as bumblebees will travel a mile or more in search of food.

3. STOP USING PESTICIDES

Pesticides are toxic to pollinators. While they may get rid of the bad bugs, they also kill the good bugs. Pesticides should not be used on plants in bloom. If you must, apply pesticides either near dusk or very early in the morning. At these times, insects are less active.

TELLING TONGUES

Although pollinators are attracted to fragrance and color, their different tongue sizes mean that they prefer different types of flowers.

■ Short-tongue bees such

NECTAR VS. POLLEN: THE STICKY DIFFERENCE

• Nectar is the sweet juice that flowers exude to attract insects. It contains complex sugars that give pollinators the energy to make their rounds.

• Pollen is the fine powder produced by the male parts (stamens) of a flower. Pollinators love it for its rich proteins and fats. As they fly from flower to flower collecting both nectar and pollen to feed to their young, they incidentally rub pollen off the flowers and onto themselves. They then carry it to their next stop—a female flower or part—and we have pollination!

Mixing pollen and nectar plants in your garden (especially among fruit and vegetables) will keep bees close to the plants that you want them to pollinate.

ENJOY MORE, LABOR LESS

Plants marked with an asterisk (*) are profiled in this book.

A GARDEN REQUIRES PATIENT LABOR AND ATTENTION. PLANTS
DO NOT GROW MERELY TO SATISFY AMBITIONS OR TO FULFILL GOOD INTENTIONS.
THEY THRIVE BECAUSE SOMEONE EXPENDED EFFORT ON THEM.
–Liberty Hyde Bailey, American botanist (1858–1954)

Superb, well-maintained gardens are usually enchanting to see, relaxing to be surrounded by, and gratifying to share. The question for many gardeners—one for all folks who live busy lives and want to maintain a garden—is how to achieve a high level of beauty and delight with less time and effort.

The answer is simple: Let "low maintenance" be a guiding principle and apply these guidelines and techniques to your garden.

SIMPLIFY

Look at your garden with an impartial eye. Ask yourself: What do I enjoy?

Simplifying doesn't mean sacrificing beauty; simplifying enhances beauty because your new choices will be easier to maintain. A tended garden is always more attractive than a weedy mess. Good maintenance is an essential component of

beauty. Consider what you are trying to achieve and where you want the most impact. Put the highest-maintenance ornamental areas close to the house, near the front walk or back patio where you can enjoy them.

As you move away from the house, flowering trees and shrub groupings will provide more visual impact. They also require less work than flower beds. Look for areas where you can eliminate perennials in favor of shrubs, add larger sweeps of plants, or even eliminate a bed or two. For example:
- Do you really want a bed of mixed perennials (that you don't have time to deadhead or weed)?
- Could you replace it with a beautiful hydrangea,* a bed of low-maintenance perennials like coneflower* (*Echinacea*), or ornamental grasses?
- Is that straggly, hard-to-mow lawn on a shady hillside an asset? Instead, plant

a ground cover like hay-scented ferns (*Dennstaedtia punctilobula*) or dead nettle (*Lamium*) to cover the slope.

New choices may require work to establish—soil prep, planting, watering, and weeding in the first year or two—but once they are, you'll have a garden that requires little maintenance.

LOVE SHRUBS

Shrubs bring structure and year-round beauty to the garden, and many are easy to maintain. Look for ones that play multiple roles—that not only bloom but also have good foliage, fruit, and bark.

Hydrangeas* are wonderful shrubs: They enjoy a dramatic, long bloom followed by spent flowers that are beautiful well into the winter, and they have bold, disease-free, green foliage.

But shrubs don't need blooms to win a place in the landscape. Redtwig dogwoods (*Cornus sericea*) and their yellow- and orange-stem cousins bring a striking flash of color to the winter landscape and have attractive midgreen foliage in season. The subtle but cheerful spring blooms are an added treat.

Traditional perennial borders require a lot of fussing. Mixing in some choice shrubs for backdrop and structure will reduce maintenance in these beds. Consider spirea for spring blooms and a fountain form, smoke bush *(Cotinus coggygria)* for bold upright branches of purple foliage, or arborvitae for upright evergreen columns.

Hedges and shrub borders play a vital role in a landscape, separating and defining spaces. Low-maintenance shrubs are those that don't require pruning. Spirea, viburnum,* and shrub willows such as the arctic willow *(Salix arctica)* have beautiful natural forms that work well in a row or staggered border. For evergreens, consider junipers or arborvitae. For a beautiful mixed hedge or shrub border, plant several different types of shrubs.

IS YOUR GARDEN A LABOR OF LOVE? SHARE A PIC AT 📷 @THEOLDFARMERSALMANAC

While you wait for the shrub border to mature, plant low-maintenance ground covers and perennials around the edges to fill in, provide blooms, and serve as a living mulch.

GET OUT OF TROUBLE
Replace fussy perennials with low-maintenance perennials such as ironweed *(Vernonia noveboracensis)*, threadleaf coreopsis* *(Coreopsis verticillata)*, and catmint *(Nepeta)*. Goldenrods *(Solidago)*, Joe Pye weed *(Eutrochium purpureum)*, and asters* *(Asters, Symphyotrichum)* are also

beautiful and easy and attract pollinators.

Choose plants that are disease-resistant and look great without frequent deadheading. Blue agastache blooms almost all summer long with no deadheading. Even among annuals, you can choose those that require less maintenance. For example, most petunias require regular removal of the sticky flowers for continued bloom, but the look-alike million bells (*Calibrachoa*) bloom all season long with only occasional cutting back.

Globe amaranth (*Gomphrena globosa*) is another easy annual with mounds of season-long color in pink, white, or purple. When the plant gets leggy in midseason, cut it in half and it'll come back strong.

In shade, grow begonias or coleus rather than impatiens, which can often be susceptible to the impatiens wilt disease.

COVER UP

Ground covers are a living mulch and a barrier to weeds. They can replace needy lawns. Planting ground covers such as ferns, heucheras, wild ginger (*Asarum*), and sweet woodruff (*Galium odoratum*) will reduce long-term maintenance and add a beautiful ground floor layer to your garden.

REPEAT

Generously sized, repeating groups of low-maintenance shrubs or plants fill spaces, smother weeds, and visually tie together your garden. Depending on the scale of the garden, start with groupings of three to five shrubs and seven to nine perennials.

RULES OF THUMB

These are the three most important ways to keep your garden simple:

1. Thoroughly mulch. Mulch conserves water, reduces weeds, and adds organic matter to the soil.

Good mulches include leaf mold (shredded tree leaves that have become partially decayed from sitting in a pile for a year or two), composted horse bedding, well-aged wood chips, and buckwheat hulls.

Stay away from raw wood chips, fresh grass clippings, and fresh manure. The decomposition of the raw materials steals nitrogen from the soil and may burn your plants. Sniff the mulch: If it has a sweet, earthy smell, it's ready for your plants.

Apply mulch 2 to 3 inches deep and keep it away from stems and trunks. Moisture in the mulch could encourage rot. Move the mulch an inch or so away by gently circling

the stem with your finger. Mulch flower beds in the spring after any self-sowing perennials and annuals have emerged. Shrubs and trees can be mulched at any time.

As the mulch breaks down, your soil is enriched with nutrients that feed your plants and organic matter that helps with water retention. Your soil will become darker and richer after several years of mulching.

2. Weed on time. Timely weeding is the key to weed control. In spring, weeds tend to overwhelm. When this happens, focus on eliminating weeds in flower or those that have already bloomed. The goal is to prevent the weeds from setting seed and producing even more generations of themselves. It is best to pull out weeds by their roots, but, in a pinch, cut off the blooms with hedge shears until you have time for a thorough weeding.

3. Water deeply and infrequently. Watering this way encourages plants to establish deep roots that will sustain them in times of drought. For more on water, see "Be Water Wise," page 206.

Follow these guidelines, and you'll see not only that gardening just gets easier but also that you'll enjoy it more!

OBSERVATIONS AND REMINDERS

CHANGES TO MAKE NEXT YEAR

CUT FLOWER CARE

Plants with an asterisk (*) are profiled in this book.

A BEAUTIFUL BOUQUET . . . IS A TRADITIONAL GIFT FOR WOMEN, BUT I HAVE
RECOMMENDED THAT BOTH MEN AND WOMEN KEEP FRESH FLOWERS IN THE HOME FOR
THEIR BEAUTY, FRAGRANCE, AND THE LIFT THEY GIVE OUR SPIRITS.
–Andrew Weil, M.D., practitioner of integrative medicine (b. 1942)

The care and arranging of cut flowers is an art, not a science: Everyone has talent for it, and "rules" can vary, even among the experts. Many of the tips here are also recommended care for blooms entered into competitive flower shows or fairs.

THE HARVEST

Prepare and bring with you into the garden a container of tepid water (100° to 110°F). Plan to cut stems during the coolest time of the day (morning or evening), before the buds fully open but when they are starting to show color, with the exception of roses.* (Entering a show? Competitions often require fully or nearly fully open flowers.) Use a clean, sharp knife; scissors might pinch the stem, eliminating its ability to conduct water. Cut the stem several inches longer than necessary to allow for trimming later. Remove any leaves

that will be in water; they tend to rot and ruin the water.

Cut roses* in their early opening stage, that is, as a tight bud with full color. A rose* will proceed to open as it ages. To remove foliage and thorns from roses* painlessly, consider getting a stem stripper.

HOMEMADE FLORAL PRESERVATIVES

FORMULA #1

2 cups lemon-lime soft drink (not diet), such as 7 Up or Sprite

1/2 teaspoon liquid chlorine bleach

2 cups water

FORMULA #2

2 tablespoons white vinegar

2 teaspoons sugar

1/2 teaspoon liquid chlorine bleach

1 quart water

HARDENING, OR CONDITIONING

A period of cool storage—3 to 12 hours—after initial cutting allows the stems to take up water and retain the flowers' freshness. Place the container of flowers in a refrigerator set at 35° to 45°F, but do not put the flowers near fresh fruit or vegetables, as these foods release ethylene gas, which will reduce the flowers' vase life. A cool cellar or basement is also suitable.

THE ARRANGEMENT

The display life of many flowers increases when they are recut while under water, prior to being arranged. When cut fresh, out of water, a stem can take in too much air, causing a blockage that keeps water from reaching the flower. (This is especially true of roses* because they have a bent neck.)

You can cut a flower in

the garden, immediately submerge the stem in warm water, and cut it again later, while holding it below the waterline.

Flowers in a vase prefer warm water (80° to 110°F); however, it is not necessary to maintain the water at this temperature.

Cut flowers last longer with a proper preservative added to the water. Use florists' preservatives or, alternatively, make some at home. The recipes on page 182 contain ingredients similar to those in a florists' preservative: lemon or vinegar to lower the pH, sugar to replace the glucose that the plant has lost and needs, and bleach and carbonation to keep the bacterial growth down.

Check your vase's water level every day. Display your flowers away from full sun, heat, hot or cold drafts, and fresh fruit.

VASE LIFE

Note your flowers' life expectancy and compatibility:

- Chrysanthemums* last for a week or more.
- Daylilies are gone after 1 day.
- Dianthuses* (carnations, pinks, sweet Williams) last 7 to 21 days, depending on variety.

SEARING THE STEM

Lobelia, milkweed, poppies, and other flowers with milky stems should be held in a flame for about 15 seconds immediately after cutting. This step seals the latex in the stem but keeps the water-conducting vessels open. Otherwise, the latex substance can leak into the water and cause it to spoil quickly. It can also affect the life of other flowers in the vase.

- Gladioluses last for 7 to 10 days.
- Lilies* may last 2 or more weeks. Note that lilies require only half the amount of food recommended for other flowers.
- Narcissuses/daffodils and others contain a type of sap that will shorten the vase life of other flowers.
- Peonies* last for 5 to 10 days. (Take only a few blooms from each peony* plant and avoid cutting stems from plants less than 3 years old.)
- Tulips* continue to grow after you arrange them, but they do not mix with daffodils.
- Snapdragons have negative phototropism: Their stems turn away from the light and the flowers can twist and turn. Stock is another flower that reacts to light when it is cut. It's important to keep these flowers straight; stake them or put them in a tall florist's bucket as soon as they are cut.
- Sweet peas, which add height to an arrangement, last 3 to 7 days. The more frequently you cut fresh sweet peas, the more they bloom!
- Sunflowers* have a vase life of 7 to 10 days.

CUTTINGS IN SEASON

(suggested; may vary)

From May into July, cut butterfly ranunculuses, narcissuses, peonies,* salvias,* snapdragons, and tulips.*

From July to September, cut amaranths, asters,* black-eyed Susans,* cosmos, dahlias,* stock, sunflowers,* statice, and zinnias.

THE MALLET MYTH

For years, florists kept mallets just for pounding woody plant stems, such as those of lilacs,* on the belief that hammering the stem end would make the flowers last longer in water. In fact, it makes the stems rot faster in the water. Put away the mallet.

If possible, cut above woody stems. If this is not possible, submerge the entire stem in water for 20 minutes to an hour before trimming.

ANGULAR VS. HORIZONTAL STEM CUTS

An angular cut allows the stem to take up water more efficiently, while a horizontal cut leaves a stem sitting flat on the bottom of a vase, thus inhibiting water intake.

An angular cut also helps if you're using a floral foam: A stem with a point is easier to insert.

MY CUTTING FLOWERS

FLOWER	DATE CUT	USAGE NOTES

HOW TO DRY FLOWERS

Plants with an asterisk (*) are profiled in this book.

THE FINEST QUALITIES OF OUR NATURE, LIKE THE BLOOM ON FRUIT,
CAN BE PRESERVED ONLY BY THE MOST DELICATE HANDLING.
–Henry David Thoreau, American writer (1817–62)

Fresh-cut flowers are delightful, but for blooms that last up to a year, dry them. Here are the basics:

Harvest flowers in the morning just before the blooms are fully open. Snip to include 5 to 6 inches of the flower's stem, depending on use: more, if a deep vase display is planned; less for a boutonniere.

Strip off all foliage from stems. This helps to speed drying.

Secure a bundle of 8 to 10 stems with a rubber band or twist tie.

Hang the bundle upside down from a hook or coat hanger in a dark, dry, well-ventilated area. Closets and attics are ideal spots; a garage works, if light does not penetrate it and air circulates in it.

In 2 to 3 weeks (less, if the weather is hot), flowers will be completely dry. Some colors may fade, but most flowers retain their original hues.

FLASH-DRYING

This method works best with large blooms—for example, hydrangeas*—and herbs.

Collect blooms as directed and gather them into bunches. Put each bunch into a brown paper grocery bag, fold over the top, and secure it with a clothespin or bag clip. Place the bag into the trunk of a car parked in the sun. If drying herbs, shake the bag daily so that the herbs do not compact; if drying flowers, check them daily to see if they are dry to the "crinkling tissue paper" stage (that's the sound that their petals should make when you rub them). Drying may be finished in as little as 24 hours.

SPECIAL EFFECTS

The lime green, cone-shape, mophead blooms of the 'Limelight' hydrangea* can be left to mature on the shrub and then stood upright in an empty (waterless) vase to dry.

The electric blue stems and flowers of 'Big Blue' sea holly are candidates for both the traditional and flash-dry methods. Cut the stems after morning dew evaporates, just before the buds open fully. Tie stems together to air-dry as directed. Expect their vivid

A VOICE OF EXPERIENCE

I have been using my car to dry herbs and flowers now for several years. I lay fresh-cut matter in shallow cardboard boxes and place these on my car seats and dashboard. If I want to flash-dry, I place them on the dashboard, leaving the windows open just a crack, weather permitting. I live in a fog zone, so this technique comes in very handy. **–Suzanne, on Almanac.com**

blue color to fade to almost gray over time. To retain the original blue color, flash-dry the bundles.

'Dragon's Breath' celosia, aka plumed cockscomb, dazzles with its red, orange, yellow, and sometimes violet, cream, and pink plumes. Harvest stems when the flowers are almost open. Hang bunches upside down in a cool, dark place for 3 to 4 weeks.

Roses* to be dried should be harvested in bud stage, when they just begin to open. Hang upside down as directed.

For pressed or flattened flowers, open to the middle of a heavy book (e.g., an encyclopedia volume). Line the facing pages with parch-

ARE YOUR PRESERVATION METHODS CUT-AND-DRIED? SHOW OTHER GARDENERS WITH A PIC ON 📌 @ALMANAC

ment or waxed paper. Arrange the petals to be face down on the parchment and close the book. Leave for 7 to 10 days to dry.

To preserve a fresh flower bouquet, bury it in sandlike silica gel, available at craft stores, in an airtight container for about a week.

BEST BLOOMS FOR DRYING

Look for flowers that have a small calyx and hold their petals tightly. (The calyx consists of the small green leaves—sepals—at the base of a bud; they enclose and protect the unopened flower.) Good candidates for drying include the following.

ageratum (floss flower)	baby's breath	hydrangea*	salvia*
	celosia	larkspur	sea holly
	coneflower*	lavender*	statice
amaranth	globe thistle	lunaria	strawflower
artemisia	gomphrena	pansy	yarrow
astilbe*	herbs	rosebuds*	

GROWING CONCERNS

DEALING WITH FLOWER DISEASES AND PESTS

Plants with an asterisk (*) are profiled in this book.

Diseases and pests are the bane of gardeners everywhere. When they appear, don't become discouraged; deal with them. Learn from the experience, adapt as needed, and plan accordingly. For more information, go to Almanac.com/gardening/pests-and-diseases.

KEY WORDS

Blight: a disease marked by rapid discoloration, withering, and death of plant parts or entire plants

Handpick: to remove pests (e.g., beetles, bugs, caterpillars, worms, snails, slugs) from a plant by hand or with an implement such as tweezers and dispose of them by drowning them in a bucket of soapy water or crushing them or their eggs

Rotation: the growing of different plants in succession on the same land, which can discourage plant pests and diseases

Soil solarization: a technique used to kill pests and diseases in the soil by covering the ground with clear plastic, in full sun, for 2 or so months in the summer before planting

DISEASES

Anthracnose: caused by fungi; favor cool/wet conditions

Signs: varies; dark leaf spots dry/fall out; foliage yellows/curls/ drops; sunken stem lesions; dark specks or pink/orange gel in lesions; twig distortion/ dieback; poor flowering; fruit/roots rot

Control/Prevention: destroy infected parts (do not compost); remove plant debris regularly; resistant varieties; good air circulation; avoid overhead watering

Aster* yellows: caused by phytoplasmas (bacteria-like microorganisms); transmitted by leafhoppers

Signs: varies; stunting/distortion; leaves yellow/purple; flowers pale or green/produce leafy growth; plants slow-growing/unusually upright, stiff

Control/Prevention: destroy infected plants (do not compost); resistant varieties; employ yellow sticky traps to monitor leafhopper numbers; use light-color/reflective mulch (such as foil); weed

Black spot: caused by a fungus that attacks roses*; favors wet conditions

Signs: dark brown/ black leaf spots with feathery edges; foliage drops; purple lesions on canes turn black/blister; poor flowering; plants stunted/weakened

Control/Prevention: destroy infected leaves (do not compost); prune diseased canes 6 to 8 inches below symptoms; remove plant debris regularly; disinfect tools; resistant varieties; good air circulation/sunlight; avoid overhead watering

Black stem, Phoma: caused by a fungus that mainly attacks sunflowers*; favors wet conditions; spread by weevil damage

Signs: black lesions on stems, also leaves/back of flower heads/crown; foliage wilts; poor flowering/seed formation; plants weakened

Control/Prevention: destroy infected plants (do not compost); tolerant varieties; control stem weevil; 4-year rotation

Blight, Ascochyta ray: caused by a fungus that attacks chrysanthemums*; favors humid conditions

Signs: one-sided distortion; flowers brown/wilt; brown or black leaf spots/stem lesions; buds/leaves/stems may rot

Control/Prevention: destroy infected parts/severely infected plants (do not compost); remove plant debris

regularly; good air circulation; avoid overhead watering; rotation

Blight, Botrytis (aka "gray mold," "fire"): caused by fungi; favor cool/damp conditions

Signs: varies; yellow/brown/gray spots with water-soaked margins on leaves/flowers; gray mold; buds remain closed; stem lesions; wilt/rot; scorched appearance ("fire") in some plants

Control/Prevention: destroy infected parts/severely infected plants (do not compost); remove plant debris regularly; disinfect tools; good air circulation/sunlight; avoid overhead watering; prevent plant stress/injury; weed; rotation

Blight, lilac* bacterial (aka "blossom blight"): caused by bacterium; favors mild/wet conditions

Signs: black spots on leaves/young stems; leaves/shoots curl;

black streaks on twigs; blackened flower buds; flowers wilt/brown; leaves/shoots/buds die

Control/Prevention: prune twigs 1 foot below symptoms/destroy infected parts (do not compost); disinfect tools; resistant varieties; prevent plant stress/injury; good air circulation; avoid overhead watering/excess nitrogen

Blight, Ovulinia petal: caused by a fungus that mainly attacks azaleas, but also rhododendrons*/mountain laurels; favors cool to mild/wet conditions

Signs: petals "freckled" with white/brown spots that rapidly enlarge; flowers slimy/brown/wilt; black, rice-size growths

Control/Prevention: destroy infected flowers (do not compost); replace soil and mulch to a depth of 1 inch; remove plant debris regularly; resistant varieties; good air circulation/sunlight; avoid overhead watering

Blight, southern (aka "mustard seed fungus," "Sclerotium crown or stem rot," "white mold"): caused by a fungus; favors warm/wet conditions

Signs: leaves/stems/entire plants wilt, brown or blacken, and may die; water-soaked lesions on lower stems; crown/bulb/rhizome rot; fluffy, white fungal mats with mustard-seed–like balls on stems bases/nearby soil

Control/Prevention: destroy infected parts/plants (if severe), white fungal mats, and surrounding soil to at least 6 inches beyond plant and 8 inches deep (do not compost); remove plant debris regularly; disinfect tools; solarize soil; resistant varieties; good drainage

Brown spot (aka "Pleiochaeta root rot"): caused by a fungus that attacks lupines*; favors moist conditions

Signs: brown/purple/black spots on lower leaves; foliage drops; brownish black lesions on stems/pods; roots rot; plants wilt/die

Control/Prevention: destroy infected plants/parts (do not compost); remove plant debris regularly; resistant varieties; employ yellow sticky traps to monitor leafhopper numbers; rotation

Bud blast (aka "rhododendron* bud and twig blight"): caused by a fungus that attacks rhododendrons*/azaleas; may spread through leafhopper damage

Signs: flower buds turn brown or black/remain closed; black, bristly growths on buds

Control/Prevention: destroy infected buds (do not compost); remove plant debris regularly; control leafhoppers

Canker and dieback, Botryosphaeria: caused by fungi that attack woody plants; favor warm/wet conditions

Signs: leaves curl/brown/wilt/don't emerge; sunken stem cankers; reddish-brown discoloration under bark; wedge-shape discoloration on branch cross-section points to center; black pustules; stunted branches; dieback

Control/Prevention: prune out infected branches to at least 6 inches beyond symptoms (do not compost); remove plant debris regularly; disinfect tools; resistant varieties; good air circulation; prevent plant stress/injury

Crown gall: caused by bacteria

Signs: pale swellings on crown/roots harden to woody, brown growths (galls); discolored leaves; dieback; poor flowering/fruiting; plants stunted/slow-growing/may wilt or die

Control/Prevention: prune out small galls/leave galls if cover most of crown; destroy severely infected plants, including roots/surrounding soil (do not compost); disinfect tools; resistant varieties; prevent plant stress/injury; avoid overhead watering; weed; 5-year rotation

Ink spot: caused by a fungus that attacks reticulated and other bulbous irises*; favors mild/wet conditions

Signs: yellow-margined, reddish brown leaf spots; brownish black powdery mass in spots; plants collapse; inky black stains on some bulbs; bulbs rot

Control/Prevention: destroy infected leaves/bulbs (do not compost); remove plant debris regularly; good air circulation; 3-year rotation

Leaf blotch (aka "measles"): caused by a fungus that attacks peonies*; favors warm/wet conditions

Signs: purple lesions on upper leaf surfaces/light brown spots underneath; reddish brown streaks on stems; olive green growths on lesions

Control/Prevention: destroy infected parts (do not compost); remove plant debris regularly; disinfect tools; resistant varieties; good air circulation/sunlight; avoid overhead watering; replace mulch at end of growing season

Leaf gall, azalea: caused by a fungus that attacks azaleas/sometimes rhododendrons* or other hosts; favors cool/wet conditions

Signs: swollen/curled leaves turn waxy pale green/pink/white; galls covered in white powder/turn brown and hard/drop

Control/Prevention: destroy galls before they turn white; prune out diseased twigs (do not compost); remove plant debris regularly; resistant varieties; good air circulation/soil

aeration/sunlight; avoid overhead watering

Leaf spot, algal (aka "green scurf"): caused by parasitic algae that usually attack leathery-leaved plants; favor warm/wet conditions

Signs: raised, green/reddish brown/gray blotches with feathery margins on lower leaves; reddish brown fuzzy growth; leaves yellow/drop; cankers; branches stunted/die back

Control/Prevention: destroy infected parts (do not compost); remove plant debris regularly; good air circulation/sunlight; avoid overhead watering; prevent plant stress; replace mulch at end of season

Leaf spot, angular: caused by bacteria; favor warm/wet conditions

Signs: water-soaked, brown/purple, angular leaf spots between veins dry/fall out; sticky, clear/white ooze; disease progresses upward

Control/Prevention: destroy severely infected plants (do not compost); remove plant debris regularly; disinfect tools; resistant varieties; good air circulation; avoid overhead watering

Leaf spot, bacterial (aka "bacterial leaf blight" of iris*): caused by bacteria; often favor warm/wet conditions

Signs: varies; water-soaked rust/black leaf spots between veins later dry/fall out, leaving holes; leaves yellow/distort/wilt/die; stem cankers

Control/Prevention: destroy infected parts/severely infected plants (do not compost); remove plant debris regularly; disinfect tools; prevent plant stress/injury; good air circulation; avoid overhead watering

Leaf spot, fungal: caused by fungi; usually favor warm/wet conditions

Signs: varies; leaf spots on lower leaves enlarge and turn brown/black; fuzzy growth or pustules in lesions; disease progresses upward; leaves die

Control/Prevention: destroy infected leaves/severely infected plants (do not compost); remove plant debris regularly; disinfect tools; resistant varieties; good air circulation; avoid overhead watering

Leaf spot, iris*: caused by a fungus that mainly attacks iris*; favors warm/wet conditions

Signs: yellow/brown leaf spots with water-soaked/reddish brown/yellow margins dry out; black specks in lesions; leaves curl/yellow/die back from tip; poor flowering; plants weakened

Control/Prevention: destroy infected parts (do not compost); remove debris regularly; resistant varieties; good air circulation/sun; avoid overhead watering; weed

Mildew, downy: caused by oomycetes (water molds); favor cool/humid conditions

Signs: varies; yellow/brown/purple angular spots between leaf veins on upper leaf surfaces; downy, usually gray-white growth on leaf undersides; defoliation

Control/Prevention: destroy infected parts/severely infected plants (do not compost); remove plant debris regularly; resistant varieties; good air circulation/sunlight; avoid overhead watering; weed

Mildew, powdery: caused by fungi; favor moderately warm/dry days with cool/humid nights

Signs: varies; white spots or flourlike coating on upper leaf surfaces; leaves drop; distortion/stunting

Control/Prevention: destroy infected parts (do not compost); remove plant debris regularly; resistant varieties; good air circulation/sunlight; spray plants with

solution of 1 teaspoon baking soda/1 quart water; prevent plant stress; avoid overhead watering

Mold, Sclerotinia white (aka "cottony rot"): caused by fungi; usually favor cool/wet conditions

Signs: varies; water-soaked, brown lesions dry/bleach; cottony growth at stem bases; black, seedlike growths; leaves/flowers wilt; lower stem/crown cankers; plants die

Control/Prevention: destroy infected plants/surrounding soil (do not compost); remove plant debris regularly; solarize soil; good air circulation; avoid overhead watering; do not overwater; weed; rotation

Rot, Armillaria root (aka "honey fungus," "shoestring root rot"): caused by fungi that attack woody plants; favor cool/wet conditions

Signs: honey-brown mushrooms at plant

base; stunted/sparse growth; dieback; leaves wilt/drop; white fungal growth under bark; black strands under bark/on roots/in nearby soil; cankers; roots rot; plants weakened/die

Control/Prevention: destroy severely infected plants, including roots/stump; remove plant debris regularly; disinfect tools; resistant varieties; prevent plant stress/injury; water during drought; do not overwater

Rot, bacterial bud: caused by bacterium; favors wet conditions

Signs: white/black spots on young leaves; gummy sap oozes from lesions; older leaves distorted with brown/yellow spots; flower buds blacken/remain closed; stalks or entire plants die

Control/Prevention: destroy infected parts/surrounding soil (do not compost); remove plant debris regularly;

disinfect tools; good air circulation; avoid overhead watering; do not overwater

Rot, bacterial soft (of iris*): caused by bacterium; enters wounds, such as from iris* borer damage; favors wet conditions

Signs: dieback starts at leaf tips; leaves yellow/wilt/separate from base; rhizomes rot; foul odor; plants may die

Control/Prevention: cut out diseased rhizome tissue/air-dry cut surfaces for 1 to 2 days before replanting; for severe infections, destroy plants/surrounding soil (do not compost); remove plant debris regularly; disinfect tools; good air circulation; prevent plant injury; control iris* borers; plant rhizomes at proper depth

Rot, Fusarium basal: caused by fungi that attack bulbs; favor warm/wet conditions

Signs: leaves stunted/discolored/wilt/die; flowers sparse/deformed; bulbs rot from base upward/scales detach; white/pink mold; sour smell

Control/Prevention: destroy infected scales/

bulblets/bulbs; remove plant debris regularly; disinfect tools; resistant varieties; avoid plant injury; provide good drainage; avoid overhead watering; avoid excess nitrogen; 3- to 4-year rotation

Rot, gray bulb: caused by a fungus that mainly attacks tulips*

Signs: bulbs turn gray/rot from top down; gray mold; tiny brown/black flattened growths on bulb/nearby soil; leaves turn red/wilt or don't emerge; plants slow-growing/die

Control/Prevention: destroy infected bulbs/surrounding soil to at least 6 inches beyond plants; remove plant debris regularly; provide good drainage; 4- to 5-year rotation

Rot, Phytophthora crown and root (aka "Phytophthora shoot blight"): caused by oomycetes (water molds); favor wet conditions

Signs: leaves discolor/wilt; dieback; oozing cankers near base; reddish brown discoloration of inner bark/wood; roots rot; plants slow-growing/stunted/die

Control/Prevention: destroy infected herbaceous plants/severely diseased woody plants/surrounding soil (do not compost); prune out branch cankers; for woody plants, remove soil near infected crown to dry tissue/replace

afterward; remove plant debris regularly; resistant varieties; prevent plant stress/injury; provide good drainage/do not overwater

Rot, Pythium root and stem: caused by oomycetes (water molds); favor wet conditions

Signs: plants stunted/yellow/may wilt in day but recover at night/die; dieback; stem bases brown/blacken; crown rot; root tips die; outer root tissue easily pulls off

Control/Prevention: destroy infected parts/plants/surrounding soil (do not compost); remove plant debris regularly; disinfect tools; solarize soil; avoid overhead watering; provide good drainage/do not overwater

Rot, Rhizoctonia root and stem: caused by fungi; favor warm/moderately moist conditions

Signs: yellow/brown leaves; reddish brown lesions/sunken cankers on lower stem/roots; roots rot; plants wilt in day and recover at night/stunted/die

Control/Prevention: destroy infected plants (do not compost); good air circulation; prevent plant stress/injury; provide good drainage; 2- to 3-year rotation

Rust: caused by fungi; some require two hosts; favor cool to moderate/moist conditions

Signs: varies; orange pustules on undersides of lower leaves/stems; spots on upper leaf surfaces; foliage distorts/dies/drops; stunting; poor flowering; plants weakened

Control/Prevention: destroy infected parts/severely diseased plants; remove plant debris regularly; disinfect tools; resistant varieties; good air circulation; avoid overhead watering; weed

Smut, white: caused by fungi; favor cool/humid conditions

Signs: varies; starts with lower leaves; white/pale yellow leaf spots turn brown, dry, and fall out, leaving "shot hole" appearance; plants weakened; in dahlias,* poor tuber development

Control/Prevention: destroy affected leaves/plants (if severe); remove plant debris regularly; disinfect tools; good air circulation/sunlight; avoid overhead watering

Viruses: caused by viral pathogens; often transmitted by aphids, leafhoppers, and other sap-sucking insects

Signs: varies; leaves with yellow/light green mottling or rings; distorted leaves/stems/flowers; flowers streaked; stunting

Control/Prevention: destroy infected plants (do not compost); remove plant debris regularly; disinfect tools; resistant varieties/certified virus-free plants; control sap-sucking insects; weed

Wilt, bacterial: caused by bacteria; favor warm/wet conditions

Signs: varies; leaves yellow/wilt/die; roots decay; cut stems may reveal dark streaks with brownish-yellow ooze; stunting; plants wilt/die

Control/Prevention: destroy infected plants/surrounding soil (do not compost); remove plant debris regularly; disinfect tools; resistant varieties; avoid overhead watering

Wilt, clematis* (aka "clematis* leaf and stem spot"): caused by a fungus that attacks clematis,* especially large-flower hybrids; favors humid conditions

Signs: spotted/black leaves; black stem lesions; sudden stem collapse, usually just before blooming; plants die back to ground

Control/Prevention: destroy infected leaves (do not compost)/prune diseased stems to just below soil line; remove plant debris regularly; disinfect tools; resistant varieties; plant 2 to 4 inches deeper than at nursery to ensure a few growth buds belowground; good air circulation; prevent plant stress/injury

Wilt, Fusarium: caused by fungi; favor warm/dry conditions and acidic soil

Signs: plants wilt (sometimes one-sided) in daytime; later, entire plant wilts/dies; stunting; yellow leaves; poor flowering; roots rot; stem cross-section reveals brown discoloration

Control/Prevention: destroy infected plants/roots/surrounding soil (do not compost); remove plant debris regularly; disinfect tools; resistant varieties; avoid excess nitrogen; in acidic soils, raise pH to 7.0; weed; 3- to 5-year rotation

Wilt, Verticillium: caused by fungi; favor warm/dry conditions

Signs: varies; leaves (lower first, sometimes on one side of leaf/plant) yellow/brown/wilt/die or don't emerge; stem cross-section shows discoloration; dieback; poor flowering; plants weakened/stunted/die

Control/Prevention: destroy infected herbaceous plants/severely infected woody plants, including roots/surrounding soil (do not compost); prune out diseased branches; disinfect tools; resistant varieties; solarize soil; prevent plant stress; control nematodes; weed; rotation

PESTS

Aphids: tiny, antennaed insects; suck sap from succulent new growth

Signs: misshapen/yellow leaves; distorted flowers; leaf drop; sticky "honeydew" (excretion) on leaves; sooty, black mold

Control/Prevention: knock off with water spray; apply insecticidal soap; inspect new plants carefully; use slow-release fertilizers; avoid excess nitrogen; encourage lacewings, lady beetles/bugs, spiders

Deer: scat is oval, pellet-like, dark brown/black; hoof prints are cloven

Signs: rough or torn appearance of leaves, twigs; deer droppings

Control/Prevention: electronic fencing; wood, wire, mesh, plastic net fencing (min. 8 feet tall to deter whitetails); cage individual plants or cover with fabric netting; use contact/area repellents; deer-resistant plants

Earwigs: small, reddish brown insects, with forceps at hind end; like moisture; active at night; prey on garden pests

Signs: small holes in leaves/flowers/fruit/stems

Control/Prevention: trap in tuna can filled with 1/2 inch of fish oil and sunk in soil slightly above ground level; remove plant debris; spread diatomaceous earth around plants

Grasshoppers: differential—black chevron markings on hind femur; two-stripe—stripes from eyes to wing tips; red-legged—red hind tibia; migratory—long wings have spots in centers

Signs: skeletonized, ragged, or hole-ridden leaves; cuts at the plant base

Control/Prevention: control summer weeds, eliminate tall grass; natural enemies include hairworms, bee flies, robber flies, ground beetles; use row covers

Iris* borers: caterpillars are 1½ to 2 inches long, pinkish; moths have brown-to-tan wings, 2-inch span

Signs: leaf tips turn brown; pinholes chewed in leaves (caterpillar/larvae entry); holes bored in rhizomes; slimy, stinky mess at plant base and rhizome

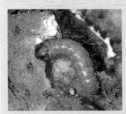

Control/Prevention: squash by hand or remove and discard affected foliage before pupation (and new moths, mating, eggs); inspect suspected rhizome damage, discard (burn/bury) affected ones; clean beds of plant debris after a hard frost

Japanese beetles: C-shape, whitish grubs become copper-color beetles with metallic green heads; feed on variety of plants

Signs: skeletonized leaves (only veins remain); chewed stems/flowers/fruit; root damage (where grubs feed)

Control/Prevention: handpick; shake off, collect, drown in soapy water; plant tansy; attract parasitic wasps, flies; spread diatomaceous earth around plants

Lace bugs: adults—tiny, oval or rectangular with lacy pattern; nymphs—smaller, dark, spiny

Signs: mottled, stippled, and discolored leaves; black (fecal) spots or cast skins (exuvia) on leaf undersides

Control/Prevention: mitigate drought; shade plants; apply insecticidal/horticultural soap/oil at egg or nymph stage

Leaf miners: yellow/white maggots become tiny flies (often black with yellow)

Signs: meandering blisters in leaves caused

by tunneling larvae

Control/Prevention: remove infested leaves; weed; use row covers; till soil early in season; rotate plantings

Leafhoppers: tiny, wedge-shape, green/brown; hop or run sideways when disturbed; adults fly

Signs: distorted/stunted plants; brown leaf edges; yellow, curled leaves; white spots on undersides

Control/Prevention: knock off with water spray; apply insecticidal soap

Lilac* borers (aka "ash borers"): white larvae, up to 1 inch long, with amber-color head capsules; 1-inch-long, wasplike moths with 1½-inch wingspan have long, yellow/black-banded hind legs and long antennae, but amber-color abdomens distinguish them from wasps

Signs: leaves wilt, turn reddish brown; branches die; affects main trunk, but also large branches; tunnels ("galleries") in sapwood can be 3

inches long and nearly ½ inch wide; irregularly shaped entrance holes, circular exit holes above; excrement ("frass") and "sawdust" outside holes; tree scars over holes

Control/Prevention: prune and destroy infected branches; dig out larvae and destroy or crush by inserting wire into galleries; use pheromone traps in spring to catch male borers; spray biological insecticides; to prevent—mulch and water regularly, avoid wounds from pruning and lawn equipment, prune older, more susceptible branches near base of plant

Lily* leaf beetles (aka "red/scarlet lily beetles"): target "true lilies"*; ½ inch long, bright red body, black legs, antennae; eggs have tan (then orange, then red) lines; larvae are plump orange/brown/yellow, sluglike

Signs: irregular holes or notches in leaves, stems, buds; irregularly shaped eggs appear on leaf undersides; next-stage larvae feed on foliage undersides and carry own excrement ("fecal shield")

Control/Prevention: handpick adults, larvae, eggs, if few; crush or knock into soapy water; neem oil; grow resistant varieties; avoid Asiatic hybrids

Mealy bugs: tiny, pinkish bodies covered by white, waxy fluff

Signs: withered leaves; "honeydew" (excretion) on leaves; sooty, black mold

Control/Prevention: knock off with water spray; apply insecticidal soap

Mice: 3 to 7 inches long; naked/slightly furry tail; 1/4-inch droppings

Signs: browsing cuts at 45-degree angle, low to ground; tooth marks resemble fork tines; gnawed bark; seedlings and sprouts "disappear" overnight

Control/Prevention: remove debris, food; destroy/eliminate homes; seal/block entries; traps

Mites, spider: minute, eight-leg, hairy bodies;

nymphs, six legs

Signs: fine webs; yellow-specked underside of leaves, later brown-edged or bronze or yellow leaves; leaf drop

Control/Prevention: rinse plants with water, mist daily; apply insecticidal soap

Moths, sunflower*: 3/8 to 5/8 inch long, shiny gray-to-brown; cigar shape with tightly clasped wings

Signs: damage to flower head; silken webbing over flower head

Control/Prevention: plant later in season; use pheromone traps, insecticide

Nematodes, foliar: microscopic roundworms that swim up stems to enter leaf pores (stomata) to feed on cells; many hosts; favor wet conditions

Signs: varies with plant; typically, starting on lower leaves, yellow/

brown/purplish, angular spots or streaks change to dark green/brown/blackish lesions between leaf veins; dead areas may drop out; distorted/curled leaves may wilt/drop; symptoms move upward on plant; stems, buds, and flowers may also be affected; poor flowering; stunted or bushy growth; in lilies,* symptoms are known as "dieback" or "bunchy top"

Control/Prevention: destroy infected leaves/plants (do not compost); remove plant debris regularly; choose resistant varieties, if available; good air circulation/spacing; avoid overhead watering/keep leaves as dry as possible; weed

Nematodes, rootknot: microscopic roundworms that feed on cells in roots; many hosts; favor warm soil temperatures

Signs: typically, roots "knotty" or galled; plants stunted/yellow/wilted/weakened; leaves and other parts may distort or die; poor flowering

Control/Prevention: destroy infested plant debris after flowering

season, including roots (do not compost); disinfect tools; choose resistant varieties; solarize soil, if possible; plant French marigolds as a trap crop; rotate plantings, if possible

Nematodes, stem and bulb (aka "stem eelworms," "bulb nematodes"): microscopic roundworm that feeds on cells in stems, bulbs, tubers/rhizomes, and leaves; many hosts; favors cool, wet conditions

Signs: typically, leaves turn yellow then brown/distort/blister/wilt/die; swollen stems, crowns, leaf bases; poor/distorted flowering; plants stunted/die; fluffy white masses ("nematode wool") may be present; discolored/distorted bulbs soften/brown/crack/die; bulb cross-section may show brown concentric rings; in tulips,* flower may bend in direction of nearby stem lesion

Control/Prevention: destroy infested plants and those within 3 feet, including soil (do not compost); disinfect tools; choose healthy, nematode-free seed/plants; rotate plantings every 5 years, if possible; plant green manures such as mustard and radish; weed

Rabbits: 15 to 19 inches long; gray or brownish; short white tail; long, tapered ears

Signs: clean-cut damage, low to ground; tooth marks wide as spoon tip

Control/Prevention: install 4-foot-tall chicken wire fence (holes 1 inch wide or less) with the bottom buried 6 inches and bend the top 1 foot of the fence away from the garden; repellents; rabbit-resistant plants; sprinkle dried sulfur around plants

Rose* stem girdler (aka "bronze cane borer"): seldom-seen adult beetles are 1/4 to 3/8 inch long at maturity, with flat body shape; feeding larvae are segmented, cream-color, with large head

Signs: swellings/galls develop near meandering

tunnels under stem bark; canes die back or break

Control/Prevention: cut stems below the wilt, examine pith, cut incrementally to white pith; examine stems in spring, remove and destroy infected canes; practice clean cultivation

Scale insects: 1/16 to 3/8 inch long; waxlike covering ("scale"); females lack wings, visible legs, antennae

Signs: leaves yellow/wilt; sticky "honeydew"; sooty mold fungi

Control/Prevention: apply insecticidal soap/horticultural oil (three times min.) over 6 to 7 days; test synthetic insecticidals before using

Slugs/snails: soft-body mollusks; snails protected by shell; both prefer cool/moist/shady conditions; active mostly at night or on cloudy/foggy days

Signs: irregular holes in leaves/flowers; gouged fruit; slimy secretion on plants/soil; seedlings "disappear"

Control/Prevention: handpick; avoid thick

bark mulch; use copper plant collars; avoid overhead watering; lay boards on soil in evening, in morning lift and dispose of pests in hot, soapy water; drown in deep container of 1/2 inch of beer or of sugar water and yeast sunk to ground level; apply 1-inch-wide strip of diatomaceous earth

Sow bugs: small, flat, brown-to-gray-to-black oval shape; segmented, armor-like plate on body parts; four antennae, 14 legs; pair of tail-like appendages at rear of body

Signs: tender transplants/seedlings "disappear" (eaten); leaf-edge holes

Control/Prevention: remove debris, e.g., leaves, grass clippings, fallen fruit, boards, stones

Squirrels, gray: 8 to 11 inches long; 1 to 1 1/2 pounds; usually gray with white underparts

Signs: chew tree buds, eat berries/succulent fruit, bulbs (whole or part); chew bark; dig in containers

Control/Prevention: fence with 1-inch wire mesh, min. 30 inches above ground, 1 foot below, 6 inches bent outward at 90-degree

angle; electrified fence—two strands, 3 inches from existing fence (one 6 inches above ground, one at fence height); to protect bulbs—lay 1-inch-mesh poultry wire in trench slightly deeper than desired depth, then add soil, plant bulb, cover plantings with additional poultry wire, add final soil; repellents; traps; to protect container plants, add a layer of gravel or stones on top of soil

Stalk borers: about 1 inch long; light brown, with narrow white stripe down full length of body and one on each side, interrupted by a dark brown/purplish midband

Signs: leaf wilt; weakened stems; tunnels in stalks and roots (split lengthwise to see)

Control/Prevention: practice clean cultivation; pinch the stem that contains the borer; remove and burn infested plants

Tarnished plant bugs: 1/4 inch, light green–to–brown; oval; yellow forewings (triangle), with black dot on lower third; nymphs are wingless

Signs: shoot distortion, bud drop, wilt, stunting, dieback

Control/Prevention: monitor with white sticky cards; sweep net sampling (brush foliage with net, count bugs); manage by mowing, weeding, eliminating debris before winter

Thrips: minute slender bodies, fringed wings; coloring varies from white/yellow to black/brown; nymphs lack wings

Signs: stunted plant growth; stippling; leaf drop; rose* petals may display dark spots/streaks, deformed buds or failure to open

Control/Prevention: knock off with water spray; use sticky traps; beat/shake branches/foliage/flowers; clip off unopened/infested buds and shoot tips; submerge in mixture of 7 parts water to 1 part isopropyl alcohol and discard; plant resistant (rose*) cultivars and those adapted to local conditions; water adequately, avoid excess nitrogen; deadhead flowers

Voles: small gray/brown rodents; two

beady eyes, small rounded ears, short tail; vegetarian; note—a *mole* is carnivorous, with paddle-like feet, no visible eyes or ears

Signs: chewed perennials (hostas), shrubs, tree bases, bulbs; partially eaten root vegetables

Control/Prevention: plant in containers; wrap/cover tree trunks; remove heavy mulch/vegetation; work gravel into soil when planting; remove bird feeders

Weevils, black vine: 3/8 to 1/2 inch long; blackish-brown, wingless body, black antennae, six legs; grubs have white body, reddish brown head, no legs; nocturnal feeders

Signs: chewed leaf edges, roots; drop from plant when disturbed, feigning death; larvae chew on basal crowns and roots

Control/Prevention: handpick; repot in "new" soil; neem products; spray with *Beauveria bassiana,* a fungus whose spores

grow through and kill the insect; pesticide for any weevil—mix diatomaceous earth into soil

Weevils, iris* (aka "flag weevil"): 1/5 inch long; black with black and yellow scales, long snout

Signs: feed on flowers, seeds, pods of wild blue flag iris *(Iris versicolor)* and purple Siberian iris; deposit eggs in ovary, which pupate in seedpod; visible when flower is in bloom

Control/Prevention: remove/destroy seedpods

Weevils, root: adults are 3/8 inch long, black, with subtle white flecking, short snout; flightless, nocturnal; larvae are 1/4 inch long, with grublike off-white body, brown head

Signs: angular notches on leaf edges; drop from plant and play dead, if disturbed

Control/Prevention: place a shallow pan of water under plant at night; weevils climb in and drown; apply beneficial nematodes as soil drench to control larvae in soil; keep moist

Verbena bud moths: caterpillar/larvae—1/2 inch long, green body, red head, black collar;

develop in seed of host plant; moth—5/16 inch long; marbled forewing in brown, tan, black

Signs: tunnels/bores into plant shoots/stalks, seeds, and buds; moths do no harm

Control/Prevention: handpick, or cut infestations, burn infested shoots and buds

Whiteflies: tiny, often clear/green, wingless nymphs become small, flylike insects with white, waxy wings

Signs: all stages suck sap on leaf undersides; leave sticky "honeydew" (excrement), sooty, black mold; yellow/silver areas on leaves; wilted/stunted plants; adults fly if disturbed; some species transmit viruses

Control/Prevention: remove infested leaves/plants; use handheld vacuum to remove pests; knock off leaf undersides with water spray in morning/evening; set yellow sticky traps; apply insecticidal soap; invite beneficial insects and hummingbirds with native plants; weed; reflective mulch

DISEASE AND PEST RECORD

DISEASE RECORD	PEST RECORD

DISEASE _____

CONTROL MEASURES _____

_____

_____

_____

DISEASE _____

CONTROL MEASURES _____

_____

_____

_____

DISEASE _____

CONTROL MEASURES _____

_____

_____

DISEASE _____

CONTROL MEASURES _____

_____

_____

DISEASE _____

CONTROL MEASURES _____

_____

_____

PEST _____

CONTROL MEASURES _____

_____

_____

_____

PEST _____

CONTROL MEASURES _____

_____

_____

_____

PEST _____

CONTROL MEASURES _____

_____

_____

_____

PEST _____

CONTROL MEASURES _____

_____

_____

_____

PEST _____

CONTROL MEASURES _____

_____

_____

FACTS ABOUT FERTILIZERS

THE BEST FERTILIZER FOR A PIECE OF LAND
IS THE FOOTPRINTS OF ITS OWNER.
–Lyndon B. Johnson, 36th U.S. president (1908–73)

Fertilizer terms can be confusing. Let us take the guesswork out of fertilizing.

THE BIG THREE

The primary plant nutrients are nitrogen, phosphorus, and potassium (N, P, and K). On the package, the number for each nutrient (e.g., 5-10-5) indicates the percentage of net weight contained within or as organic additives. For example, a 100-pound bag of 10-10-10 contains 10 pounds of each element. The rest is filler, which gives the fertilizer bulk and makes it easier to spread.

Nitrogen (N) promotes strong leaf and stem growth and dark green color. To increase available nitrogen, add aged manure to soil or apply alfalfa meal (which also feeds soil organisms), fish meal (also a good source of potassium), or blood meal. Nitrogen is released quickly; add it to soil in spring. Be aware that proportions are not equal: 10 pounds of blood meal supplies the same amount of nitrogen as 10 to 20 bushels of manure, but blood meal does not provide the benefits of the organic matter in manure.

Phosphorus (P) promotes root and early plant growth and helps with setting blossoms and seed formation. The most readily available sources are fast-acting bonemeal or slow-release rock phosphate. Still, unless they are sandy and acidic, most non-agricultural soils contain sufficient amounts of phosphorus. In soil, excess phosphorus can inhibit beneficial organisms called mycorrhizal fungi.

Potassium (K), aka potash, regulates the flow of water in plant cells and promotes plant root vigor and disease and stress resistance. Plants deficient in potassium may display stunted leaves. Most soils contain potassium, so its ratio number tends to be the smallest.

Complete, all-purpose, or balanced fertilizers contain all three nutrients (e.g., 10-10-10). The ratios can be important. For example, if plants produce

---

RULES OF GREEN THUMBS

• If soil has no specific needs, a 5-5-5 fertilizer provides the nutrients for healthy growth.

• Bonemeal worked into soil around newly planted bulbs keeps them springing up for several years.

• Flowering annuals burst into bloom when foliage-producing nitrogen is held back. The tonic that they need is 5-10-10.

• To remain green, many evergreens need high nitrogen, plus several trace elements. Evergreen food may have a ratio of 30-10-10, plus doses of copper, molybdenum, and iron.

lush green growth but no flowers, the soil may contain too much nitrogen. A 3-20-20 fertilizer (low in nitrogen) would be appropriate. Alternatively, plants bedded in cold soil may need a boost for root growth—specifically, phosphorus in a 10-50-10 mix.

ORGANIC VS. SYNTHETIC

Organic fertilizers come from sources such as manure, blood

MORE IS NOT BETTER

Be aware: Excess phosphorus and potassium may pose a threat to the environment in the form of water runoff. This can induce algae blooms in lakes and ponds, possibly eventually killing fish and other animals.

meal, cottonseed meal, feather meal, and crab meal. They encourage healthy soil biology that is rich in microbial activity.

Synthetic fertilizers are lab-made and derived from compounds like ammonium nitrate, ammonium phosphate, superphosphate, and potassium sulfate. They expedite plant growth and can contribute to bloom rate in flowering plants. They are great for a boost but do little to improve soil health, texture, or fertility. Applying too much can "burn" foliage and damage plants. These are high in salts and can be detrimental to beneficial microorganisms. Also, being water-soluble, they can leach into water sources.

In general, organic fertilizers need time to enrich the soil, so they're best applied in the fall, thus making nutrients available in spring. Some consist of an organic mix and small amounts of synthetic fertilizers in order to provide long-term benefits as well as immediately available nutrients. Note that the N-P-K ratio of an organic fertilizer is typically lower than that of a synthetic one. By law, the ratio label can list only nutrients that are immediately available.

GRANULAR VS. SOLUBLE FERTILIZERS

Granular fertilizers are solids that must be worked into soil. They need time (and water) to dissolve and become available to plants. Slow-release fertilizers are a subset of granular formulations; a portion of the fertilizer is not immediately available to plants. Nutrients are meted out over several weeks. Therefore, they are applied less frequently.

Sometimes called "liquid feed," soluble fertilizers are ready-to-use solutions or packaged dry-milled materials to be dissolved in water. These tend to be quick-release fertilizers that are high in nitrogen and result in fast green growth. To build the long-term health and fertility of soil, we recommend granular organic fertilizers. Supplementing with a water-soluble fertilizer ensures that plants have the nutrients that they need when they need a boost (during active growth).

WHEN TO FERTILIZE

When correcting a nutrient deficiency based on a soil test, fertilize well before you plant so that the fertilizer can be worked deep into the soil. Otherwise, fertilize ground soil in spring before planting annual flowers and as soon as dormancy breaks and growth begins for perennials, shrubs, and ornamental trees. Mix fertilizer several inches deep in the soil for annuals. Work it lightly into the soil around perennials.

FERTILIZING CONTAINER PLANTS

For thriving outdoor flowerpots and containers, a continuous supply of nutrients and fertilizer is essential.

1. Incorporate slow-release fertilizer into potting mix. (If the mix contains fertilizer, skip this.)

2. Supplement the slow-release fertilizer with a water-soluble (liquid) one. Choose one with an equal ratio of N-P-K or use an organic option such as fish meal emulsion or liquid kelp. These deliver nutrients directly to plant roots.

3. If plants need a pick-me-up due to stress or heavy flower production, feed plant leaves ("foliar feed") directly in the morning or early evening. Avoid this when temperatures are above 90°F or when the sun is beating on plants; the fertilizer will burn leaves. Deadhead old blooms and cut back damaged foliage. Spray water-soluble fertilizer on leaf tops and undersides. (Or, water with diluted seaweed solution or spray the solution directly onto the leaves.) The spray delivers nutrients directly to where photosynthesis takes place. Results can be dramatic.

MY FERTILIZER RECORD

DATE	PLANT	FERTILIZER	NOTES

BE WATER WISE

Plants with an asterisk (*) are profiled in this book.

HOW OFTEN IT IS THAT A GARDEN, BEAUTIFUL THOUGH
IT BE, WILL SEEM SAD AND DREARY AND LACKING IN ONE OF ITS
MOST GRACIOUS FEATURES, IF IT HAS NO WATER.
–Antoine-Joseph Dezallier d'Argenville, French gardener and writer (1680–1765)

Gardeners anywhere can face periodic drought, as well as high water bills and seasonal water restrictions. Water-saving practices not only make good "green" sense but also save time, energy, and effort. The basic techniques are easy to apply in a new garden or an existing one.

GOOD SOIL IS ESSENTIAL

Fertile soil with good drainage is the most important factor for a successful, water-thrifty garden. If you are building new beds, add a 50-50 mixture of compost or aged manure and topsoil. This will nourish the plants. Plus, less compact soil will make better use of both water and nutrients. In an established garden, adding or mulching with compost will improve fertility.

IRRIGATE INTENTIONALLY

If you water by hand or hose, do so just on the soil around the plants; overhead watering can invite moisture-loving fungal diseases. Newly set plants need more frequent watering than established ones. The soil should be moist but not wet, and the only way to determine this is to test the dirt with your finger.

Soaker hoses and drip irrigation systems allow you to control water; they deliver a specific amount exactly where it is needed, while regular hoses tend to spray a fine mist over a large area.

Soaker hoses release water from along the full length of the hose. These work best in small, level gardens where plants are spaced closely together.

Drip irrigation systems are better for large gardens with a variety of plantings. An automatic timer attached to your system will ensure that your garden is watered on a regular schedule.

Rainwater can be captured in containers and/or directed to plants located at lower levels in your yard. Dig small basins around plants and trees to catch runoff or place a rain barrel under your gutter downspout.

MULCH

Mulch is a must: It improves soil fertility, slows evaporation and erosion, and discourages weeds. Compost, shredded dead leaves, grass clippings, and bark chips are natural mulches that gradually break down and add nutrients to the soil. Apply mulch 2 to 3 inches deep but not touching the stems of plants, a situation that can encourage decay and disease.

LOSE ANY GUILT ABOUT WILT

Temporary wilting during the heat of midday does not mean that a plant needs water. Some plants go through an obvious midday slump, which is an indication of the plant's natural adaptation to its environment. Visit your garden again in the early evening and see if the wilted plants have regained some turgidity. If they have come back—that is, if they look perkier—do not water. Plants are highly adaptable. They have the ability to draw water from deep in the soil. Periodically, take a trowel and dig down several inches into the zone where the roots are most active. If the soil is moist, there would be no benefit from watering.

RETHINK THE LAWN

Keep it small—or not at all: Consider growing ground covers. Water the lawn only when it's necessary. Here's how to know this: Step on the grass. If it springs back, it doesn't need water.

OBSERVE NATURE

Take inspiration from Mother Nature's wide variety of plants that cope splendidly with drought. They tend to have deep root systems and may have thorns, hairs, or silvery foliage to keep leaves cool, reduce water loss, and reflect sunlight.

Look at the plants thriving naturally in your region. These plants will be the foundation of

LET YOUR CURRENT INSPIRATIONS FLOW WITH A PIC ON **f** @THEOLDFARMERSALMANAC

your water-wise garden. Consider those with long bloom times and interesting foliage as well as color and form.

Among the low-water lovers are daisylike flowers, descended from tough prairie plants; these thrive on little water, once established. Also try black-eyed Susans,* coneflowers,* coreopsis,* feverfew, and tansy.

Many plants native to desert and Mediterranean-zone soils adapt widely, including agaves, cacti, and yuccas.

Drought-resistant ornamental grasses, such as tall fescues and variegated *Miscanthus sinensis*, create a fountainlike effect without water.

YUCCA

PUTTING THE GARDEN TO BED

Plants with an asterisk (*) are profiled in this book.

SUMMER, FALL, WINTER, SPRING,
THE SEASONS ROTATE AS EACH BRINGS
ITS SPECIAL BEAUTY TO THIS EARTH OF OURS.
WINTER'S SNOW AND SUMMER'S FLOWERS
FROZEN RIVERS WILL FLOW COME SPRING,
THERE IS A RENEWAL OF EVERYTHING.
–Edna Frohock, American poet (1907–97)

Gardens need help to make it through long, cold winters. Fortunately, preparing the garden doesn't cost much money, but you do have to spend time on it. The effort is worth it: Your perennials, trees, shrubs, and flower beds will be in good shape to weather snow, subzero temperatures, and those sudden thaws.

BEAT THE FROST

You can start preparing about 2 weeks before the first frost. (See pages 34 and 35 for frost dates or get your local dates on Almanac.com/frostdates.) This allows you to acclimate any plants you are taking indoors and locate bales of straw and other mulch materials—for instance, burlap, even old sheets. (They make good plant protectors.) An early start also gives you time to dig up tender summer-flowering bulbs—caladiums, gladioluses, and tuberous begonias—before the first freeze.

Allow all bulbs, tubers, and corms to air-dry, then pack them in dry peat moss or vermiculite and store them in a cool, dry location.

GO TO WORK AFTER A FREEZE

The first freeze of fall is your signal to get busy. Remove dead annuals as soon as you can, before they turn brown and crispy. Leave the dead foliage on healthy perennials for insulation; stems and leaves catch the snow. Plus, remaining dried seed heads are a great source of food for winter birds.

Lift cannas* and dahlias* after a killing frost.

KEEP WATERING

Soil that is like a moist, wrung-out sponge when the ground freezes gives lawns, shallow-rooted woody plants, and flowering perennials a better chance of survival. Trees and shrubs, too, especially newly planted ones, need water to get through the winter. Evergreens especially need moist soil because their leaves and needles continue to lose water throughout the winter. Although plants go dormant, they still use water to maintain themselves. The same goes for the lawn. Water every 7 to 10 days, if rainfall is not sufficient, until the ground freezes.

LOVE LEAVES

Before spreading mulch,

gather fallen leaves from the lawn. Their removal prevents them from matting and smothering the turf. The easiest way to gather leaves is to run a mower over them. If your mower has a bagger, attach it to pick up the shredded leaves. Then dump them in perennial beds and vegetable patches and around shrubs. Depending on your climate, a 2- to 4-inch covering is sufficient. Any leftover leaves can be added to compost piles or stored until spring, when they can be incorporated into new beds.

MULCH

Winter mulch protects against wide temperature fluctuations in the soil and prevents extremely cold temperatures from harming plants. You want to keep everything dormant until spring truly arrives. Mulch will maintain a cold soil even when temperatures hit 50°F in February or when the snowpack melts temporarily. Apply winter mulch after the ground has frozen but before severe temperatures or heavy snows occur. Applying mulch too early delays the freezing of the ground and invites disease and rodents. (They love to munch on succulent buds and the stems of your favorite plants.) Keep mulch a few inches away from tree and shrub trunks to keep rats and mice from gnawing on the bark.

READY THE ROSES*

Some plants, like roses,* need to have a thicker layer of leaf insulation to help them to stay dormant and avoid winter injury.

In areas north of Zone 5, once frost has killed the foliage on your hybrid tea roses,* prune them back to 1 foot tall. Flowers are generated on new growth, so all of the buds on the sides of each cane will generate new shoots with flowers come spring. Keep only four to six canes; if you leave more than six, flower numbers

**TIME TO GO BEDDY-BYE?
SHOW US HOW YOU
TUCK IN YOUR GARDEN
FOR WINTER ON** [instagram icon]
@THEOLDFARMERSALMANAC

will increase but the average bloom size per flower will be reduced. Dust hybrid teas with fine sulfur, available at most garden centers. Sulfur helps to control mites and mildew; mice can't stand the taste.

In more moderate zones, cover the graft unions of grafted roses* (including hybrid teas) with soil to insulate them from low temperatures. After a freeze or two, mound 12 inches of soil over the rosebush base. Potting soil from summer containers can be put to good use this way. Then, in spring, work the old soil into the ground.

If you use Styrofoam rose* cones for insulation, remove them on sunny days when the temperature is above 25°F. It gets hot inside the cones, and buds will sprout.

Nongrafted roses,* such as rugosas and antiques, don't need to be covered. Just mulch the ground around them with a couple of inches of straw or shredded leaves.

Climbing roses* need to be protected. Pull down the canes, lay them on the ground, and cover them with at least 6 inches of soil. Mound soil around the plant base, too. If your winter temperatures typically go below −10°F, leave the canes in place and insulate them with a thick covering of straw wrapped with burlap or old sheets.

HAUL IN THE HOSE

When your garden is all tucked in, unhook all hoses, drain the water from them, and cover water spigots with insulation if they are not self-draining.

CONTINUE COMPOSTING

In mild regions, where the weather is warm enough, the composting process will continue over the winter because compost generates its own heat. Where temperatures remain below or near freezing throughout the winter, composting still occurs, but slowly; it's more like freeze-drying than composting. Regardless of whether the organic matter is breaking down, the compost bin is a good place to store it until spring. Secure the base and lid to deter mice.

EMPTY ALL POTS

If winter temperatures are likely to drop below freezing, empty the potting soil out of all of your clay pots. Soggy soil in a pot that's left out for even one night of freezing can crack or shatter the container (water expands when frozen). Work the soil into the garden. Saving it for next year's potted plants is penny-wise but dollar-foolish, because it is full of roots and difficult to work.

MOW BEFORE SNOW

Although your lawn doesn't grow much in the fall, take the time to give it one last mow. If left too tall, it serves as an ideal environment for insects and diseases. Tall grass traps moisture and becomes a haven for diseases like snow mold, which kills grass and leaves huge brown splotches on the lawn. This can be a problem in any region where snow cover persists for a month or two during the winter.

PROTECT TREES

Rodents and other animal pests often chew on fruit trees, ornamental trees, and shrubs when their winter food supplies dwindle. This makes tree wraps essential for winter. Plastic collars, applied in fall, keep burrowing pests from nibbling on tree roots and bark. Take the wraps off in spring, or they will quickly strangle the tree once active growth resumes. Tree wraps also protect trunks from sunscald and the splitting and blistering that can occur when bare trunks are exposed to repeated freezing and thawing. This is especially important in the many regions of the northern United States and Canada where bitter-cold winter temperatures are interrupted several times per season by weather patterns that cause bark to thaw.

CLEANUP CHECKLIST

AFTER THE FIRST FREEZE OF FALL . . .	NOTES
REMOVE DEAD ANNUAL PLANTS.	
LIFT AND STORE CANNAS* AND DAHLIAS.*	
WATER PLANTS, TREES, AND LAWN.	
MOW AND/OR RAKE LEAVES FROM THE LAWN.	
SPREAD SHREDDED LEAVES ON GARDEN BEDS AND/OR COMPOST PILES.	
PRUNE HYBRID TEA ROSES* TO 4 TO 6 CANES, EACH 1 FOOT TALL.	
DUST HYBRID TEA ROSES* WITH SULFUR.	
AFTER A FREEZE OR TWO, MOUND 12 INCHES OF SOIL OVER HYBRID TEA AND GRAFTED ROSEBUSH* BASES.	
MULCH THE GROUND AROUND NONGRAFTED (RUGOSA AND ANTIQUE) ROSES.*	
PROTECT CANE ROSES* (SEE PAGE 210).	
MOW LAWN ONE LAST TIME BEFORE WINTER.	
UNHOOK HOSES, DRAIN, AND SHUT OFF AND/OR COVER TO INSULATE SPIGOTS.	
EMPTY POTS OF POTTING SOIL.	
AFTER THE GROUND HAS FROZEN . . .	
MULCH BEDS (KEEP A FEW INCHES AWAY FROM TREE AND SHRUB TRUNKS).	
WRAP TREE TRUNKS.	

LORE AND MORE

INTERPRETING PLANT NAMES

Plants with an asterisk (*) are profiled in this book.

**IF YOU DO NOT KNOW THE NAMES OF THINGS,
THE KNOWLEDGE OF THEM IS LOST, TOO.**
—Carl Linnaeus, Swedish botanist (1707–78)

The scientific name of a plant gives clues to its history and original uses. Swedish botanist Carl Linnaeus began the modern system of classification and nomenclature in the 18th century. He introduced a system for classifying plants using a two-word name, or "binomial," that consists of a genus name and a descriptive species name. Sometimes, further description is needed and a subspecies name or variety name is added. He mostly used Latin to create these names, but other languages, such as Greek, have sometimes been used as well.

In 1867, scientists began to formulate standardized international codes with intricate sets of rules for naming all living and ancient plants and related organisms. The scientific names of even modern genetically engineered plant varieties have these highly structured codes and centuries of precedent behind them.

Knowing the meanings of these Latin terms takes the mystery out of plant names. Note that this list is not comprehensive.

aestivalis	summer
alatus	winged
altus	tall
amoenus	pleasant, charming
angustifolius	narrow-leaved
aquaticus	grows near water
arborescens	treelike
asper	rough
aureus	golden
australis	southern
autumnalis	of autumn
baccatus	berry- or pearl-like
barbatus	bearded or barbed
bellus	beautiful
brevis	short
caeruleus	blue
campanulatus	bell-shape
campestris	growing in fields
candidus	white
canescens	grayish
capillaris	hairlike
cardinalis	bright red
carneus	flesh-color
caudatus	tailed
cinnamomeus	cinnamon brown
coccineus	scarlet
compactus	dense
contortus	twisted
cordatus	heart-shape
coriaceus	leathery
corniculatus	horned
cuneifolius	wedge-shape leaves
digitatus	finger-shape
dulcis	sweet
edulis	edible
elatus	tall
erectus	upright
esculentus	edible
fasciculatus	clustered, bundled
ferrugineus	rust-color
flavens	yellowish
fulvus	brownish yellow
germinatus	twin
gibbosus	humped, swollen on one side
glabratus	smooth
globulatus	bell-shape flowers

214

grandifolius . . . . large leaves
hastatus . . . . spear-shape
hirsutus . . . . . . hairy or shaggy
humifusus . . . . sprawling
humilis . . . . dwarf
inodorus . . . . without odor
junceus . . . . rushlike
kewensis . . . . . relating to Kew
   Gardens (England)
labiatus . . . . lipped
lacteus . . . . milky
laevigatus . . . . smooth
lanosus . . . . woolly
latiflorus . . . . . broad-flowered
laxiflorus . . . . . loose-flowered
lignosus . . . . like wood
limosus . . . . . of muddy places
lucidus . . . . shiny
luteus . . . . muddy yellow
maculatus . . . . spotted
mirabilis . . . . wonderful
natans . . . . floating
nemoralis . . . growing in woods
niger . . . . black
nitens . . . . shining
niveus . . . . snow-white
noctiflorens . . . night-flowering

occidentalis . . . . western
officinalis . . . . a formerly
   recognized medicinal
oleraceus . . . . from a vegetable
   garden
pallens . . . . pale
paludosus . . . . marshy
paniculata . . . . clustered flowers
parviflorens . . . small-flowering
patens . . . . spreading
pauciflorus . . . . . few-flowered
plumosa . . . . feathery
pratensis . . . . growing in
   meadows
pubens . . . . downy
pumilus . . . . dwarf, small
puniceus . . . . . reddish-purple
quadrifolius . . . . . . four-leaved
quinquefolius . . . . . five-leaved
radicans . . . . rooting
regalis . . . . royal
repens . . . . creeping
reptans . . . . crawling
reticulans . . . . netlike
riparius . . . growing near a river
roseus . . . . rose*-color
rotundifolius . . . . . round leaves

rubens . . . . red
ruderalis . . . . . growing among
   rubbish
rugosus . . . . wrinkled
sabulosus . . grows in sandy soil
sativus . . . . cultivated
scandens . . . . climbing
sericeus . . . . silky
setosus . . . . bristly
speciosus . . . . beautiful
spinosus . . . . with spines
stellatus . . . . starlike
stramineus . . . . . . straw-color
strigosus . . . . stiff-bristled
tenuis . . . . slender
tinctorius . . . . . used for dyeing
tomentosus . . . . like felt
tuberosus . . . . with tubers
urens . . . . stinging
vacillans . . . . swaying
velutinus . . . . velvety
vernalis . . . . of spring
verus . . . . true
villosus . . . . with soft hairs
violaceus . . . . violet
viridis . . . . green
vulgaris . . . . common

THE LANGUAGE OF FLOWERS

Plants with an asterisk (*) are profiled in this book.

A FLOWER IS NOT A FLOWER ALONE; A THOUSAND THOUGHTS INVEST IT.
–A Victorian Flower Dictionary: The Language of Flowers Companion *(2011),*
by Mandy Kirkby

The symbolic language of flowers has been recognized for centuries. Mythologies, folklore, sonnets, and plays of the ancient Greeks, Romans, Egyptians, and Chinese, as well as William Shakespeare's works, are peppered with flower and plant symbolism.

Nearly every sentiment imaginable can be expressed with flowers. Learning the symbolism of flowers became popular during the 1800s. Most Victorian homes had guidebooks for deciphering the "language," although definitions shifted among sources. Typically, flowers were used to deliver messages that couldn't be spoken aloud. The recipient of a rose* declaring "devotion" or an apple blossom showing "preference" might return to the suitor a yellow carnation* to express "disdain." Flowers could also be used to say "yes" or "no": Flowers given with the right hand meant "yes"; using the left hand meant "no."

The condition and presentation of flowers was important. If given upside down, the message being conveyed was the opposite of what was traditionally implied. The ribbon bore meaning, too: Tied to the left, the flowers' symbolism applied to the giver; to the right, the sentiment described the recipient. Of course, a wilted bouquet delivered an obvious message!

The meanings and traditions associated with flowers have changed over time, and different cultures assign varying ideas to the same species, but the fascination with "perfumed words" persists. This chart reflects mainly Victorian symbolism.

SYMBOLIC MEANINGS OF FLOWERS

Amaryllis . . . . .Pride	Clematis* . . . . Mental beauty
Anemone . . . . .Forsaken	Columbine* . . . . Foolishness
Aster* .Love, daintiness	Columbine,* purple . . . . Resolution
Bachelor's button . . . . Single blessedness	Columbine,* red . . . . .Anxious, trembling
Begonia. . . . . Beware	Coreopsis* . . . . Cheerfulness
Black-eyed Susan* . . . . .Justice	Crocus, spring . . . . Youthful gladness
Bluebell. . . . . Humility	Cyclamen . . . . Resignation, diffidence
Carnation *(Dianthus*)* . . . . Love	Daffodil . . . . Unequaled love
Chrysanthemum,* red . . . . I love you	Dahlia,* single . . . . Good taste
Chrysanthemum,* white . . . . Truth	Daisy. . . . . Innocence, hope
Chrysanthemum,* yellow. . . . . . . Slighted love	Daylily. . . . . Chinese emblem for mother

216

BEGONIA

BLUEBELL

EDELWEISS

Edelweiss . . . . .Courage, devotion

Forget-me-not . . . . True love memories

Gardenia. . . . . Secret love

Geranium, oak-leaved. . . . . . . True friendship

Gladiolus . . . . Remembrance

Heliotrope . . . . .Eternal love, devotion

Hollyhock* . . . . Ambition

Honeysuckle. . . . . .Bonds of love

Hyacinth, blue . . . . Constancy

Hyacinth, purple . . . . Sorrow

Hyacinth, white . . . . Loveliness, prayers

Hyacinth, yellow . . . . Jealousy

Hydrangea* . . . . .Gratitude for being
understood

Jasmine,* white . . . . Sweet love, amiability

Jasmine,* yellow . . . . Grace and elegance

Lady's slipper . . . . .Capricious beauty

Larkspur. . . . . Lightness, levity

Lavender* . . . . Distrust

Lilac* . . . . .Joy of youth

Lily, calla. . . . . Beauty

Lily-of-the-valley* . . Sweetness, purity, pure love

Marigold. . . . . Despair, grief, jealousy

Morning glory . . . . Affection

Myrtle. . . . . Good luck and love in marriage

Nasturtium. Patriotism

Pansy. . . . . Thoughts

Peony* . . . . .Bashful, happy life

Poppy, red. . . . . .Consolation

Rhododendron* . . . . Beware

Rose,* dark crimson . . . . Mourning

Rose,* pink. Happiness

Rose,* red. . . . . Love, I love you

Rose,* white . . . . I'm worthy of you

Rose,* yellow . . . . . . .Jealousy, decrease of love,
infidelity

Salvia,* blue . . . . .I think of you

Salvia,* red . . . . Forever mine

Snapdragon . . . . .Deception, graciousness

Speedwell . . . . .Feminine fidelity

Sunflower,* dwarf . . . . Adoration

Sunflower,* tall . . . . .Haughtiness

Sweet pea . . . . Delicate pleasures

Tulip,* red . . . . Passion, declaration of love

Tulip,* yellow . . . . .Sunshine in your smile

Violet . .Loyalty, devotion, faithfulness, modesty

Yarrow. Everlasting love

Zinnia . . . . Thoughts of absent friends

LADY'S SLIPPER

MYRTLE

YARROW

BIRTH MONTH FLOWERS

Plants with an asterisk (*) are profiled in this book.

THE MORE YOU PRAISE AND CELEBRATE YOUR LIFE,
THE MORE THERE IS TO CELEBRATE.
–Oprah Winfrey, American entrepreneur (b. 1954)

CARNATION

JANUARY: CARNATION,* SNOWDROP

PRIMROSE

FEBRUARY: VIOLET, PRIMROSE

DAFFODIL

MARCH: DAFFODIL, JONQUIL

DAISY

APRIL: DAISY, SWEET PEA

HAWTHORN

MAY: LILY-OF-THE-VALLEY,* HAWTHORN

HONEYSUCKLE

JUNE: ROSE,* HONEYSUCKLE

DELPHINIUM

JULY: DELPHINIUM,* WATER LILY

POPPY

AUGUST: GLADIOLUS, POPPY

MORNING GLORY

SEPTEMBER: ASTER,* MORNING GLORY

COSMOS

OCTOBER: MARIGOLD, COSMOS

CHRYSANTHEMUM

NOVEMBER: CHRYSANTHEMUM*

NARCISSUS

DECEMBER: NARCISSUS, HOLLY

–courtesy of the Texas A&M Cooperative Extension and FlowerInfo.org

OBSERVATIONS AND REMINDERS

CHANGES TO MAKE NEXT YEAR

INDEX

Note: **Boldface** references
indicate boxes or tables.

A

Abelia, 156
Agastache, aka anise hyssop
for bees, 176
for color, 157
for hummingbirds, **174**
for low maintenance, 180
how to use, 11
when to start from seed, **38**
Agave
for hummingbirds, **174**
for low water, 207
Ageratum, aka floss flower
for drying, **187**
when to start from seed, **37**
Alyssum, aka sweet alyssum
for containers, **20**
for pollinators, 176
when to start from seed, **37**
Amaranth *See also Globe*
amaranth
as an architectural plant, 14
for cutting, 184
for drying, **187**
when to start from seed, **37**
Anemone, Japanese, **160**
Anise hyssop *See Agastache*
Annuals
defined, **12,** 13–14
fertilizing, **202,** 204
for birds, 172
for containers, **20**
for hummingbirds, **174**
how to use, 11, 14, 157, 180
when to start from seed, **37**
Arborvitae, 179
Artemisia, aka wormwood
for color, **161**
for drying, **187**
Asclepias *See Butterfly weed*
Aster *(Aster;*
Symphyotrichum),
42–44
birth month flower, **218**
for bees, 177
for birds, 172
for cutting, **160,** 184
for low maintenance, 179
for perennials, 12, 17
how to use, 11
Astilbe *(Astilbe),* 45–47
for containers, **20**
for drying, **187**
Azalea *See Rhododendron*

B

Baby's breath
for drying, **187**
in a bouquet, 89
Bachelor's button, **37**
Baptisia, aka false indigo, 13
Barrenwort, **157**
Basil, holy, aka tulsi, 176
Bats, 16, 176
Bayberry, northern, 175
Beautyberry, 172–173
Bee balm *(Monarda),* aka
wild bergamot, 48–49
for containers, **20**
for hummingbirds, **174**
for pollinators, 176
how to use, 11, 12
when to start from seed, **38**
Bees
as pollinators, 11, 14, 16,
176–177
house for, 176
plants for, 158, 163, 166;
see also Flowers chapter
profiles
Begonia
end-of-season care, 208
for containers, **20**
how to use, 14, 180
Bellflower
easiest to grow, **161**
in a bouquet, 89
longest-blooming, **161**
Bergamot, wild *See Bee*
balm
Bergenia, **20**
Biennials, **12,** 13
Birds
benefits for, 16–17
plants for, 166, **170,**
172–175, **174,** 208;
see also Flowers chapter
profiles; Hummingbirds
Birth month flowers, **218**
Black-eyed Susan
(Rudbeckia), aka
Gloriosa daisy, 50–52
easiest to grow, **160**
for birds, 172
for cutting, 184
for low water, 207
for pollinators, 176
how to use, 11, 12
longest-blooming, **160**
native plant (large
coneflower), 17
when to start from seed, **38**

Blanket flower, aka
gaillardia, **38,** 176
Bleeding heart *(Dicentra),*
53–54
easiest to grow, **160**
for containers, **20**
for shade, **157**
native bulb (Dutchman's
breeches), 18, **54**
Bloodroot, 17
Blue anise sage, **157**
Blue mist *See Bluebeard*
Bluebeard, aka blue mist
benefits of, **170**
flowering shrub, 166
Bluestar, 17
Browallia, aka bush violet
for containers, **20**
for shade, 14
how to use, 11
Bulbs *See also Flowers*
chapter profiles
care in advance of winter,
208
native, 17–18
planting advice, 163, **202**
spring-blooming, 11,
162–163
Bush violet *See Browallia*
Butterflies
attracting, 11, 14, 17, 156,
158, 166, 168, 169,
170, 176; *see also*
Flowers chapter profiles
characteristics, 177
Butterfly weed, aka asclepias
See also Milkweed
how to use, 11
Mexican, for color, 158
most beautiful, **160**

C

Cacti, 207
Caladium, 208
Calamint, 158
Calendula
for pollinators, 176, 177
how to use, 11
when to start from seed, **37**
Canada lily, 17, 113
Canna *(Canna),* 55–59, 208
Carnation *See Dianthus*
Carolina allspice, aka
strawberry shrub,
sweetshrub
benefits of, **170**
flowering shrub, 166–167

Catmint
for low maintenance, 179
when to start from seed, **38**
Celosia
for drying, 187, **187**
when to start from seed, **37**
Chrysanthemum
(Chrysanthemum),
60–62
and Ascochyta ray blight,
191
birth month flower, **218**
vase life, 183
Cinquefoil, shrubby *See*
Potentilla
Clarkia, 176
Clematis *(Clematis),* 63–65
and clematis wilt, 196
for color, **157**
for hummingbirds, **174**
Cleome, aka spider flower
for moist soil, 14
for pollinators, 176
how to use, 11
Coleus
for containers, **20**
for low maintenance, 180
when to start from seed, **37**
Columbine *(Aquilegia),* 66–67
for hummingbirds, **174**
how to use, 11
most beautiful, **161**
when to start from seed, **38**
Compass plant, 17
Compost
how to make, 28–29
how to use, 12, 20, **21, 24,**
25, 31, 36, 163, 180,
206, 209, 210
Coneflower *(Echinacea),*
68–71
for birds, 172
for containers, **20**
for drying, **187**
for hummingbirds, **174**
for low maintenance, 178
for low water, 207
for pollinators, 176
how to use, 11, 12, 178
longest-blooming, **160**
when to start from seed, **38**
Coneflower, large
(Rudbeckia), 17
Conifers, dwarf, 11
Containers
care in advance of winter,
210

fertilizing in, **204**
for seed-starting, 30–32
plants for, **20**
potting mix recipe, 21
self-watering, 21
sizes and capacities, **21**
soil for, 20
types of, 20
Coreopsis (*Coreopsis*), 72–73
for containers, **20**
for low maintenance, 179
for low water, 207
for pollinators, 176
how to use, 11, 13
when to start from seed, **38**
Corydalis, yellow, 157
Cosmos
birth month flower, **218**
for cutting, 184
for pollinators, 176
how to use, 11
when to start from seed, **37**
Cotoneaster, 173
Crape myrtle, dwarf, 156
Crocus, 11, 162–163
Cup plant, 17
Currant, 173
Cut flowers, 182–184, **182, 183**

D

Daffodil
birth month flower, **218**
for cutting, 184
for spring bloom, 163
how to use, 11
Dahlia (*Dahlia*), 74–78
end-of-season care, 208
for cutting, 184
how to use, 11, 88
Daisy See also *Ox eye daisy*
birth month flower, **218**
for pollinators, 177
how to use, 11
when to start from seed, **38**
Daylily
classification of, 112
for containers, **20**
how to use, 11, 13
vase life, 183
Dead nettle, 23, 178
Delphinium (*Delphinium*), 79–81
birth month flower, **218**
for cutting, **161**
for hummingbirds, **174**
when to start from seed, **37, 38**

Desert lily, 18
Dianthus (*Dianthus*), aka carnation, pink, sweet William, 82–84
birth month flower, **218**
for pollinators, 176
longest-blooming, **161**
vase life, 183
when to start from seed, **38**
Dicentra See *Bleeding heart*
Diseases, 32, 180, 190–196
Dogwood, redtwig See *Redtwig dogwood*
Drip irrigation, 10, **102,** 206
Dry flowers, how to, 186–187
Dusty miller, **20**
Dutchman's breeches, 18, **54**

E

Earthworm soil test, 23
Elderberry, 173
Evening primrose, **20**
Evergreen plants
arborvitae, 179
azalea, 124
bayberry, northern, 175
broadleaf, 11
dianthus, 84
end-of-season care/ watering, 98, 105, 208
holly, 173
juniper, 179
lavender, 104
nitrogen and, **202**
rhododendron, 126
viburnum, 145

F

False indigo See *Baptisia*
Ferns
for low maintenance, 178, 180
native plants, 18
Fertilizers, 202–204
for containers, **204**
for seedlings, 32
granular vs. soluble, 204
ingredients, 202–204
kelp and seaweed, 32, **204**
organic vs. synthetic, 203–204
when to apply, 32, 204
Feverfew, 207
Firecracker plant, Vermillionaire, **174**
Floss flower See *Ageratum*
Flowering tobacco, aka nicotiana, white

shooting stars
as an architectural plant, 14
when to start from seed, **37**
Footprint soil test, 38
Forget-me-not, 13
Foxglove (*Digitalis*), 85–86
for hummingbirds, **174**
how to use, 11, 13
when to start from seed, **38**
Frost
and when to start from seed, 30, **37,** 38, **38**
preparation for/ protection from, 208–209
Frosts and Growing Seasons
Canadian, **35**
U.S., **34**
Fuchsia, **20**

G

Gaillardia See *Blanket flower*
Garden balsam, **174**
Gardens
care in advance of winter, 208–210
container, 20–21
low-maintenance, 178–180
native, 16–18
planning, 10–11
Geranium, cranesbill, 11, **157**
Gladiolus, 184, 208, **218**
Globe amaranth, aka gomphrena
for dry soil, 14
for drying, **187**
for low maintenance, 180
when to start from seed, **37**
Globe thistle, **187**
Gloriosa daisy See *Black-eyed Susan*
Glory-of-the-snow, 163
Goatsbeard, 46
Goldenrod, 172, 179
Gomphrena See *Globe amaranth*
Grasses, ornamental, 207

H

Hardening off seedlings, 32
Hawthorn, **218**
Hedges
how to use, 11, 170, 179
potentilla as, 168
shrub roses as, 169

Heliopsis, **38**
Hellebore, **160, 161**
Herbs
for drying, 186, **187**
for pollinators, 176
Heuchera, 11, 180
Hibiscus
Rose of Sharon shrub, 168, **170**
when to start from seed, **38**
Holly, 173, **218**
Hollyhock (*Alcea*), 87–89
for hummingbirds, **174**
how to use, 13
when to start from seed, **38**
Honeysuckle
birth month flower, **218**
for hummingbirds, **174**
for pollinators, 177
Hosta
for containers, **20**
how to use, 13
Hummingbirds, plants for, 11, 156, 173, **174;** see also *Flowers chapter profiles*
Hydrangea (*Hydrangea*), 90–95
benefits of, **170**
for color, 157, 167
for drying, 186, **187**
for low maintenance, 178
Hyssop, anise See *Agastache*

I

Iceland poppy, **161**
Impatiens
and wilt disease, 180
for hummingbirds, **174**
Indian pink, 17
Iris (*Iris*), 96–99
and bacterial leaf blight, 193
and bacterial soft rot, 194
and ink spot, 192
and iris borers, 197
and iris leaf spot, 193
and iris weevils, 200
for cutting, **161**
for hummingbirds, **174**
for spring bloom, 162
how to use, 12
Ironweed, 179

J

Jack-in-the-pulpit, 18
Japanese anemone, **160**

Japanese meadowsweet *See Spirea*
Jasmine *(Jasminum)*, 100–102
  for hummingbirds, **174**
Joe Pye weed
  as a soil indicator, **23**
  easiest to grow, **160**
  for low maintenance, 179
Jonquil *See Daffodil*
Juniper, 179

K
Kelp solution, for fertilizer, 32, **204**

L
Lady's mantle
  how to use, 11
  most beautiful, **160**
Lamb's-quarter, **23**
Lambs' ears, **161**
Language of flowers, 216–217
Lantana, 156
Larkspur
  for drying, **187**
  for pollinators, 176
Latin names, translated, 214–215
Lavender *(Lavandula)*, 103–106, 132
  for color, 158
  for drying, **187**
  for pollinators, 176
Lenten rose, **160**
Lights for seed-starting, 31–32
Lilac *(Syringa)*, 107–110
  and lilac bacterial blight, 191
  and lilac borers, 197
  for color, 157
  for cutting, **184**
  for pollinators, 177
Lily *(Lilium)*, 111–114
  and lily leaf beetle, 197
  Canada lily, 17, 113
  vase life, 184
Lily, day *See Daylily*
Lily, desert, 18
Lily, Peruvian *See Peruvian lily*
Lily, southern swamp, 18
Lily-of-the-valley *(Convallaria)*, 115–116
  birth month flower, **218**
  to gauge soil temperature, **58**
Lilyturf, **157**

Limestone, aka lime, 21, 24, 26
Little sweet Betsy, 18
Lobelia
  for containers, **20**
  for cutting, **183**
  for shade, 14
Lunaria, 13, **187**
Lupine *(Lupinus)*, 117–119
  and brown spot, 191
  for pollinators, 176, 177

M
Mallow, musk, **160**
Mallow, tree, **161**
Maltese cross, **20**
Manure, **21**, **24**, 25, 36, 163, 180, 202, 203, 206; *see also Flowers chapter profiles*
Marigold
  birth month flower, **218**
  for containers, **20**
  when to start from seed, 37
Mexican butterfly weed, 158
Mexican petunia, 156
Mexican sage, purple
  for color, **160**
  for cutting, **161**
Mexican sunflower, 14
Mildew, **32**, 193, 210
Milkweed *See also Butterfly weed*
  for cutting, **183**
  when to start from seed, 38
Million bells, 180
Monkey flower
  for hummingbirds, **174**
  for moist soil, 14
Morning glory
  birth month flower, **218**
  for containers, **20**
  when to start from seed, 37
Moss rose *See Portulaca*
Mud cake soil test, 36
Mulch, 180, 206, 208–209
Musk mallow, **160**

N
Narcissus *See Daffodil*
Nasturtium
  for containers, **20**
  how to use, 11
Native plants
  for pollinators, 11, 176
  vs. non-natives, 16–17
  you might not know, 17–18
Nectar vs. pollen, **177**

Nicotiana *See Flowering tobacco*
Nitrogen
  in compost, 28–29
  in fertilizer, **202**, 202–204
  weed indicators of, **23**
Nodding ladies' tresses orchid, 17

O
Obedient plant, **161**
Orange sedge, **161**
Orchid, nodding ladies' tresses, 17
Ox eye daisy
  as soil indicator, **23**
  for cutting, **160**

P
Pansy
  for containers, **20**
  for drying, **187**
  when to start from seed, 37
Penstemon
  for hummingbirds, **174**
  for shade, **157**
  most beautiful, **161**
Peony *(Paeonia)*, 120–123
  and leaf blotch, 192
  for cutting, **184**
  how to use, 13
Perennials
  defined, 12, 13
  end-of-season care, 208–209
  for birds, **172**
  for color, 156–158
  for containers, **20**
  for hummingbirds, **174**
  for low maintenance, 178–180
  how to use, 11
  native plants, 17
  survival traits, **160–161**
  when to fertilize, 204
  when to start from seed, 38
Peruvian lily
  for color, 157, 158
  for cutting, **161**
Pests, 196–200, 210
Petunia
  for containers, **20**
  when to start from seed, 37
Petunia, Mexican, 156
pH, 12, **21**, 24, 25
  plant preferences, **26**
  testing, 22–23
Phenology, 58, 131

Phlox
  for butterflies, 177
  for color, **160**
  for cutting, **160**
  how to use, 11, 13
  most beautiful, **160**
  when to start from seed, **37**, **38**
Phosphorus
  in fertilizer, 202–204, **203**
  to boost roots, **32**
  weed indicators of, **23**
Pink *See Dianthus*
Pink, Indian, 17
Pollen vs. nectar, **177**
Pollinators *See also Bees; Birds; Butterflies; Hummingbirds*
  how to attract, 176–177
  native, 16–17
Poppy
  birth month flower, **218**
  for color, **161**
  for cutting, **183**
  longest-blooming, **161**
Portulaca, aka moss rose, 14, 20, **37**
Potassium
  in coffee grounds, 21
  in fertilizer, 202–204, **203**
  weed indicators of, **23**
Potentilla, aka shrubby cinquefoil
  benefits of, **170**
  flowering shrub, 167–168
Primrose, **218**
Pruning *See also Flowers chapter profiles*
  flowering shrubs, 170

Q
Queen Anne's lace, 177

R
Ranunculus, 184
Red-hot poker, **174**
Redtwig dogwood
  for birds, 175
  for low maintenance, 178–179
Rhododendron and azalea *(Rhododendron)*, 124–126
  and azalea leaf gall, 192
  and bud blast, aka rhododendron bud and twig blight, 192
  and Ovulinia blight, 191

222

Rose *(Rosa)*, 127–132
  and black spot, 190
  and rose stem girdler, aka
    bronze cane borer, 199
  benefits of, **170**
  birth month flower, **218**
  end-of-season care,
    209–210
  flowering shrub, 168–169
  for color, 157
  for cutting, 182
  for drying, 187, **187**
Rose, Lenten, **160**
Rose, moss *See Portulaca*
Rose of Sharon
  benefits of, **170**
  flowering shrub, 168
Russian sage
  for color, **160**
  how to use, 13

S
Sage *See Salvia*
Sage, Russian *(Perovskia)*
  for color, **160**
  how to use, 13
Salvia *(Salvia)*, aka sage,
    133–136
  autumn sage, 134, 158
  blue anise sage, **157**
  for color, 156, 157, 158,
    160, 161
  for containers, **20**
  for cutting, **161,** 184
  for drying, **187**
  for hummingbirds, **174**
  for pollinators, 176, 177
  how to use, 13
  Mexican sage, purple,
    160, 161
  when to start from seed, **37**
Scabiosa
  for color, **157**
  when to start from seed, **37**
Sea holly, 186, **187**
Seaweed as fertilizer, 32, **204**
Sedge, orange, **161**
Sedum
  easiest to grow ('Autumn
    Joy'), **160**
  how to use, 11, 13
  native plant (wild
    stonecrop), 17
Seeds
  how to start, 30–32
  how to test viability, **30**
  lighting for, 31–32
  starter soil recipe, 31

when to sow annual,
    37, **37**
when to sow perennial,
    38, **38**
Serviceberry, 175
Shrubs *See also Flowers*
    chapter profiles; Hedges
  arborvitae, 179
  bayberry, northern, 175
  beautyberry, 172–173
  bluebeard, aka blue mist,
    166, **170**
  care in advance of winter,
    208–209
  Carolina allspice, aka
    strawberry shrub,
    sweetshrub, 166–167,
    170
  cotoneaster, 173
  currant, 173
  elderberry, 173
  evergreen holly, 173
  for color, 156, 157
  for low maintenance,
    178–180
  how to use, 10, 11,
    156–157
  hydrangea, 167, **170,** 178,
    186–187
  juniper, 179
  placing and planting,
    168, 180
  potentilla, aka shrubby
    cinquefoil, 167–168, **170**
  pruning flowering, 170
  redtwig dogwood, 175,
    178–179
  rose, 157, 168–169, **170**
  rose of Sharon, 168, **170**
  serviceberry, 175
  smoke bush, aka
    smoketree, 169, **170,** 179
  spirea, aka Japanese
    meadowsweet, 169,
    170, 179
  sumac, 175
  summer flowering,
    166–170
  summersweet, aka sweet
    pepperbush, 170, **170**
  viburnum, 175, 179
  when to fertilize, 204
  willow, arctic, 179
Site selection, 10–11
Smoke bush, aka smoketree
  benefits of, **170**
  flowering shrub, 169
  for low maintenance, 179

Snapdragon
  for containers, **20**
  for cutting, 184
  for hummingbirds, **174**
  for pollinators, 177
  when to start from seed, **37**
Snowdrop
  birth month flower, **218**
  for spring bloom, 162
  how to use, 11
Snow-in-summer, **161**
Soil *See also Fertilizers*
  and water use, 206–207,
    208
  condition indicators, **23**
  fixes (amendments), **24**
  for bulbs, 163
  for seed-starting, 30, 31
  pH, **21,** 22–23, 24, 25, **26**
  quality, 24–25
  recipes, 21, 31
  solarization, 190
  tests, 22–23, 36, 38
  texture, 24
  top-, 24–25
Southern swamp lily, 18
Speedwell, aka veronica
  for containers, **20**
  for hummingbirds, **174**
Spider flower *See Cleome*
Spider lily, 18
Spirea, aka Japanese
    meadowsweet
  benefits of, **170**
  flowering shrub, 169
  for low maintenance, 179
Squill
  Siberian, 163
  striped, 163
Statice
  for containers, **20**
  for cutting, 184
  for drying, **187**
  when to start from seed, **37**
Stock
  for cutting, 184
  when to start from seed, **37**
Stonecrop, wild, 17
Strawberry shrub *See*
    Carolina allspice
Strawflower
  for drying, **187**
  when to start from seed, **37**
Sumac, 175
Summersweet, aka sweet
    pepperbush
  benefits of, **170**
  flowering shrub, 170

Sunflower *(Helianthus)*,
    137–140
  and Phoma black stem, 191
  and sunflower moths, 198
  as an architectural plant, 14
  for birds, 172
  for pollinators, 176
  vase life, 184
  when to start from seed, **37**
Sunflower, Mexican, aka
    tithonia, 14
Sunflower, swamp, **160**
Sweet alyssum *See Alyssum*
Sweet pea
  birth month flower, **218**
  for containers, **20**
  for cutting, **160,** 184
Sweet woodruff, 180
Sweetshrub *See Carolina*
    allspice

T
Tansy, 207
Tickseed *See Coreopsis*
Tithonia, aka Mexican
    sunflower, 14
Topsoil, 24–25
Torenia, aka wishbone
    flower, 14
Tree wraps, 210
Tree mallow, **161**
Trillium, 18
Tulip *(Tulipa)*, 141–144
  and gray bulb rot, 194
  for cutting, 184
  how to use, 11
Tulsi *See Basil, holy*

V
Verbena
  how to use, 11
  when to start from seed, **37**
Vermillionaire firecracker
    plant, **174**
Veronica *See Speedwell*
Viburnum *(Viburnum)*,
    145–147
  for birds, 175
  for low maintenance, 179
Vines, **20,** 63–65, 100–102,
    148–151, **218**
Viola, aka violet, **38, 218**

W
Wallflower, 176
Water
  and compost, 29
  and containers, 20–21

and seed-starting, 31–32
and wilting, 206–207
efficient use of, 206–207
in advance of winter, 208
low-water plants, 207
ways to, 10–11, 180
Water lily, **218**
Weed
as soil indicators, **23**
control, 180
White shooting stars *See*
Flowering tobacco

Wild bergamot *See Bee*
balm
Wild ginger
for low maintenance, 180
native plant, 17
Willow, arctic, 179
Wind
and planting, 11, 16
effect on container plants,
21
effect on seedlings, 32
Winter aconite, 162

Wishbone flower, aka
torenia, 14
Wisteria *(Wisteria)*, 148–151
Woodsia *See Ferns*
Wormwood *See Artemisia*

Y
Yarrow
as a soil indicator, 23
for drying, **187**
for pollinators, 177
how to use, 11, 13

most beautiful, **161**
when to start from seed,
38
Yucca *(Hesperaloe),* **174**
Yucca *(Yucca),* 207

Z
Zinnia
for cutting, 184
how to use, 11
when to start from seed,
37

PHOTO CREDITS

Abbreviations: GI: Getty Images. PX: Pixabay. SS: Shutterstock. WM: Wikimedia. **Cover and Title Page:** See Flowers chapter profiles. **Editor's Note:** brainstorm1962/GI. **Contents:** 4: schnuddel/GI. 6: dokosolo/SS. **Ground Rules:** 8–9: kschulze/GI. 11: PX. 13: PX. 14: PX (all). 17: American Meadows (top left). bookguy/GI (top center). MiaZeus/GI (top right). Juniper Level Botanic Gardens, NC (bottom left and bottom right). Joyfnp/GI (bottom center). 18: PX (top left). Kenneth_Keifer/GI (top center). jlwhaley/GI (top right). PX (bottom left). stevelenzphoto/GI (bottom center). kongxinzhu/GI (bottom right). 21: Pilat666/GI. 22: Liliboas/GI. 25: elenaleonova/GI. 28: OceanProd/GI. 31: ArtRachen01/GI. 36: Ravi Natarajan/GI. **Flowers:** 40–41: Edita Medeina/SS. 42: PX. 44: PX. 45: Aleks Images/SS. 47: Nadya-So/SS. 48: Tatyana Mut/SS. 50: PX. 52: SelectSeeds.com. 53: PX. 55: Michel VIARD/GI. 57: PX. 59: PX. 60: Savina Nataliia/SS. 63: Peter Kvasnicak/SS. 64: PX. 66: ValentinAgapov/SS. 68: Meindert van der Haven/GI. 71: Dragoncello/SS. 72: All for you friend/SS. 74: Junko Nishimoto/SS. 77: Eden Brothers. 78: J. Parker's. 79: Proven Winners. 81: PX. 82: neotemlpars/SS. 83: PX. 85: guentermanaus/SS. 87: PX. 89–92: PX. 94: PX. 96: PX. 99: PX. 100: PX. 103: PX. 105: Angela Luchianiuc/SS. 107: PX. 109–110: PX. 111: IMNATURE/GI. 112: Benjamina/SS. 114: SHSPhotography/GI. 115: Natamischa/SS. 117: Cristina Ionescu/SS. 118: schnuddel/GI. 120: windcatcher/GI. 123: brytta/GI (left). PX (right). 124: anakumka/SS. 127: Andrew Twigg/SS. 129–130: PX. 133: Rattachai Boonbai/SS. 135: PX. 136: Pinrath Phanpradith/SS. 137: PX. 139: PX. 141: PX. 143: PX. 145: PX. 147–148: PX. 151: PX. **Inspiration:** 154–155: Martin Wahlborg/GI. 156: JLPC/WM (left). Prenn/WM (center). Proven Winners (right). 157: Cindy Dyer/WM (left). Proven Winners (center and right). 158: Jamain/WM (top left). White Flower Farm (top center). Proven Winners (top right). Stan Shebs/WM (bottom left). Peter T. Lin/WM (bottom center). Roland/WM (bottom right). 161: TracieMichelle/GI. 162–163: Netherlands Flower Bulb Information Center (all). 166: Nature Hills Nursery. 167: Gardenia (top). Proven Winners (bottom). 168: Kingsbrae Garden/Flickr (left). Brighter Blooms (right). 169: Brighter Blooms (left). Proven Winners (right and bottom). 170: Kaknes Landscape Supply. 172: PX (left and center). Dragoncello/SS (right). 173: PX (top left). Milcho Petrov Milev/SS (top center). Proven Winners (top right and bottom left). Mark Robinson/WM (bottom center). USDA (bottom right). 174: PX (all). 175: PX (top left). Famartin/WM (top center). Goddard_Photography/GI (top right). Alex Hauner/WM (bottom left). Oneconscious/WM (bottom center). Proven Winners (bottom right). 177: AriasPhotos/GI. 179: fotolinchen/GI. 183: zozzzzo/GI. 184: PX. 187: RozochkaIvn/SS. **Growing Concerns:** 188–189: seaonweb/SS. 190: Rutgers University (anthracnose). Missouri Botanical Garden (aster yellows). 191: Sunflowernsa.com (phoma black stem). William Jacobi, Colorado State University (lilac bacterial blight). Bob Stewart/Twitter (ovulinia petal blight). UMD Extension (Southern blight). 192: Robin Rosetta (bud blast). University of Florida/IFAS (crown gall). Joe Boggs (ink spot). OSU Extension (azalea leaf gall). 193: HGIC Clemson University (algal leaf spot). David B. Langston, University of Georgia/WM (bacterial leaf spot and powdery mildew). Oklahoma State University (iris leaf spot). 194: University of California Pest Management Program (sclerotinia mold). Joseph O'Brien USDA Forest Service (armillaria root rot). OSU Plant Clinic (fusarium basal rot). 195: Everett Hansen (phytophthora crown and root rot). Michigan State University (pythium root and stem rot). North Carolina State University (white smut and bacterial wilt). 196: PX (aphid). Karen Snover-Clift, Cornell University/Bugwood.org (fusarium wilt). PX (earwig). Howard F. Schwartz, Colorado State University/Bugwood.org (verticillium wilt). 197: Wisconsin Horticulture (iris borer). PX (Japanese beetle). Muddy knees/SS (leaf miner). PX (lily leaf beetle). 198: AjayTvm/SS (mealy bug). University of Missouri Extension (spider mite). J. P. Michaud, K-State Research and Extension (sunflower moth). gardening.which.co.uk (stem and bulb nematode). 199: Oregon State University (rose stem girdler). BARAKAT2011/WM (scale insects). Mike Boone/WM (stalk borer). 200: Lyle Buss, University of Florida (thrips). DreCampbellFarm.com (black vine weevil). skitterbug/iNaturalist.com (verbena bud moth). 203: Amy Newton-McConnel/GI. 207: kamira777/GI. 209: SbytovaMN/GI. **Lore and More:** 212–213: Alfribeiro/GI. 215: PX. 217: PX (all). 218: PX (all).

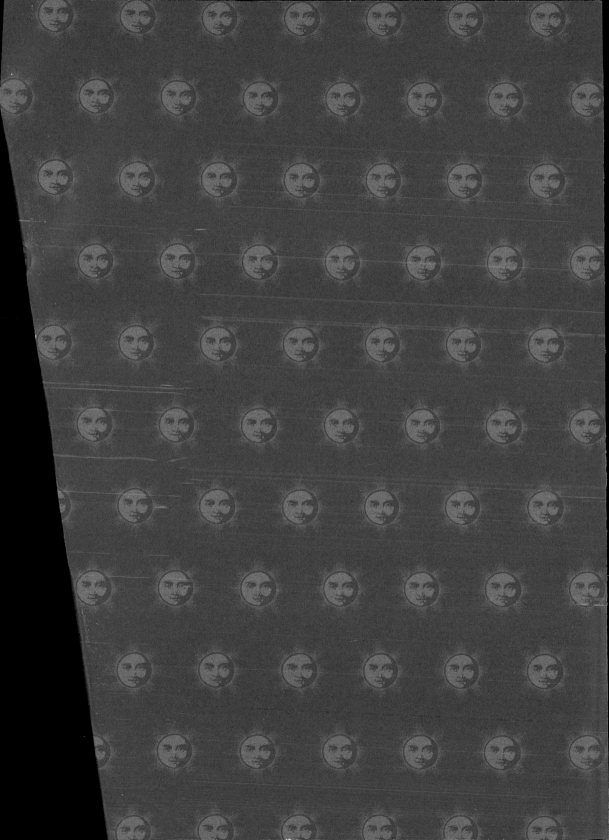